CW01272530

THE
IMPACT
ENGINE

Every organization has a vision and goals.
The path to reaching these goals is the **strategy**.
Think of the strategy as the chess queen—
the most powerful piece on the board deciding
the direction and priorities of the organization.

For an organization to get things done, it must build strong delivery capability. Picture the **delivery engine** as a gear that powers an organization's ability to execute.

When you combine a winning strategy with the capability to enable high-powered execution, you get an **IMPACT Engine** designed to drive progress toward the organization's vision. This book puts you behind the wheel of the IMPACT Engine—developing the mindsets, systems, and processes to accelerate organizational value delivery.

THE IMPACT ENGINE

Accelerating Strategy Delivery for PMO and Transformation Leaders

LAURA BARNARD

"Implementing Laura Barnard's IMPACT Engine System in two organizations exponentially improved accountability, efficiency, staff growth, and mission IMPACT, helping us achieve outsized results. Barnard's unique approach focuses on solving business problems rather than simply standing up a project management office. I encourage fellow executives to see this book as a window into a better execution system that can transform an organization's culture and processes, strengthening its people and its IMPACT on the world."

JOEL ALBIZO, CEO, American Planning Association

"A super-helpful recipe to elevate the performance of any PMO or enterprise transformation effort, and drive high-IMPACT mission success."

MIKE HANNAN, CEO, Fortezza Consulting; Co-Founder, Project Management for Change

"More than just a step-through process from strategy to execution, Laura Barnard's *The IMPACT Engine* emphasizes the crucial mindset change that sets it apart from other books. She demonstrates that you can and must know where to steer, adopting a solution-oriented approach that unleashes your team's potential to deliver value quickly and effectively. If you manage projects, regardless of your organization's structure, this book is essential. Get *The IMPACT Engine* and set your direction...fast!"

J. KENDALL LOTT, CEO, M Powered Strategies; Co-Founder, Project Management for Change

"If you need to transform strategy into action that makes an IMPACT, this is your golden guidebook."

DAWN MAHAN, Founder and CEO, PMOtraining.com

"Finally! A step-by-step guide for PMO leaders that dispenses with dogmatic theory—and gets results."

JESSE FEWELL, Consulting CEO and Chair of PMBOK® Guide 8th Edition

"Realize the full potential of your business through better approaches designed to elevate business value."

ANDY JORDAN, President, Roffensian Consulting

"I've personally seen delivery leaders go through the IMPACT Engine process and go from burned out to burning bright! This system just works every time."

STUART EASTON, CEO, TransparentChoice

"A seminal work for PMO and strategy leaders navigating complex organizational landscapes. This book doesn't just theorize; it equips you with pragmatic strategies and real-world tactics to drive sustainable business outcomes. *The IMPACT Engine* is not merely a book; it's a catalyst for change."

MICHAEL SHOST, Global PMO Leader and Innovation Pathfinder

"The IMPACT Engine System is comprehensive, practical, and proven. You are led through a logical sequence of steps that results in faster, better business outcomes that are aligned with the organization's strategy, providing undeniable value for the organization, and ultimately earning you a seat at the table as the organization's Strategy Navigator."

BETH MAY, COO, Project Management for Change

"A mind-shifting book filled with 'aha' moments. If you are a consultant building project capability for clients, you can use this step-by-step framework to elevate your IMPACT and grow your business in the process."

GREGOR ANDROJNA, IES student; PMOexpert, PMO Consultant

"I've applied Laura Barnard's IMPACT Engine System to more than six PMOs across three different companies and now coach others to do the same. This program is a game-changer. Whether you're struggling with where to start, what to prioritize, or how to set up your PMO, this is the right guidebook, at the right time, with the right coach. You'll save time, energy, and your sanity while helping you achieve measurable business results!"

ANDREA CIRELLI, IES student and coach; Senior Director, MassDOT PMO

"*The IMPACT Engine* encapsulates the essence of accelerated strategy execution and robust delivery capabilities. The principles in this book provide a clear, actionable path to success, resonating with strategic initiatives and transformative projects. Laura Barnard's insightful approach offers practical guidance and inspiration for anyone seeking to make a significant IMPACT."

BADR MOHAMMED BURSHAID, Chairman,
Global Project Management Forum

"You'll find yourself reviewing this book again and again to 'broaden your focus beyond project execution'—and you'll establish and sustain a disciplined cadence that enables you to deliver more value."

WILLETTA LOVE, IES student; Associate Director, Strategy Office,
American Psychological Association

"By emphasizing the value chain and strategy lifecycle, Laura Barnard positions the PMO as a crucial player in driving organizational transformation and operational excellence. Her focus on practicality, collaboration, and impactful results sets a new standard for excellence in organizational management."

SAADI ADRA, CEO, ADVISORS; 2016 PMI Snyder Award Winner;
2022 World PMO Influencer

"*The IMPACT Engine* masterfully bridges the gap between strategic intent and execution excellence. This book is a beacon for PMO, transformation, and strategy leaders aiming to navigate the complexities of organizational change with grace and efficacy."
THOMAS KENNEDY, IES student; Senior Manager, PMO

"The bible on how to run a PMO! Read this book if you want to succeed in project delivery."
PETER BADGER, IES student; Head of Program Management

"The IMPACT Engine System offers a fresh perspective and a comprehensive approach to not only establishing your PMO but also ensuring sustainable value."
JENI PITMAN, IES student; General Manager, Transformation Office, InvoCare

"Laura Barnard's transformative approach has revolutionized the way I guide people through change. With empathy and understanding, she masterfully supports individuals and organizations on their journey to unlock their full potential and achieve their strategic goals. Barnard's expertise showcases the power of creating a positive, collaborative environment that empowers organizations to thrive."
APRIEL BIGGS, IES student; PMO Executive; Certified Enterprise Agile Coach

"A great insight into how to set up or turn around PMOs and ensure they deliver strategy in a structured yet flexible way."
NICOLETE FRIEDMANN, PMO Practice Lead

"Recommended for every PMO—whether you are a one-person PMO or you have staff to assist you."
JETTE JEPSEN, Continuous Improvement Manager

"A comprehensive guide that seamlessly navigates the complexities of project and portfolio management."
VICTOR CHIDONGO, IES student; Head of PMO, Momentum Metropolitan Holdings Africa

"The key to creating and delivering a repeatable, step-by-step approach to take your PMO to the next level while providing immense business value."
BRENDA LINDBERG, IES student; IT PMO Director

"Gives you the arsenal of skills and tools to develop yourself and your team as strategy leaders and IMPACT Drivers in the organization."
MONIE MANUGUE, Director, Delivery Management

"*The IMPACT Engine* is an essential guide for both aspiring project managers and seasoned PMO leaders. Through compelling stories and proven strategies, Laura Barnard provides a clear path to help us make a transformative IMPACT on our organizations. This book is a must-read for anyone looking to drive success, optimize their PMO's performance, and take their project management skills to the next level."
REBECCA SEAGO-COYLE, PMO Leader

"Exceptional! This action-oriented book will change the way you think about and build your PMO. Buy it! You will have NO REGRETS!"
JOAN RAUSCH, IES student; PMO Leader

"With her emphasis on the step-by-step approach, Laura Barnard gives a clear perspective on how to build the mindset to excel through the transformation journey. *The IMPACT Engine* is written so that anyone can understand and follow the path to greater IMPACT, performance, and goal realization in the organization."
MARGARET GUNNION, IES student; Project Manager

"Filled with action-taking steps and resources, this book is everything you need to guide you on the journey of building a PMO and delivering your organization's strategy."

JEANNE BROCK, IES student; ERP Systems Manager

"I believe any leader—PMO, change agent, project manager, etc.—can benefit from this book."

VICKIE SASSER, IES student; Scrum Master 3

"An opportunity to get out of the old-school PMO mindset and elevate your team and organization."

TAMERA RYNSHOVEN, IES student; Director, IT Program Management Office

"A step-by-step method to setting up a team to deliver strategy that is steeped in competence, practical experience, and laser-focused guidance."

VIJAY CHAVDA, IES student; Operations Director

"An extraordinary source of inspiration, motivation, and encouragement. What attaches the reader most is Laura Barnard's generosity of heart, which shines through in the abundance of information she doesn't hesitate to share, her passion, and her immense desire to make us IMPACT Drivers!"

JEANICK DEBROSSE, IES student; PMO Director, Groupe ProFin

"With over 30 years focused on all things PPM, I can truly say I'm in awe of what Laura Barnard has accomplished with her excellent book. I truly wish I had this book available during my 10 years at Gartner so I could have just said to clients, 'Read this book before you do anything else.' Barnard makes it clear that it is people first, process second. She also makes it very clear that the process itself has to ADD value rather than just control and report on activities. Thank you for the job well done."

DONNA FITZGERALD, Executive Director, NimblePM,Inc.

Copyright © 2024 by Laura Barnard

All rights reserved. No part of this book may be reproduced, stored in a retrieval system or transmitted, in any form or by any means, without the prior written consent of the publisher or a license from The Canadian Copyright Licensing Agency (Access Copyright). For a copyright license, visit accesscopyright.ca or call toll free to 1-800-893-5777.

All stories are real stories; some names and identifying details have been changed to protect the privacy of individuals.

Cataloguing in publication information is available from Library and Archives Canada.
ISBN 978-1-77458-452-1 (hardcover)
ISBN 978-1-77458-453-8 (ebook)

Page Two
pagetwo.com

Printed and bound in Canada by Friesens
Distributed in Canada by Raincoast Books
Distributed in the US and internationally by Macmillan

24 25 26 27 28   5 4 3 2 1

IMPACTEngineBook.com

This book is for you, the courageous change agent on a journey to help your organization achieve great things. I've been where you are. I see you now and I wish I had me when I was you. Together, we will elevate your influence and IMPACT while you accelerate the delivery of your organization's strategy. You are never alone on this journey. I've got you.

Contents

I Wish I Had Me When I Was You 1

STAGE ONE NEW ROLE, NEW MINDSET 11

1 Your Strategic Opportunity 15
2 You Are an IMPACT Driver 37
3 The IMPACT Engine System 47

STAGE TWO ASSESS THE ORGANIZATION 65

4 Bring Them with You 69
5 Give Them What They Want 91

STAGE THREE DEFINE HIGH-IMPACT SERVICES 125

6 Solve the Right Problems 129
7 Create Solutions Across the Strategy Lifecycle 143
8 Determine Your "Worth It Factor" 173

STAGE FOUR **PLAN THE IMPACT JOURNEY** 187

9 Develop the IMPACT Delivery Framework 191
10 Become the Stakeholder Whisperer 205

STAGE FIVE **DELIVER SUSTAINABLE VALUE** 229

11 Create a Delivery-Focused Culture 233
12 Lead the Change 249

STAGE SIX **EVOLVE YOUR IMPACT ENGINE** 273

13 Drive Continual Value Delivery 277
14 Take Your Seat at the Table 295

Acknowledgments 305
Sources 307
Detailed Table of Contents 309

I Wish I Had Me When I Was You

IN 1999, I was at the heart of the internet boom building my first project management office (PMO) delivering e-commerce websites for brick-and-mortar stores. I had no idea what I was doing.

Internet search engines were very new and there wasn't a lot of information on "how to set up a PMO." In fact, I wouldn't even have known what to search for at the time, as the PMO concept was still a relatively new one, at least to me. I had to figure things out on my own by asking a lot of questions, identifying challenges, and defining solutions to them. I learned early on that the power of getting to the heart of what the executives *wanted* was going to be key to my success. Don't get me wrong—it was tough with a steep learning curve. But it was also immensely rewarding, even if I was running on caffeine and adrenaline.

That first PMO may have been the easiest. I didn't have an overwhelming amount of information bombarding me, from various sources all over the world, about all the things a PMO "should" do. Back then it was simple—I had to ask good questions and trust my instincts. I figured out what needed to get done and knew I still had a lot to learn.

Over time, as I continued to immerse myself in learning everything I could about PMOs and strategy delivery, things got worse.

The more I worked with my team to apply my learning from various courses and the industry standards that theorists were creating, the more roadblocks we hit. With every new template or process we put in place, we heard a big fat "no thanks" from our stakeholders. I didn't understand why we were facing a wall of resistance when everything we created was in their best interests and was what we "should" be doing, but the colleagues I was working so hard to help believed we were slowing projects down instead of speeding them up. They saw "too much work" instead of "we're here to make things easier." All the best practices and standards we were using were designed to ensure every possible scenario was covered, but they felt overburdensome to the people they were meant to help. We were told by the experts that this kitchen-sink approach was what "good" looked like. But instead of progress, it loaded us down with box-checking, heavy governance, and endless complaints.

I knew I had to find a better way—especially if I didn't want to find myself out the door. So I asked better questions and learned that over my years of trying harder and harder to follow the theory, I had shifted to giving people what I thought they *needed* instead of what they *wanted*. So I did the only thing I knew to do. I went back to what had worked so well in the beginning. I switched gears in favor of what key stakeholders said they wanted: to move fast, show tangible results, and drive real organizational value that made things easier for them. I did what my lifelong best friend Bryana calls "turning common sense into common practice."

What happened when I made this shift? Resistance decreased, projects got done faster, and business leaders were seeing measurable improvements not just in the deliverables, but also in the business benefits achieved for the cost of those projects. I loved it, and they loved it. This practical give-people-what-they-want approach was working.

Most importantly, I learned that what drove most of my success then and now was shifting my focus to driving better business outcomes, while weaving organizational change management techniques into project delivery. And the best part is that this felt so much easier than the every-box-must-be-checked approach I had been taught.

Looking back, I wish I'd had a mentor to help steer me in the right direction and avoid some of the frustrations I faced. I didn't—but you do. You get the benefit of my three decades of hard-won lessons, first in your shoes and then with clients and students across industries. My goal is to make your path smoother by distilling decades of experience into actionable advice that gets at the heart of what executives want, shows you how to gain their trust, and enables you to deliver real value—as *they* define it.

This book is for you if you are building your first delivery team and are unsure where to start. It's for you if you've been doing this for a while and are building your next delivery team and wondering why stakeholders don't understand the value that project management can bring to the table. It's for you if you are building internally focused project delivery capability and don't consider it "strategically focused." It's for you if you know you should have a seat at that leadership table but can't quite figure out how to be taken seriously or get invited into those critical business conversations.

And yes, it's for you if you aren't even sure if this team that you're building should be a project/program/portfolio management office, a strategy delivery office, a business transformation office, an Agile management office, a product management office, a... yeah, there's a lot of names for this thing we do.

Finally, it's for you if you know that the skills and expertise in delivering results that you have to offer are extremely valuable and you simply need a clear path to build or elevate your team and organization to deliver more IMPACT.

In 2013, I founded my company with a clear goal in mind: to help delivery leaders like you fast-track their success by sharing what I had learned about building PMOs, business transformation functions, and other strategy delivery teams right the first time, while avoiding the mistakes that stop so many in their tracks. After almost two decades of leading transformation and change inside organizations, I knew the importance of setting up the entire strategy lifecycle for greater success and higher return on investment (ROI), and I wanted to help others achieve this goal more easily as well.

Our approach, in all of the years that I've been running my company, has had a 100 percent success rate. Those aren't the typical industry results—because this isn't the typical industry guidance. It's a unique approach to drive IMPACT that I'll share with you in this book. If you do the work, you will see the results. This is the IMPACT Engine System.

The IMPACT Engine System

The IMPACT Engine System (IES) is a step-by-step program to accelerate the entire strategy lifecycle—from initial strategic planning through to high-powered, measurable results. It starts with vital mindset shifts that clarify your value proposition, and presents a detailed delivery system to help you create the team that drives strategy implementation and gets you a seat at the leadership table. Refined through countless missions across global sectors with our clients and students, the IES road map has been stress-tested under intense conditions. It's a proven approach forged in the fire of real-world delivery challenges.

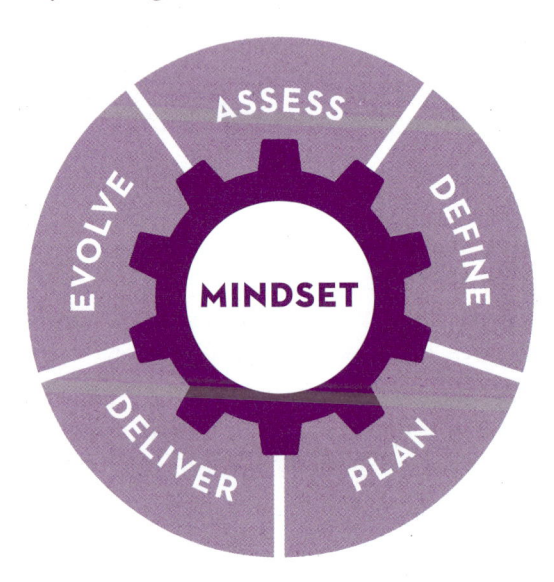

The IMPACT Engine System takes you through six stages, creating a disciplined cadence that enables you to deliver measurable value to your stakeholders.

1 **New Role, New Mindset:** Position yourself for success by developing the optimal IMPACT Driver Mindset and discovering the secrets to high-IMPACT strategy delivery.

2 **Assess the Organization:** Build strong stakeholder relationships and unlock their highest priorities that, when addressed, will have your stakeholders begging for more.

3 **Define High-IMPACT Services:** Earn credibility fast with high-IMPACT solutions that get to the root of the organization's pain points.

4 **Plan the IMPACT Journey:** Complete your IMPACT Delivery Model to guide the organization toward greater value realization for the strategy.

5 **Deliver Sustainable Value:** Drive exceptional business results that strategically position your team at the center of organizational value delivery.

6 **Evolve Your IMPACT Engine:** Iterate your way to IMPACT following the adaptive continuous value delivery model so shifting business needs don't derail success as you become the Strategy Navigator and earn that seat at the leadership table.

The IMPACT Engine System is based on what I learned (mostly the hard way) building PMOs, driving strategy delivery functions, and helping companies transform as a professional working inside organizations, and from the thousands of ambitious professionals who, since I founded my company, have helped me perfect this system by asking great questions, providing feedback, and sharing their wins. It can work for you too, because you will work *with* your organization and the people in it. You will be building, improving,

Knowledge alone is not power. It's the application of that knowledge that drives real IMPACT.

accelerating, and creating more value for your organization—even if you only apply a small portion of what you learn here. Now let's talk about what it's going to take to see the results.

Action Steps Worth Doing

Knowledge alone is not power. It's the application of that knowledge that drives real IMPACT.

All too often, we see people drown themselves in knowledge, but fail to make any real change in their lives. The classes bought, the memberships joined, and the access to people willing and able to help—all squandered. Too often, we only do the first half of the work by learning what needs to get done to see results, but not applying it. We've all been there. We might get great inspiration from a class we take or book we read and then, as we get back into our regular routine, we may not take the time to apply what we've learned. The busy takes over.

As you embark on this journey, understand that from your very first steps in this process, I'm going to challenge you to think bigger about your role and how you can provide value in your organization—and I'm also going to give you downloadable action-taking resources, or as my friend Dawn Mahan calls them, Thinking Tools—to apply what you learn. (Find these resources at IMPACTEngineBook.com.) The resources are cumulative; each download builds on the one before. And the faster you start applying your learnings, the faster you will see results—before you have a chance to go back to the old way of doing things.

Even if you aren't building a strategy delivery team right now, there are things you'll explore in this book that you can test out, apply, and learn from quickly—and you will discover ways to do that. I've even applied much of what I am going to teach you here to nurturing my marriage, raising a teenager, advising friends going through tough divorces, and even simply running my own business better. There are so many secrets in these pages that can make your life easier. Be on the lookout for the everyday application so you can find creative ways to practice what you are learning in and outside the office.

To see results, you must learn then apply, learn then apply. Use the resources to keep you focused, keep you going, give you the step-by-step guidance you need to show real tangible value, and watch the extraordinary results unfold for you and your organization. This process has been helping delivery leaders around the world get recognized in big ways and get game-changing results much faster than they thought possible, and I want you to join them. I'll remind you to activate that knowledge in some "Think" and "Do" action steps at the end of each chapter, and reference the downloadable resources you can use to apply what you are learning to your real-world scenario.

If you do not have a real-world scenario to apply these learnings to at work, or would like more detailed guidance and support beyond what a book can offer, you may want to skip ahead and join the IMPACT Engine System implementation program, where we have a detailed case study and many more resources and guidance you can use to apply every step of the comprehensive program (and work toward your certification in the process). Learn more at IMPACTEngineBook.com.

I wish I had me when I was you, and now I've made it my mission to save you from the headaches, frustration, and overwhelm that I experienced when in your shoes. And I'm also on a mission to elevate the role of PMO and strategy delivery professionals globally. We're going to do great work together as you go through this book, but it doesn't stop there. Let's keep talking online, in our communities, on social media, with our friends, with our colleagues (and maybe even with our teenagers).

You will find some pages in this book that highlight a quote to remind you of key concepts you are learning. You may find it helpful to take a picture of these quotes and post them on your wall or share them on social media to keep the conversation going about the importance of accelerating strategy delivery globally. I'd love to see you there (don't forget to tag me)!

Let's make a bigger IMPACT in all our organizations!

You belong at the leadership table, and I am going to help you get there. We'll start with Stage One: building the right mindset about strategy delivery and the role you can play. Get ready for a game-changing moment in your journey.

STAGE 1

NEW ROLE, NEW MINDSET

MINDSET

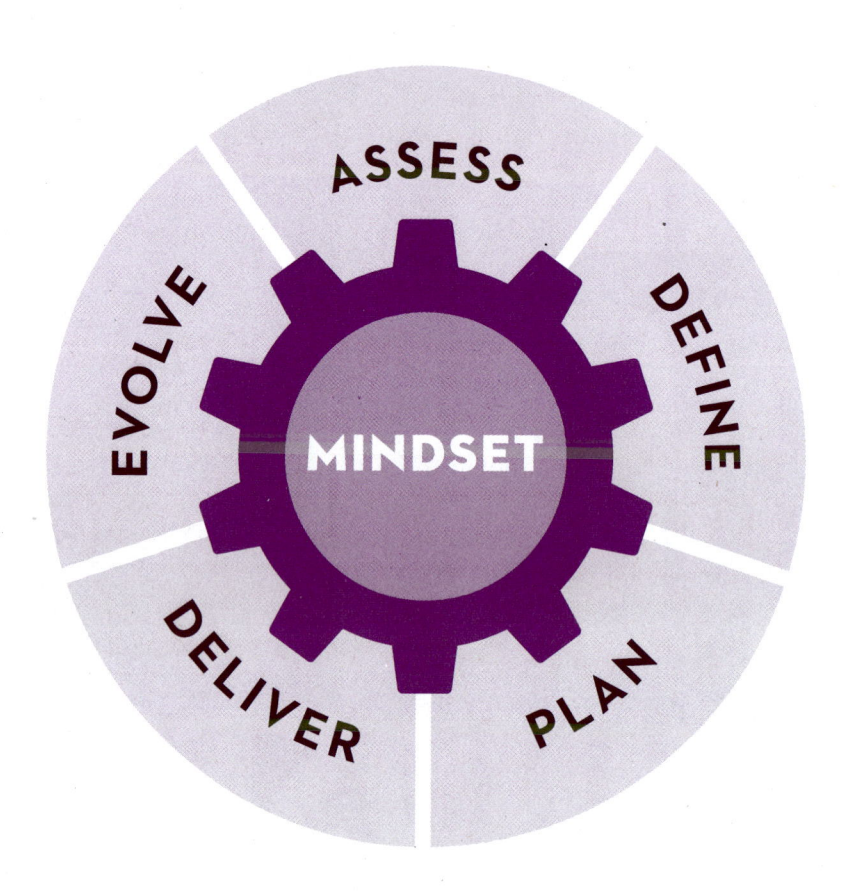

- ASSESS
- DEFINE
- PLAN
- DELIVER
- EVOLVE

Before you can *be* successful you have to *know* what success looks like—not just to you, but to the leaders who put you in this role.

That may require you to shift some of your current beliefs and understandings about your role, why you were hired, and your value proposition to the organization. I will show you how to align your thinking with the stronger business outcomes your executives want—which is step one to getting your seat at the table with them.

In Stage One: New Role, New Mindset, you will gain a clear understanding of the value you are capable of delivering. That's the foundation on which you will build capacity to help your organization execute on its strategy, with the highest possible return on investment, as quickly as possible.

I will show you the chessboard that is the game of organizational strategy delivery, and prepare you to make a series of chess moves that strategically position you to address the biggest business pain points quickly and help your organization take advantage of strategic opportunities. Get ready; you might be surprised to learn where those big opportunities are hiding.

Next you'll look at your role and the shift you may need to make to position yourself as the leader of this new type of business-focused department, driving value in a way that your business leaders will recognize and reward.

And then I'll get you rolling on the details of the IMPACT Engine System, the motor that will drive results. Along the way, I'll share some of the successes of our clients and students to show you what's possible for you.

Let's do this!

Your Strategic Opportunity

IT WAS Samantha's first week on the job as the leader of the newly formed project management office. After seven years as a project manager, she knew she was ready for more. When she interviewed for this role, her new boss made it clear that project management was broken in their company and that the executives were looking for a new approach to get projects done. "Projects take too long and cost too much," he told her on her first day. "You need to fix project management fast."

The CEO had recently attended a conference where he'd heard his peers talk about the success that they had in implementing a PMO. He figured if it was working for those companies, it might work in his company. But what he knew for certain is that what they were doing now wasn't working. The executive team was sure the business strategy was solid, so ineffective execution was seemingly to blame for their challenges. As soon as they threw the strategy over the fence to the delivery teams, things seemed to fall apart.

This was Samantha's first time in a role like this and she was eager to prove her value quickly. She immediately got to work creating a detailed process to ensure a consistent approach to project delivery. But her excitement was short-lived. As she started researching how to deliver good project management at scale, she found herself lost in a maze of conflicting information. The books she consumed gave her long lists of templates to create and processes to develop, and her notebook was filling up with a rainbow of sticky notes on all the things she had to do *today*.

Samantha's confidence began to falter, and she started to question her ability to succeed in this role—especially since her request to add resources to her team was denied because the executives wanted to "see progress first" while she was also running the two most important projects for the company. Ugh. She would have to do this by herself, and so she spent many evenings poring over standards guides to document the right methodology and create a compliance framework to ensure everyone followed the process.

When it came time for her 90-day check-in with the boss, Alex, Samantha walked into the meeting with a tired but victorious smile on her face. She had burned the candle at both ends, but she had pulled off so much.

"So, Samantha, what have you been working on for the past three months?" Alex asked.

Samantha leaned forward in her seat with a twinkle in her eye. "Well, I've been researching the best practices for setting up a successful PMO, and I've put together a PMO charter and a set of templates based on what I found."

Alex sat back in his chair and nodded. "OK." Eyeing her binder, he said, "Can you walk me through some of the templates you've created?"

Samantha eagerly flipped through the pages of the binder, pointing out each of her templates and the detailed methodology while explaining how they would be used. Alex listened patiently, nodding along as Samantha spoke. After she finished her presentation, he said, "But how is this actually going to solve our execution problems?"

Samantha's smile faded for a moment. She had been so focused on creating the templates and methodology that she hadn't had time to think through how they would be rolled out. She figured that once people saw the new process, they would be as excited as she was to put the templates to use—after all, she saw how the absence of these resources led to unnecessary confusion and reinventing the wheel each time a project was done.

"As soon as we implement this structured process, we'll be able to get all the projects in on time and on budget," Samantha explained. "We'll create an audit checklist and ensure that every project is following each step, so we know they are doing it right. And we need to make it clear that compliance with the new processes is critical to the success of the projects. Consistency is key!"

"OK, but we better make some progress quickly because the C-suite is complaining that nothing has changed over the last three months," Alex said. "And you know the IT department has been trying to take over project delivery for the whole company, so if we don't move fast, we won't get the chance to show the value of the PMO."

"I understand and I'm on it!" Samantha scooped up her template binder and hurried out. As she strode back to her desk, she realized she hadn't even had the chance to ask about the new customer project he'd just added to her plate. She was going to be working all weekend to catch up.

The Typical Advice and Typical Results

Samantha's story might be painfully familiar. You might have this book in your hand because you watched the webinars, read the books, attended the classes, or even hired a consultant, and nothing you've tried has truly delivered the competitive advantage your organization needs to the satisfaction of your business leaders. On the other hand, you may have been fortunate enough to find this book before you could fall into the trap of following the typical industry advice.

What's wrong with the typical industry advice? Well, if you follow it, you will get the typical results. And the typical results won't get you very far in your organization or your career.

According to a 2018 survey by the Project Management Institute, about half of PMOs failed to meet their original objectives.

McKinsey & Company has found that an overwhelming 74 percent of executives don't have faith that their company's transformative strategies will succeed. Research by PwC's consulting business unit, Strategy&, found that only 8 percent of leaders rated their companies as effective at both strategy and execution. And since these statistics came out several years ago, I've seen hundreds of examples that indicate things have been getting worse in many organizations. PMOs and other strategy delivery teams are failing faster thanks to the dwindling patience of business leaders combined with global and market influences that require results yesterday. And when they start like Samantha's, many don't even get off the ground.

In 2010, Gartner released a report saying that approximately 50 percent of PMOs fail because they focus too much on processes and tools and too little on value. I had a chat with one of the authors, Donna Fitzgerald, now a dear friend, and sadly, the numbers haven't gotten much better. She said that at the 2013 Gartner PPM Summit, Gartner pointed out that 68 percent of stakeholders perceive their PMOs to be bureaucratic, and I hear this complaint in companies around the world still to this day. This has to change.

You might be reading this book because you're fearful of becoming one of those statistics. You might be the person who replaced the last person that was a part of those statistics. Or you might be feeling just like Samantha.

Don't worry. I've got you.

Stop following the typical advice if you want to stop getting the typical results. The key to your success is not going to be found in piecing together snippets of advice from across the internet. Much of that advice says that templates and tools are the secret to your success. This is not true. In all my years of experience in this space, I've never heard an executive say, "Wait! Can you come back when you have five more templates for me to fill out?" Nope, hasn't happened. Not once. Why?

Because they don't care about your templates or your process.

Does that mean you shouldn't have them? No, but it does mean you need to be smart about what you do, in what order, and when and how you implement them. I'll help you follow the right path to ensure you're solving the right problems, the right way, and fast, so your business leaders aren't wondering what you've been doing all this time. Yes, we will even talk templates... but not yet.

It's Not You, It's the Process

Three months later, as Samantha enthusiastically trained each department and gave them the project management methodology and templates to use, she hit a wall. No one wanted to work with her, and she struggled to convince business leaders of the value of her new methodology. Despite her best efforts to sell the value of following a good process, she couldn't get the support she needed, and complaints started coming in from all over the organization.

When Alex called her into his office at the six-month mark, Samantha knew things weren't going well, but was sure she could convince him that her hard work was paying off. After rushing from the printer with the latest versions of all the templates, checklists, and beautifully crafted methodology, she ran down the hall to Alex's office. She made it to his door and took a deep breath. And then she peered through the doorway, saw his face, and froze in a wave of anxiety. After a moment, he noticed her hesitation and said, "Come in, Samantha. Please take a seat."

As she sat down, her heart raced. Samantha had heard from her friend Robert, who'd heard it from his boss, that Alex was thinking about making a change. She wasn't sure if this was just a rumor or if she was about to get fired.

"We have a problem," Alex said. "Several team members have complained that you are hard to work with and that everything you have asked them to do is just slowing them down and now projects are taking even longer. No one wants to work with the PMO." The weight of his words hit Samantha like a ton of bricks.

"I don't understand," she said, her voice shaking slightly. "I keep telling everyone about how the templates and methodology will help them address this total chaos. Why don't they get that the problem is a lack of consistency?"

Alex leaned back in his chair. "Samantha, we need to see tangible results, not just a bunch of templates and processes. I see people going in the other direction when they see you coming."

Samantha was so frustrated. She had put so much effort into this over the last several months, and now her boss was questioning the value. No, he was questioning *her* value.

She knew it would be weeks before she could get back on Alex's calendar. "They just need training," she pleaded, "and I need some help selling the benefits of these tools."

Alex leaned forward, placing his hands on the desk. "I will see what I can do. But you need to deliver results, and quickly. The success of the PMO—and you running it—depends on it."

Samantha nodded and swallowed hard. She knew that the next few months would be critical. She went back to her desk and called her husband to give him the bad news that their upcoming vacation was not going to happen.

Countless times I've seen people in Samantha's shoes hit this wall. They focus so much on perfecting the process that they don't spend the time to understand what pain points the teams are experiencing and want solved. This process-first approach leaves a large gap between what the stakeholders find valuable and what delivery leaders focus on. Samantha hit resistance because of this gap.

Here's what she didn't know that would have saved her a lot of time and frustration: the more time you spend *selling the value* instead of *showing the value* of the solutions you provide, the more resistance you will hit. No one wants to be sold to—and if you're doing it right, you won't need to sell to them at all.

You must create a pull for your solutions, not a push. To create that pull, you must understand what your stakeholders value. They don't want templates, they want results. You must shift your focus to the results.

When this resistance is mounting, people will find someone to blame. Samantha's stakeholders saw her as the enemy and instead of giving her a chance, they attacked her so they wouldn't have to make any changes. If she wasn't credible, they could ignore her, so

You must create a pull for your solutions, not a push.

they made her the problem when she truly wanted to help but didn't know how.

Many experts suggest that resistance to change is normal and to be expected, and they offer a host of tactics to overcome that resistance including becoming a salesperson to convince everyone you're right and they just need to listen to you. Do not buy into such backward notions. When change management is done effectively, you will not hit resistance. You will learn how to avoid it in Stage Two: Assess the Organization.

Trapped in the Triangle

A few weeks later, Alex had good news: the IT department had agreed to use Samantha's methodology. But he warned that his reputation was on the line, so she had to make it work.

Samantha dove in, protecting the triple constraint triangle of "on time, on scope, and on budget" to make sure there were no changes along the way. She felt a rush of confidence—finally things seemed to be falling into place.

Six months later, another meeting with Alex. Before she could share her progress, he gave her bad news: executives weren't happy. Critical projects missed key features and business goals were not being met. They blamed the PMO for not achieving desired outcomes. It was starting to feel like everyone had an ulterior motive.

Samantha was confused. She'd hit the metrics she was using to define success—on time and on budget—which of course meant she had to say no to those scope changes. Alex explained that despite her efforts, they'd missed market opportunities and lost customers waiting on critical features. Now the Chief Technology Officer (CTO) had all the ammunition he needed to take over project delivery and blamed the PMO for the failures. She was sure now that the CTO had been setting her up to fail right from the start.

Samantha was crushed. It seemed like no matter what she did, she wasn't successful. That night, feeling disheartened, she sat down and worked on her résumé. She had given her all, but it seemed that nothing she did could satisfy the expectations of the organization's business leaders.

Samantha learned the hard way that delivering projects according to the triple constraint is not enough. Hitting timelines and budgets doesn't guarantee business value. Executives care most about outcomes aligned to growth and goals. Delivery teams must understand and work toward the business outcomes executives want.

Samantha's scenario is, unfortunately, all too common. Delivery leaders often work tirelessly to complete projects on time and on budget, and are shocked to learn that despite making progress on those metrics, business leaders remain unsatisfied.

The reason for this disconnect is that many executives, without realizing it, complain about missed timelines and budgets which masks their larger frustrations. While those quantitative measures can be useful, the core problem often lies elsewhere—in missed market opportunities, dissatisfied customers, or products lacking key features that were not identified in the original scope.

Your organization's business leaders care more about outcomes that align with strategic goals and deliver real value that goes beyond the triple constraint to focus on the business results.

The Real Delivery Gaps

We know that what gets measured gets done. However, the metrics organizations use to evaluate their delivery teams often fail to reflect the true business goals those teams should be working toward.

For example, project managers are hired for their certifications, sending the message to those project managers that their value is tied to the credentials they've earned. So they double down on applying as much of what they learned in their training as possible to every project, thinking more is better. Project managers become perfectionists of process instead of drivers of business value.

Delivery teams are not often taught to measure the business value of the projects they deliver, so they measure what they *are* taught to measure: progress. They tie the success of a project to the triple constraint triangle instead of to how those projects are moving the needle for the strategy. Remember what Alex told Samantha? Even though the projects were on time and budget, they missed critical features to achieve the necessary business value.

Many organizations use a technique called Earned Value Management (EVM), which is a misnomer because it measures progress against original planning estimates, not value. EVM tracks how much money is spent to produce project deliverables over time, relative to how much time and money planners thought it would take to produce those deliverables. EVM assumes that if deliverables are completed according to the original plan and schedule, it signifies valuable progress being made. However, EVM does not actually measure whether meaningful business value was created for all of that effort. It was never designed to assess if the project outputs generated the ROI, improved services, or produced other benefits the organization truly cares about. EVM simply tracks how closely spend and activity is occurring as planned. Yet many delivery teams erroneously consider EVM and other progress metrics as the definitive indicators of project success, and the gap between execution and business value grows wider.

Business value includes the tangible and intangible benefits an organization seeks—growth, profitability, market share, operational efficiency, customer satisfaction, effect on society, and so on. It goes beyond project outputs to focus on outcomes that align to organizational goals. Don't become a perfectionist of process. Instead, become a driver of business value.

If you talk to the executives who are ultimately responsible for achieving business results, you will find they don't understand why delivery teams aren't always thinking about the business results or how to measure them. Consequently, the executives often get frustrated and try to speak the language of the project managers, when they should be educating the project managers on more meaningful metrics that would elevate everyone's understanding of how the true project value is aligned with results. Important questions about the projects achieving their desired outcomes are replaced with questions about time and budget, and no one knows if they are any closer to achieving their business goals. Further, some executives don't even know that there are better questions to ask in the first place, or that "on time" and "on budget" are indicators of how well a project is meeting time and cost expectations, but they won't necessarily be indicators of successful business outcomes. It's like a sports coach getting frustrated with players for not winning games when all the coach emphasizes is proper technique and conditioning drills rather than strategy, teamwork, and scoring goals.

Making things even worse, many projects are set up for failure because the executives have not clearly defined success. Delivery teams are told to "get it done" but without a clear picture of the desired outcomes. In their desire to "just get going," the team starts a flurry of disorganized activity while desperately trying to understand how to be successful. Without a clear picture of success, or a strategy well defined and communicated, project managers fall back on their training and define their own success by that triple constraint.

This widens the gap between strategy and execution, frustrating everyone involved.

The delivery teams are trying to stick to the schedule they developed, even as key resources are pulled in too many directions and the scope is unclear. To add to this chaos, many business leaders don't sufficiently define the project's scope and goals at the start. It's only when the work is well under way, when they are finally giving this work their attention, that they realize the direction won't meet their business needs. So they change requirements midstream, forcing delivery teams to rewrite plans while also trying to stick to the original schedule, even though staff and hours are limited.

This creates a push and pull between the executives who define the strategy and the teams that are responsible for delivery. The delivery leaders resist project changes fiercely to protect the timeline and budget. But what these leaders don't realize is that they shouldn't be saying no because they don't actually own the project—the business does. And while the Agile movement embraces such

Don't become a perfectionist of process. Instead, become a driver of business value.

scope changes, many Agilists also fail to ask the right questions about business outcomes, often resulting in excessive iteration caused by a similar lack of clarity about whether their actions are harming the desired business outcomes more than helping.

Whether time is wasted debating late changes or iterating on them, the result is often the same: projects are pushed so far out that they start to lose their real value or ability to achieve a meaningful return on investment.

In other cases, projects get delivered on the original timeline, with a loosely defined scope, and within the original budget, but the desired business outcomes that should result from the project do not materialize. The delivery team members are busy patting themselves on the back for "on time, on budget" delivery by restricting scope change, while the executives, having failed to meet their business goals, are trying to save their jobs.

Executives don't always realize the role they play in their own demise. And delivery teams don't understand why they are seen as blockers of progress and not offered a seat at the table to help the organization achieve its business goals. Each side feels unheard and misunderstood by their counterparts and frustrated that it's so hard to achieve success.

You might be thinking, "Yeah, but I don't own the projects once they are over. It's up to operations to make sure they deliver value." By the time things are handed off to operations, though, it's too late. Rather than wait until after the project is complete to determine it was off track from the start, your team must set the strategy up for success before projects begin. In fact, you're the only team that can do it, because when projects are completed, project managers are off to the next project before you can blink. You and your team are usually the only people in the organization with a cross-project perspective.

Some believe Agile environments address this, with product teams retaining accountability. However, while product owners carry responsibility for delivering value, they may lack the necessary project management skills to deliver the underlying projects in a way that achieves the required business results. Moreover, dedicating teams long-term is a luxury most organizations can't afford, given the pressing need to kick off new initiatives. When you align stakeholders from the start of the strategy lifecycle, your organization is set up for the greatest chance of success in achieving its business goals. And even here, while Agile does address this alignment imperative at the project and product level, when you look across the portfolio, you may find that overall project throughput is slower than it needs to be for the organization to achieve all of its strategic goals.

When you can get this alignment right at the project, product, and portfolio level, you become the Strategy Navigator, earning you a seat at the table to steer the whole strategy from start to finish.

Start at the Start

Most guidance on how to "close the strategy-to-execution gap" focuses primarily on fixing project execution. But that's too late. To drive real IMPACT, you must get involved earlier in the strategy lifecycle.

Your role is to set up success from the start by aligning people, processes, and metrics to business goals. This enables maximum return on investment—the top priority for executives.

Most execution training doesn't teach leaders to build services that support the entire strategy lifecycle or that strategic ROI is your goal. Let's change that paradigm now.

A successful strategy consists of three components.

1 **Definition:** Defining the strategy and the desired strategic outcomes.

2 **Execution:** Executing on that strategy while maintaining focus on the outcomes.

3 **Realization:** Ensuring that the strategic outcomes are realized.

THE STRATEGY LIFECYCLE

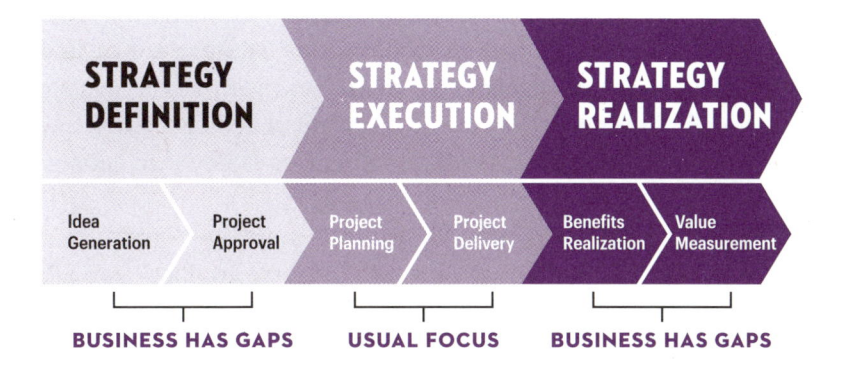

STRATEGY DEFINITION	STRATEGY EXECUTION	STRATEGY REALIZATION
Idea Generation / Project Approval	Project Planning / Project Delivery	Benefits Realization / Value Measurement
BUSINESS HAS GAPS	USUAL FOCUS	BUSINESS HAS GAPS

These are the phases I spell out in the Strategy Lifecycle Worksheet in the downloadable action-taking resources. Regardless of the methodology used, every strategy follows these three phases. To achieve the objectives of the strategy, you generate ideas and approve projects, plan and deliver those projects, then measure that completed projects achieve the intended business results.

The problem, as we've seen, comes when the strategy isn't achieving those intended business results. From the point of view of the executives, the strategy is sound, but it's not getting the expected results, so they assume the fault lies in the execution phase. As a result, delivery leaders are often told that "project management is broken," so they focus on training staff, creating processes and templates, and implementing tools to "fix" that broken project management. However, when this is done, most organizations are disappointed to see that nothing really improves in a measurable or sustainable way. The reason is that this focus on the execution process alone doesn't address the most important parts of the strategy lifecycle: setting the strategy up for success and making sure the value intended for that strategy is achieved.

Let me explain what's really happening. Things might start off well, or at least that's how it seems. The strategy is defined, turned over to the delivery teams to execute, and everyone is off to the races. However, when all projects derived from the strategy are treated with equal priority, resources get divided across every project equally, resulting in projects either crawling forward or stalling completely. Project managers are constantly fighting for resources to get anything done.

Many organizations attempt to implement an Agile framework like Scrum, thinking it will solve resource conflicts through practices like daily stand-ups, sprint planning, and retrospectives. However, while these techniques can help allocate resources at the team level, initiative-level Agile approaches do not fully address the deeper strategic issues of shared resource allocation across initiatives to accelerate the entire portfolio. As a result, delivery managers start begging business leaders for more resources, but because nothing is moving, the executives are reluctant to add more money and resources to solve the problem because they aren't convinced the resources are "fully utilized." This causes what appears to be a resource management problem when the delivery team is simply trying to do too many simultaneous projects for the resources they have.

You don't have a resource management problem—you have a shoving 10 pounds of projects into a 5-pound bag problem. And even when resource managers think it's only 5 pounds of projects, they're trying to maximize utilization of those resources (inputs) instead of trying to maximize the value delivery cadence (outcomes). What you need to do is shift your focus from begging for resources for a pile of stalled projects to making sure projects are prioritized by their value to the organization and started only when you have the resources to do them in a way that maximizes the cadence of value delivery. If you did nothing else but make this shift, you would be on your way to improving your organization's ability to deliver on the strategy. And we're not even through Chapter 1. But even this shift isn't enough to leap the chasm between how business leaders define strategy and how delivery teams execute that strategy. There are more gaps to consider.

Set Up Strategy Delivery for Success

Now, let's look at it from the role of the delivery organization you have been asked to set up.

Even if projects are prioritized initially, you still may find that executives are pressuring their staff to start all the projects at once because "we have the funding now" instead of staggering the work in a way that drives the fastest throughput across the portfolio. Such fractional resource assignments prevent the delivery teams from focusing on their most important work because they are constantly responding to the squeakiest wheel and trying to show progress on all the projects under way, all while responding to their own manager who keeps redirecting them to other work.

Executives are widening this gap between strategy and execution even further by failing to take the necessary time to ensure the delivery teams truly understand the company's strategy. According to *Harvard Business Review*, 95 percent of the typical workforce does not understand their company's strategy.

In other words, it's likely that many people doing execution work in your organization don't know why they're doing what they're doing. If that's the case, how is the workforce supposed to deliver the strategy in a way that ensures the goals of that strategy are met?

Just as a road trip is unlikely to arrive at its desired destination as planned if the driver does not have access to the map directing their journey, an organization's strategic goals are at risk if the workforce is driving in the dark with no understanding why their day-to-day work matters to reaching those objectives.

With slow progress, executives look around and instead of asking, "What got done today?" they find themselves asking, "What *didn't* happen today?" That's when frustrated executives double down on pressuring delivery leaders to "fix project management," and because they aren't sure what else to do, the delivery leaders add *more* templates, *more* tools, and *more* processes, slowing things down even further, just like Samantha did.

Unfortunately, everything is still a number one priority, the strategy is still unclear to the people responsible for delivering that strategy, resources are still overallocated, managers still keep redirecting staff, and projects still don't meet goals. The projects cost more than the benefits they were designed to achieve, and nobody's measuring value anyway, so who knows if the projects were worth doing in the first place? All of that means that results not only don't improve, but often, get even worse. The vicious circle continues. No one learns any lessons in the process, and frustrations grow.

Even when the resources are not overallocated, the fact that they are fractionally assigned means everything they're fractionally assigned to will be far slower. Some resource managers will pat themselves on the back when everyone is at 90 to 100 percent utilization and think that everything is optimal because no one is overallocated. However, the resources are task-switching so much that they aren't getting much of anything done quickly or with quality. That task-switching can cost the organization up to 40 percent loss in productivity according to the American Psychological Association.

The reason this is happening is that most leaders focus on fixing execution instead of setting their strategy up for success right from the start. In 61 percent of organizations, there's a failure to bridge the gap between strategy formulation and its day-to-day implementation. They can't close the strategy-to-execution gap because there's more than one gap. It's as if leaders are trying to build a house without a solid foundation.

This is where you come in.

To break this vicious circle, you must broaden your focus beyond project execution. Don't get stuck like Samantha trying to "fix project management," rearranging furniture when the floor is about to fall into the basement, by focusing all of your efforts on strategy execution. Instead, optimize the entire strategy lifecycle—from strategy definition to execution to realization of business value.

Shift left on the strategy lifecycle to strategy definition, instead of starting in strategy execution, to front-load success by aligning initiatives to strategy before projects start. Bridge communication gaps between stakeholders throughout the process. Maintain line-of-sight from tasks to overarching objectives.

By linking execution to business value and enabling strong hand-offs between genuinely focused teams, you can drive strategic IMPACT. This big-picture perspective is key to improving project outcomes and achieving organizational goals.

You might be thinking, "This is great, but you're adding more work to my already full plate!" This isn't about more reactive work, though—it's about starting at the start to prevent problems proactively.

When you support the full strategy lifecycle, you'll get the seat at the table and the respect that you deserve. Your organization will see your true worth.

You were put in this role because executives aren't getting the desired results. They blame execution, but you know now that this is usually a downstream effect of upstream issues such as poor prioritization, fractional resource assignments that dilute execution focus, and a misplaced emphasis on resource utilization over the value delivery cadence.

Your job is setting up the strategy for success from the start across three phases: definition, execution, and realization. Do this right, and execution challenges become fewer and more manageable and business outcomes improve. When you front-load success, the strategy delivery flows smoothly. Your work will become easier, your value greater, and your results undeniable. No more selling—your contributions will speak volumes. This is the power of the IMPACT Engine System—simplifying strategy delivery and accelerating results. With the right framework, your potential is limitless.

Now I'll show you the key to limitless thinking.

How Might We?

We have a rule in my house. We don't use the word "can't." It's a limiting word that has no place in a limitless world. This mindset shift applies to our personal lives and professional lives, and it will make a difference in your ability to apply what you learn in this book. Limiting beliefs are normal, but you need to learn how to identify them and address them proactively.

In the IMPACT Accelerator Mastermind, my group coaching and leadership development program for delivery leaders just like you, we regularly identify and knock down the "Yeah, but..." monster. That's the monster that climbs up onto your shoulder and tells you that you can't do something. That monster will give you a million reasons why you should stay right where you are, doing exactly what you're doing, and that it's too hard or it's not worth it to change.

You know what I'm talking about, and it's perfectly OK that you have one of those monsters. We all do. It kept our ancestors safe from lions and tigers and bears. But it has no place in your corporate world.

If you ever get stuck, instead of thinking about how impossible something may feel, just ask, "How might we?" I learned the power of this question from my dear friend and colleague Mike Hannan during his tenure as CEO of our nonprofit, Project Management for Change. He taught our team of dedicated volunteers to ask this question when they were brainstorming ways to creatively evolve the way we delivered our signature event, the Project Management Day of Service (PMDoS®). I immediately saw the power in asking the question in precisely this way instead of a variation like "How can we?" or "How should we?"

I'll say it again: "How might we...?" Each of these three words has an important purpose.

- **How (solution):** Shifts to a solution-oriented mindset.
- **Might (possibilities):** Broadens thinking to what's possible.
- **We (collaboration):** Builds a sense of shared mission.

If you ever get stuck, just ask, "How might we?"

If you find yourself thinking that something I suggest in this book won't work for you, keep in mind that what I'm teaching you has worked for thousands of your peers in organizations across all industries and all around the world. You just need to ask, *"How might we make this happen?"*

This is also a great place to collaborate with your peers, team members, executives, and others to ask the question together—it is "we," after all, not just "me," so invite your colleagues into the possibilities conversation.

You are exactly where you need to be, and you are the exact right person to end the vicious circle. The IMPACT Engine System will help you do it. But first we need to make more of the foundational mindset shifts that IES is built upon. When you make these mental shifts, you'll see friction reduce and resistance disappear, and you will be seen as far more valuable to your organization. You will experience the power of elevating how you think before you elevate what you do.

You are going to become an IMPACT Driver.

MAKE AN IMPACT

Think: How are you thinking differently about playing a bigger game to support the full strategy lifecycle?

Do: Download your Strategy Lifecycle Worksheet (from IMPACTEngineBook.com) to brainstorm opportunities to set strategy delivery up for greater success.

You Are an IMPACT Driver

SAMANTHA ALMOST knocked me over as she rushed up after my keynote. I saw her shining bright smile among all the nodding heads in the crowd. The second I finished, that human light bulb zipped over in a blur. Thank goodness for my balanced stance, as killer stilettos and an enthusiastic audience member can be a precarious combo for a hugger!

"I get it now! I know why everything I've tried hasn't worked! Why didn't I see this before? My job is on the line, and I have been so frustrated and overwhelmed not knowing what to do. I finally see why I've hit a wall. But how do I fix it? Please help!" Samantha pleaded. "Oh, by the way," she added, finally releasing me from the hug, "I'm Samantha and I'm really excited to meet you!"

After listening to Samantha share her story, I gave her some of the same advice I'll share in this book. Then I smiled and said, "I'm going to ask you to stop thinking of yourself as a project leader and start thinking of yourself as an IMPACT Driver. You may not understand exactly what that means yet, but trust yourself, trust the process, and know that you've got this." That advice changed everything about how she saw her role—and it can for you too.

One month after Samantha made this critical mindset shift, she shared in our IMPACT Accelerator Mastermind group: "I'm already having completely different conversations with my stakeholders. I have full support from the executive team to proceed with this new approach to creating services that are aligned to their pain points. I even got approval to hire *three* team members to start delivering on the services to address the root causes we identified!" Yes, that's right: she went from begging for help to getting the full support of her leaders in a month. A month after that, she was leading the governance board meetings with her executives to deliver on the organization's strategy. She now had her seat at the table, and she wasn't even through her first cycle of the IMPACT Engine System.

Samantha's story is one of many that shows the value of getting your priorities straight. Let me tell you about Aaron and Chase, two highly accomplished former Big Four consultants, who recognized their potential and wanted to play a bigger game in their careers, but needed a clear road map to reach their goals. They may have been skilled consultants, but even experts need a road map!

The executives at their firm, a fast-growing disruptor in the financial industry, understood the importance of staying ahead and sought ways to elevate their game to continue thriving in the competitive market. As they built out their enterprise project management office (EPMO), Aaron and Chase quickly realized that many of the executives were looking for the EPMO to be a "spy" designed to control information in the departments, but they believed there had to be a better way to enable people to do their best work without the EPMO hovering over their shoulder. What if they could create a team that helped organize the chaos while accelerating the results? They needed help navigating the complex chessboard of a large executive team with conflicting priorities and different ideas of success. After they walked me through their concerns and aspirations for this EPMO, I introduced them to the IMPACT Engine System. They began to realize the power of supporting the entire strategy lifecycle so they could adapt to the dynamic changes happening within their organization. They thought, "Could we really become the navigators of the organization's strategy?"

As organizational changes unfolded, we assisted Aaron and Chase in positioning their team strategically, giving them the next chess move they needed to make as the functional and organizational changes seemed to swirl around them with business leaders who were all moving at a frenetic pace. As each chess piece was moved, I'd tell them what was about to happen next and why.

About 30 days later, Aaron started sharing the latest changes that his leaders had just announced and said to me, "You predicted what would happen with near pinpoint accuracy!" I just smiled and said, "Ah, OK, so now let's talk about what's next." As if it was not a surprise to me at all—because it wasn't. In disbelief, Chase looked at Aaron and said, "Is she clairvoyant? How in the world is she seeing around these corners?"

It was easy to predict the future when I knew what to look for, and the secret to their success was going to be learning how to anticipate the future needs of the executives. This would enable them to proactively prepare and present their strategies to the new company president—the necessary chess moves to position them as the go-to team to drive organizational change.

In only a few short months, Aaron and Chase earned their rightful place at the right hand of the company president overseeing the delivery of the organization's reinvention to stay competitive in the marketplace. Their influence and IMPACT continue to grow, and they are only scratching the surface of their potential.

When I asked their permission to use their story in the book, they said it should come with a disclaimer reading "Results are not typical." I laughed and agreed at first. But then I thought of other students who had companies fighting to hire them. Some got promotions faster than expected. Some moved on to bigger roles. All of them saw their careers take off. It dawned on me that these results *are* typical for people who use the IMPACT Engine System. If they can do it, you can too.

What you need first is perspective: to help accomplish your professional goals while positioning your team to support the entire strategy lifecycle, you're going to shift your mindset about your role.

The IMPACT Driver Mindset

Whether it was the more significant transformation Samantha experienced or the subtle but well-timed strategic moves that allowed Aaron and Chase to earn their seats at the table, a shift had to happen for them to step into the full potential of their new leadership roles.

You, too, need to make a shift to go on this journey. Your role is about more than just checking boxes, creating templates, ensuring compliance, and perfecting processes. Your role is about driving more IMPACT for the organization. Until you make that change in perspective, you will see the same friction and challenges that Samantha initially experienced, and yes, some of the naysayers may even make it about not liking *you* to make it easier to reject what they believe you represent.

To implement the IMPACT Engine System, you need an IMPACT Driver Mindset.

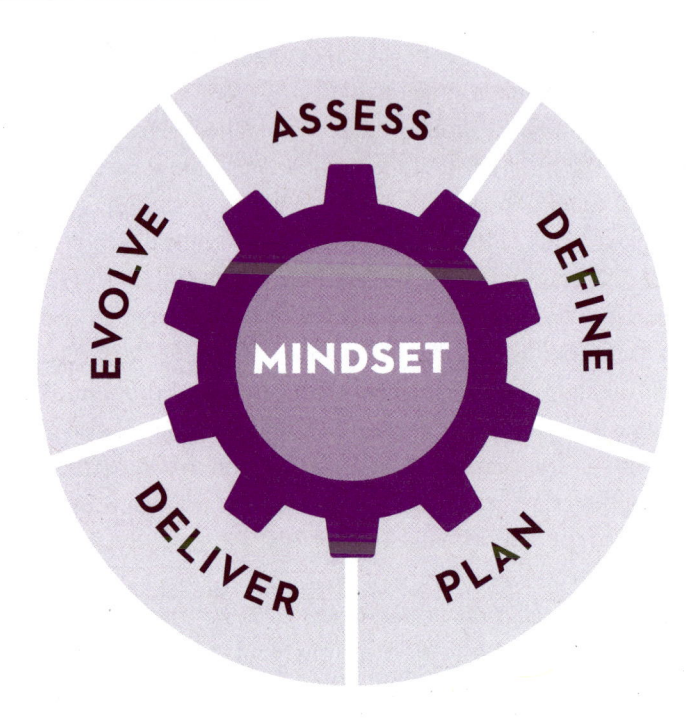

As you work through this book, you will start to see things differently. It might be subtle at first, but by the time you finish the book, you'll see your role and the work you do in an entirely new way. Over time this change will be so strong that it will permeate what you say and do and how you lead others on this journey of delivering your organization's strategy.

What you are experiencing is what we refer to as the IMPACT Driver Mindset. You'll see these mindset shifts woven throughout the content in each chapter to support your evolution in your role as a leader and change driver. The initials of these mindset shifts spell the word "IMPACT," and they make up the central gear that makes the IMPACT Engine turn. Everything you do from this point forward hinges on you maintaining this mindset.

Here is what that looks like—and for each point, don't just nod and smile and read on; stop and ask yourself how *you* will do it.

I: Instill Focus

You will solve strategic business problems, not just tactical project problems. This requires deeply understanding your organization's vision and rallying people behind goals that focus their efforts like a laser on driving targeted business outcomes.

M: Measure Outcomes

You will expand your definition of project success to go well beyond simply tracking project progress using the triple constraint (time, scope, cost) and Earned Value Management. You will develop metrics and mechanisms for ensuring you are achieving not just the inputs and outputs for each project, but the intended outcomes. It will be clear that you are not only making progress but also achieving business results.

P: Perform Relentlessly

You will know that there is more to delivering projects than implementation methodology. You will focus on streamlining and optimizing strategy delivery across the project portfolio while ensuring you do not fall victim to methodology wars or to applying every tool in the toolbox to every project to the detriment of achieving successful project outcomes.

A: Adapt to Thrive

You will bring people with you through the change process so that you can accelerate business results together while creating a nimble and flexible environment for all strategy delivery work to be achieved.

C: Communicate with Purpose

You will facilitate effective and transparent communication, removing overhead and administration for information sharing and collaboration so that stakeholders have the information they need, when they need it, to make decisions that are educated and informed.

T: Transform Mindset

You will elevate the way you think about your role to become the strategic business partner your executives need by their side instead of waiting for your stakeholders to "get" the importance of the work you do. This will secure your seat as the Strategy Navigator guiding your organization on the journey of transformation.

You Are a Navigator

It's important to understand that being an IMPACT Driver does not mean you're in charge of everything. It does not mean you're making all the decisions. It does not mean you're creating a controlling organization where everyone needs to do what you tell them.

Although it would be awesome if more people would just do what they're told because we know better (or do we?), that isn't how people work. And you need to know how people work and dial in to their intrinsic motivation so that they want to do this work with you. That comes a lot easier when you let *them* get in the driver's seat.

Throughout this process, you're going to learn how to bring people with you through change, and an important part of that is learning to let someone else be in the driver's seat while you navigate. Let your stakeholders be a part of the process, come to their own conclusions, make the decisions, and help you get to better business outcomes. This goes a long way to helping you build engagement and support from those stakeholders. You want them invested in the process and in getting to the outcomes *with* you. You can be the navigator, but you need to let them do some of the driving.

A navigator is a facilitator. Have you ever watched a professional facilitator at work? The good ones do a combination of guiding the conversation, gently influencing the outcomes, and helping people come to their own conclusions on the best path forward. Facilitators don't control much. They guide participants in the direction they know they need to go. You, too, will be a guide. And by guiding, you will get there a lot faster than by pushing.

I learned this lesson very early in my career. I was a young and hard-charging professional and, because I think in Gantt charts, I could see how the plan needed to play out. I was still doing technical work when Andy, a manager in our department, pulled me aside. He said, "We can't keep up with you!"

"What do you mean?" I said, confused and a little impatient.

"Imagine the alphabet. When we're trying to figure out how to solve a problem, you need to take us one letter at a time. We're still up at C and you're all the way down at Q and we don't know how you got there," he explained. "I mean, you're right," he added with a smirk, "but if you want us to come with you, you have to lead us there step by step."

You must take them one letter at a time. By playing the role of facilitator, you're still driving the change, but you're doing it from a place that invites your stakeholders on the journey with you. Help them draw conclusions instead of giving them all the answers. Encourage and validate when their input is in alignment with your plan to help the organization deliver value faster. This will help them become more invested in the process, and you in leading them through it. Plus, they likely have some helpful ideas!

Everyone can become an IMPACT Driver.

Sometimes, to be an IMPACT Driver you need to be in the passenger seat with your road map in hand.

Notice how you feel right now. Are you seeing places where you can elevate how you think about your role and drive even more business value? If you can't see them yet, don't worry. Much of what you are going to learn and apply throughout this process is different from what you may have learned or come to believe.

The IMPACT Driver Mindset provides the mental framework to position you to navigate strategy for your organization. Next, the IMPACT Engine System will give you the road map to build the business capability that can make that strategy happen. It outlines what to do, in what order, why it matters, and how to assemble the team and systems that will drive strategy delivery in a way that positions the organization to achieve the highest return on investment as quickly as possible.

Everyone can become an IMPACT Driver. Organizations can thrive. We can change the world through the IMPACT we deliver.

All you need to do is trust yourself, trust the process, and apply what you learn to make an IMPACT. You've got this!

MAKE AN IMPACT

Think: What limiting mindsets will you need to replace to shift to the role of IMPACT Driver?

Do: Download your IMPACT Driver Mindset Worksheet to evaluate the mindset shifts you will make on this journey.

The IMPACT Engine System

IN 2014, I met Joel, a company CEO who wanted to build project management capability to help his team deliver on the organization's strategy. One part of helping him achieve this goal was to set up a project management office. Joel had chosen Andrea E., a junior team member, to do the job. Andrea didn't have a project management background, but what she lacked in experience, she made up for in openness to learning and excitement for the opportunity. That's all I needed to know. We trained the whole organization on project management fundamentals, and my company guided Andrea on a journey of creating a sustainable PMO that would help the organization achieve substantial value for their members and community.

Years later, Joel called me. He had joined a new organization as CEO, and he asked my company to support his transformation journey by applying the IMPACT Engine System once again. As he introduced us to his leadership team, Joel reflected on the journey of working with our team at his last organization. He said, "We had no business accomplishing all that we did as an organization of our size."

Joel introduced me to his leadership team and a select group of staff that he wanted to take through a yearlong project management competency development program while they delivered the organization's most important strategic initiatives. He asked us to be on the lookout for a shining star in the group who could lead what would ultimately become their strategy delivery office. As we spent time with this team, there was one person who stood out as always finding ways to share his perspective with his peers on how what they were learning would help the organization elevate their ability to define and deliver strategy.

Mike W. was in a more senior leadership role than Andrea had been when I worked with Joel the first time, but like her, Mike did not have any formal project management training or experience. What we saw in the training and coaching process made it clear that Mike was the perfect fit to lead the strategy delivery office. Throughout our time together, he applied several cycles of the IMPACT Engine System and secured his seat at the table as an integral part of how the organization delivers strategy. After a year in the role, Mike was featured in a leading industry magazine about this new role called the Strategy Delivery Office Leader. We couldn't be more proud of him and the entire organization's progress and IMPACT.

That name for a delivery organization might be new to you, but we've found that when we ask our client executives, like we did with Joel and his leadership team, to name the organization in a way that represents what they want it to do, they usually don't say project management office. That's only the middle piece of the full strategy lifecycle. They want the whole strategy delivered successfully. When you present your IMPACT Delivery Proposal in Stage Four, consider a conversation with your executives about the right name for this delivery function and let them be in the driver's seat on naming it.

Even though it was their first time doing this kind of work, Andrea and Mike demonstrated that success comes to those willing to put in the effort. You do not need to have project management experience to do this job well. You do not even need to be senior in your organization to do it well. You just need a desire to learn and a willingness to trust the process. And then follow that process not just once, but again and again.

The process is the IMPACT Engine System. To put it in business terms, IES is an iterative value delivery framework designed to continuously elevate your team's capabilities and services to accelerate the IMPACT of your organization's strategy.

IES will help you build a new delivery organization, whether you call it a PMO, transformation group, strategy delivery team, or any of the other derivatives of "the team that delivers on the organization's goals." You can also use IES to elevate an existing delivery capability if the executives' desired business outcomes are not being achieved. And yes, you can even use IES to rescue a team that may end up in the next round of layoffs or being disbanded in the next company reorganization if something doesn't change fast.

As you apply what you learn in each of the IES stages, you will create a much stronger alignment between the people defining the strategy and those delivering it. Executives will understand how to set up the strategy (and you) for success right from the start, and you will be armed with a new mindset and a step-by-step framework that enables easier and faster value delivery.

The IMPACT Delivery Cycle

The IMPACT Engine System is designed to be an iterative approach. Key to that approach is the IMPACT Delivery Cycle. Let's start with an overview; then I'll unravel this cycle in more detail in the chapters that follow.

1 In the first iteration of the IMPACT Delivery Cycle, you will go through each stage—starting with Assess, followed by Define, Plan, Deliver, and Evolve—over about a 90-day period, or roughly one quarter of the year. Why 90 days? Because you need to show results quickly, and quarterly cycles likely align well with how your leaders already operate. I will guide you on how much time to allocate to each of these stages later on in this chapter. Can you do it faster than 90 days? Absolutely. This timeline

assumes you will not be able to dedicate 100 percent of your focus to this work. The more you can focus and apply what I am teaching you, the faster you can go. But don't skip steps or you will end up back at the beginning wondering why your stakeholders don't support you.

2. Once you have gone through the cycle to complete the Deliver stage for the first time, you will have created a minimum viable product (MVP): an initial solution that begins to address the root cause of one or more of the business challenges or opportunities identified by the business leaders and other stakeholders. That MVP is the starting point of what you can accomplish and a way to whet your stakeholders' appetite by showing them what's possible.

3. In the Evolve stage, you will collect initial feedback from your stakeholders who are using that first solution you put in place. Their feedback will influence what you do during the next cycle so you can keep iterating your way to IMPACT.

4. At the beginning of the next quarter, you'll start your next IMPACT Delivery Cycle at the Assess stage, incorporating feedback from the last Evolve stage, and continue your journey through ongoing cycles of value delivery over the coming quarters. Essentially you take what you learn in each IMPACT Delivery Cycle and feed that into your IMPACT Delivery Road Map to influence what you do in the next cycle.

Yes, it's an agile approach to delivering value. But it's not a "big *A*" Agile PMO (or transformation group or whatever your company calls it). Why? Because no team designed to elevate delivery of the organization's strategy should be named by a specific implementation framework or methodology. Your organization is much more than Agile or Waterfall or even Water-scrum-fall. It is more than templates, tools, and frameworks, more than a single approach to implementing projects. You are creating an engine designed to guide your organization in the delivery of its strategy. It's about driving that strategy to make a bigger IMPACT. The team you are building now will become the IMPACT Engine for your organization, pointed squarely in the direction of the organization's vision.

Now, let's take a brief look at each stage of the IMPACT Delivery Cycle so you can see how you'll get there.

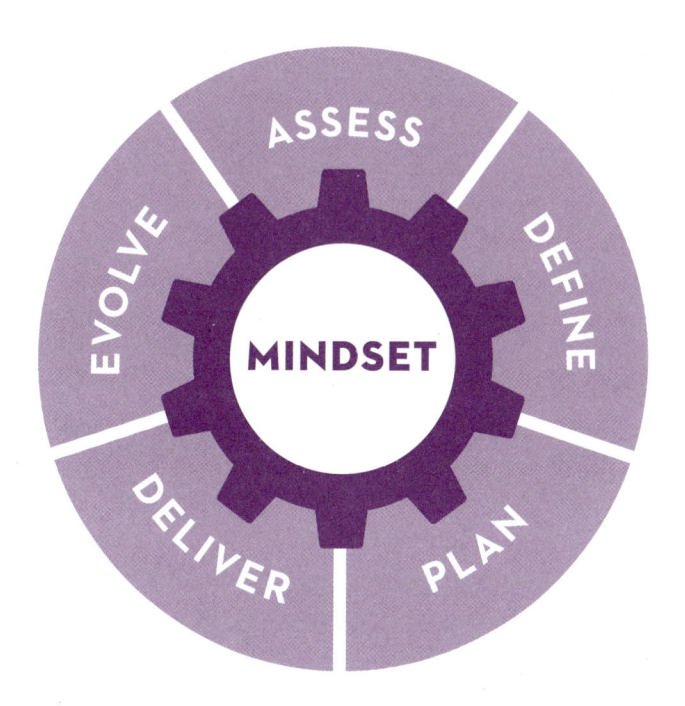

Stage One: Mindset

The mindset work that you have already started here in Stage One will stay with you throughout the entire program. That's why it's anchored in the middle of the graphic. It is the gear that turns the cycles of the program. The mindset shifts you make and the techniques you apply to align your thinking with the outcomes you need to drive for the organization are woven throughout each of the following stages.

Stage Two: Assess

As you meet with stakeholders and encourage them to express their challenges and opportunities for improvement, you develop trusted relationships and unlock their highest priorities with ease, simply by asking good questions, giving them space to talk, and listening to them explain their pain points. This begins to build a foundation of trust. Then, when you deliver the services your stakeholders begged for, these relationships will form the basis of your coalition of support to prevent change resistance.

Stage Three: Define

You build credibility fast by identifying the root causes of the pain points identified in the Assess stage. Then you define the solutions that will be delivered to address the challenges and opportunities your organization has across the entire strategy lifecycle to achieve bigger business results with a higher return on investment.

Stage Four: Plan

You create a clear and compelling business plan (*not* a charter) for the department you are creating that helps you elevate your team to the same level as other business-focused departments and shows how you are driving measurable business value for the organization. Then you lay out your IMPACT Delivery Model in alignment with the most pressing challenges that your stakeholders know they want fixed.

Stage Five: Deliver

You deliver the solution defined in Stage Three that strategically positions your team at the center of strategy delivery and secures your seat at the table to drive future organizational success. As you bring stakeholders with you through the change process, you prevent their resistance to change and address any new challenges that arise with an adaptive management approach.

Stage Six: Evolve

Once you have delivered the solution in Stage Five, you expand your focus to ensuring your delivery approach is nimble and adaptive so shifting business needs don't derail success. You use what you learned in the Deliver stage to evolve your IMPACT Delivery Model to respond to the needs of the organization. With a success under your belt, you begin the shift to becoming the organization's Strategy Navigator.

Going forward, I want you to think of the team and services you are building as an IMPACT Engine. An IMPACT Engine drives the highest possible return on investment for your organization's strategy. That is what your business leaders care about. That is something they can understand and get behind, and you'll never have to convince them to support you.

Once you've gone through one full cycle of the IMPACT Engine System, you will have created a minimum viable product: one solution that addresses one or more of the business challenges or pain points identified by the business leaders and other stakeholders. This is a crucial component of the IES process. You can't do everything all at once, no matter how much you want to. If you're going to build an IMPACT Engine, you must start by focusing on the MVP that provides recognizable value and can be delivered quickly.

The MVP Approach

"I can't figure out how everyone in here is making so much progress so quickly! What am I doing wrong?" Arjun said in a shaky voice during an IMPACT Accelerator Mastermind coaching session. "Everyone seems to be getting wins so early, even people who started later than me! I can't seem to get through the Define stage because there are so many things that need fixing."

"OK," I said, "let's look at what might be holding you back. Talk to me about where you are in the process."

Arjun hesitated for a moment and then continued, "Well, there are so many issues happening and there's pressure to get big results fast, so I have been working on putting several services in place to address these problems. But it's not working out as I expected. I feel overwhelmed, and they just keep adding more to my plate as new problems crop up."

I leaned forward and responded, "I see. Trying to do everything at once often leads to exactly how you're feeling—overwhelmed. And it actually slows down progress. By trying to build out all the services at once, you're spreading yourself thin. Nothing is going to get done, and your impatient business leaders are going to be even more upset while they continue to add to the chaos."

Arjun nodded. "That's so true. The CEO has me leading projects, which means I'm spending a lot of time working *in* my PMO, not just *on* my PMO" (something I'd taught the Mastermind group and that you will learn in Chapter 13). "With so many projects happening at once, I have limited time to make progress on building out the PMO. We have important delivery deadlines and that means I'm barely scraping by doing a little bit every night."

With a gentle tone, I said, "Right. I know your business leaders want to see value quickly, and they don't realize they are preventing you from making progress. But doing it all at once is not going to work. You don't have a lot of time to show value, so you need to pick the most important thing and do that, and only that, first." I smiled reassuringly. "Instead of overwhelming yourself with everything at once, you can break up your services into manageable pieces. They will be busy taking advantage of the first thing you delivered while you work on the next thing and then the next."

Arjun's face brightened. "But how do I focus on delivering one specific service when so many things are broken?"

"Go back to the beginning of Define," I said. "Take all those pain points from your stakeholders and conduct the Root Cause Analysis. You're playing whack-a-mole with symptoms instead of getting to the root cause. I bet you can fix one thing and make several of their pain points go away at once. It just has to be the right one thing—a real root cause, not a symptom of the chaos."

A new understanding washed over Arjun's face. "Ah. By fixing one issue they have now, I can earn their support and even add resources, so I don't have to do this all myself in the next cycle."

"Precisely!" I said, genuinely excited. "It's about taking incremental steps and consistently demonstrating the IMPACT of your efforts. You don't need to talk to every stakeholder or define every service before you move on, and you don't want to wait until you have everything planned out before you deliver your first piece of measurable business value. If you do that, you'll get shut down before you've had a positive IMPACT."

I could see knowing smiles from some of the students who had been in the program for a long time because they knew what I was going to say next. "The secret is putting one pot of water on the stove instead of trying to boil the entire ocean at once. One pot of water is manageable and it's easy to see when you've made progress."

The old-school approach of spending a year or more building the services needed to help your organization achieve its goals doesn't work. To gain credibility and trust with your business leaders, you must start showing that you understand the pain points that need to be addressed from the perspective of the business stakeholders, and then show tangible progress quickly.

To hit the ground running, it's tempting to do a quick scan of the project templates, tools, methods, and current portfolio of projects, and then start fixing what appears to be broken. This is a mistake. What you don't know and can't see is about to bite you hard. That approach fails to do the important engagement work to build strong partnerships with the stakeholders and misdirects you to put bandages on symptoms instead of discovering the root causes that are the reason for pain points. The MVP Approach changes all that.

When you start with a minimum viable product for the first cycle, you talk to key stakeholders and prioritize their pain points together, so you can address their most pressing pain points first. Then you conduct a Root Cause Analysis of the symptoms, to find out what vicious circles are perpetuating the problems they see. From there, you'll know what to focus on for your MVP.

When you start simply, stay focused, and begin with the MVP, you give your stakeholders a taste of what's possible and show them you are exactly the right person to take them where they want to go. By engaging them in this process and showing value quickly, you build credibility and gain critical support.

And how do you know where to go after the MVP? Like Arjun's, your organization probably has plenty of pain points that you can identify together as opportunities to improve. In your first cycle through, you will create an IMPACT Delivery Model that shows your stakeholders the services you'll deliver over the coming years, so you can roll right into the next cycle of value delivery.

Iterate Your Way to IMPACT

Arjun's struggle is not unique. Many leaders get stuck because they have set the bar so high that they can't reach it. They gather all the inputs they could possibly gather and make an endless list of everything they could possibly do. Of course, they feel completely overwhelmed because they have all this work to do. And then business leaders start asking questions like, "What have you done for me lately?" "When are we going to see results?" "We poured all this money and resources into you and your team, and nothing has improved."

You don't have time to waste with this struggle.

Instead, you are going to use an iterative implementation approach that is aligned with your organization's current business management flow. By creating quarterly cycles of value delivery, you address the impatience of your stakeholders and make it easy for them to see the value you are driving. There is more movement, and the small victories add up quickly into visible results.

As you can see in the downloadable IMPACT Engine Planner, I recommend the following breakdown for your first IMPACT Delivery Cycle. The time estimates are designed to prevent you from getting stuck or trying to solve everything at once.

Mindset (1 Week)

Congratulations! You are almost through Stage One. You understand the ways that you can drive value across the full strategy lifecycle, and you understand the IMPACT Driver Mindset shifts you'll make as you apply the IMPACT Engine System in your organization. Even if it took you weeks to get to this point, you're here now and you can follow this plan to get you the rest of the way through an IES cycle.

Assess (2 Weeks)

Give yourself two weeks to conduct your initial conversations and collect the business challenges and opportunities. Start with executives first because they are ultimately accountable for the business results and are the decision-makers who, if they feel ignored, can yank your leadership opportunity away. You don't need to talk to everyone in these two weeks. Use this time for a concentrated focus on interviews and engagement, then continue to have conversations with stakeholders as a normal part of your ongoing relationship-building process. At the end of this stage, you will bring these leaders together to share your findings and engage them in determining what challenge or opportunity to address first.

Define (3 Weeks)

Allow yourself three weeks in the Define stage the first time through to conduct your Root Cause Analysis and then identify solutions to address the root causes of the challenges and opportunities your stakeholders shared with you. At this point, you're only deciding what services will address the root causes and for whom, not building them yet. You will know from the Assess stage which one your executives prioritized first. That list of solutions to the root causes is the beginning of your IMPACT Delivery Model.

Plan (2 Weeks)

Allow yourself two weeks to update your initial IMPACT Delivery Model to show when and how you will address the desires of your business leaders, the outcomes your solutions will drive, and the IMPACT this will have on the organization. You will create an IMPACT Delivery Road Map to specify in which upcoming quarterly cycle you expect each of the challenges and opportunities to be addressed with the solutions you've defined, giving your leaders another opportunity to prioritize the delivery of these capability improvements before you deliver your first solution.

Deliver (4 Weeks)

Give yourself four weeks to build and deliver your MVP while you bring your stakeholders with you through the change process. The first part of this time will be spent creating the resources, process, and structure for the service; the rest will be piloting that service with your first stakeholder group. You'll start to see how this first solution is improving strategy delivery, and you'll use the insights you gain to inform the next stage.

Evolve (1 Week)

You need a week to measure the results of this first cycle to evaluate how the MVP is working, discover where you might need to shift to create more value, and define your focus for the next cycle—which may include expanding this MVP service to more stakeholders, adding more features to it, or creating your next service.

After the first cycle, you will have created many of the foundational components that will allow you to get to the delivery stage faster in subsequent cycles. When you deliver your MVP, you buy yourself some time and build credibility while showing your executives that you're here to rapidly solve business problems, not just project problems. Then you can look at the next set of services on your road map and simply follow the IMPACT Engine System approach to Assess, Define, Plan, Deliver, and Evolve.

The Evolve stage sets you up to iterate your way to IMPACT while giving you space to shift slightly, or even pivot, based on what you've learned. Because you are regularly engaging with your business leaders, you will know if the demands of the business are evolving. That's why these cycles are small and focused—they allow you to adapt so your organization can thrive.

This adaptive and highly responsive model is exactly what your business leaders want and need to maintain a healthy business. It positions you as a future predictor who anticipates what your business leaders will want next and adapts your plans to support them. They will start to think you are reading their minds, and it will allow you to quickly become the "right hand" to your business leaders as they make the decisions necessary to ensure the organization thrives. As a result, it will be only natural for them to invite you to the table to help drive this natural organizational evolution.

Before we go any further, I'm going to share with you one thing that may seem obvious but can sometimes be a big gotcha for our Mastermind students when they are just getting started.

The Perfection Trap

How many times have you noticed that projects get stalled in the requirements phase because the team wants to be sure that no requirement is missing? They spend a lot of time analyzing and iterating while deadlines are missed, and customers are disappointed because teams can't get unstuck. They are paralyzed. You might have even helped teams get out of analysis paralysis. And guess what? It applies to the work you are doing too. Chasing the ideal world of a perfect team delivering the perfect services will only lead you to paralysis. And paralysis leads to disappointed stakeholders.

This is why the Agile movement gained so much momentum early on—executives were frustrated that everything was taking so long. We now know that many Agile transformations fail for the same reasons traditional PMOs and any other organizations responsible for strategy delivery fail. Just changing your implementation approach isn't enough to fix the root causes. You need to redefine success to get early wins.

Perfection gets in the way of progress.

Instead of shooting for perfection, apply the 80/20 rule. In Stage Three: Define, you will identify the 20 percent of services that will drive 80 percent of the value, so be sure those services are included in the first several iterations. This is a lot easier to do when you are focused on addressing the root causes of all the symptoms you see affecting strategy delivery; there are usually far fewer root causes than symptoms.

Don't worry about building the perfect process right out of the gate. Get something up and running that tackles the most obvious root cause tied to the highest-priority pain points. Learn and refine as you go. You can always expand services later. In fact, you will have to expand services later because once you solve one problem, others will be uncovered.

For example, you might discover that the root cause of stalled projects is that the executives aren't prioritizing. However, they can't prioritize because they don't even have a list of all the projects that are happening in the organization. Start with that. In your minimum viable product, give them a list of the projects inclusive of all those hidden pet projects that are stealing resources from the higher priorities. Doing the investigative work to find all those hidden projects and then getting the executives together to look at the list is plenty of work already!

As a bonus, I bet you'll hear them say, "I had no idea all of this work was happening." And guess what that leads to? A much easier job prioritizing now that they see how much work is really going on. I always find it funny how shocked executives are when they see the full list of projects happening in their organization for the first time. But this is natural. After a decade of running my own company, I can relate. I understand that there's no way I could know everything going on in my organization because that's what I have hired a team to handle. However, I do need to make sure that the big projects that are taking their focus are prioritized in alignment with our business strategy.

The list of projects doesn't need to be perfect. Even an incomplete list will demonstrate value by providing transparency and that will get traction. Momentum beats stagnation.

Perfection does not equal progress. In fact, perfection gets in the way of progress. You need progress to build credibility and you don't have long to do it.

Done is better than perfect. A good enough service now is better than a perfect service never. Prioritize and iterate. Deliver incremental improvements over time. You can always add more columns to your dashboard after your leaders see the list and start asking questions, so you know what matters most to them. Let the questions they ask and the complaints you hear drive your improvements.

While you always want to keep your vision of a future state in mind, don't underestimate the power of starting small and building from there. Take the first step. Deliver an MVP. Make an IMPACT. Then make it even better.

And if you ever get stuck, remind yourself: experience is not required.

Experience Not Required

If you happen to be one of the many readers going through this process for the first time, you might have heard your "Yeah, but..." monster telling you there's no way this book will work for first-timers. Maybe you moved into this role from another part of your organization or have been recently promoted into a new role and need to prove yourself quickly. Good.

First, I'm glad you realize you must show value fast. That's important.

Second, if you are doing this for the first time, excellent! This book is perfect for you. We've used this process to help countless first-timers do really big things quickly—like Mike and Andrea, at the beginning of this chapter. You can too.

The common connection between Mike and Andrea is their CEO, Joel. He's my favorite CEO because he does exactly what the chief executive needs to do to support everything that you're going to learn in the IMPACT Engine System.

You may not have this level of engagement and support from your executives yet, and that's OK. Just know that your job is to make your business leaders look good, and the secret to earning their support is showing them exactly how you are going to help them achieve their goals. When that is clear, it's easier for them to support you, and you won't have to spend one minute "selling" your executives on your approach.

Stage Two: Assess is designed to bring your stakeholders with you—and when you do, you'll get all the buy-in and support you need for your changes.

Trust yourself. Trust the process. It's time to make an IMPACT.

MAKE AN IMPACT

Think: What would it feel like to have your first cycle of the IMPACT Engine System done in 90 days?

Do: Download your IMPACT Engine Planner and complete your week-by-week plan for your MVP cycle. Then block off time on your calendar and commit to protecting that time so you can do this important work!

STAGE

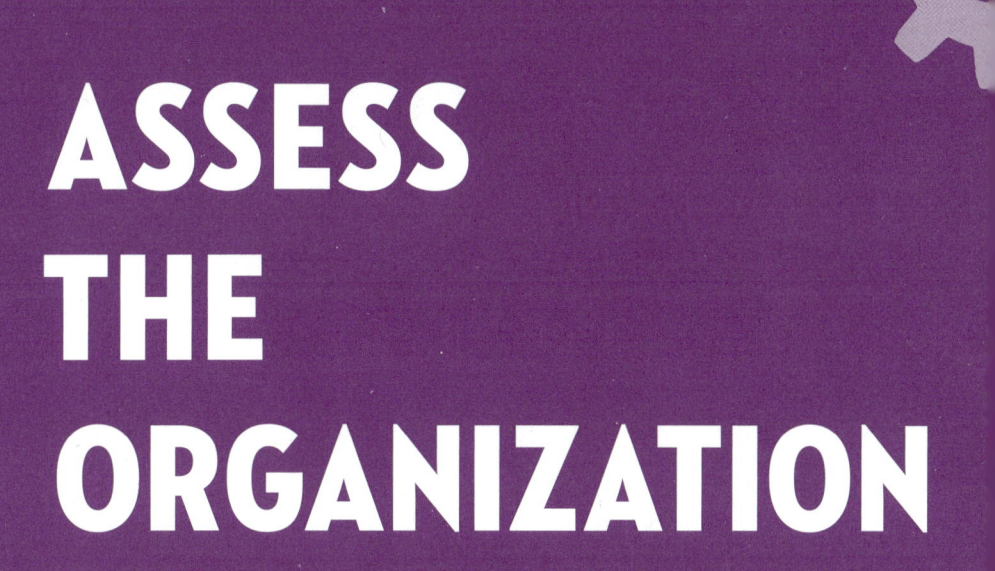

ASSESS THE ORGANIZATION

MINDSET

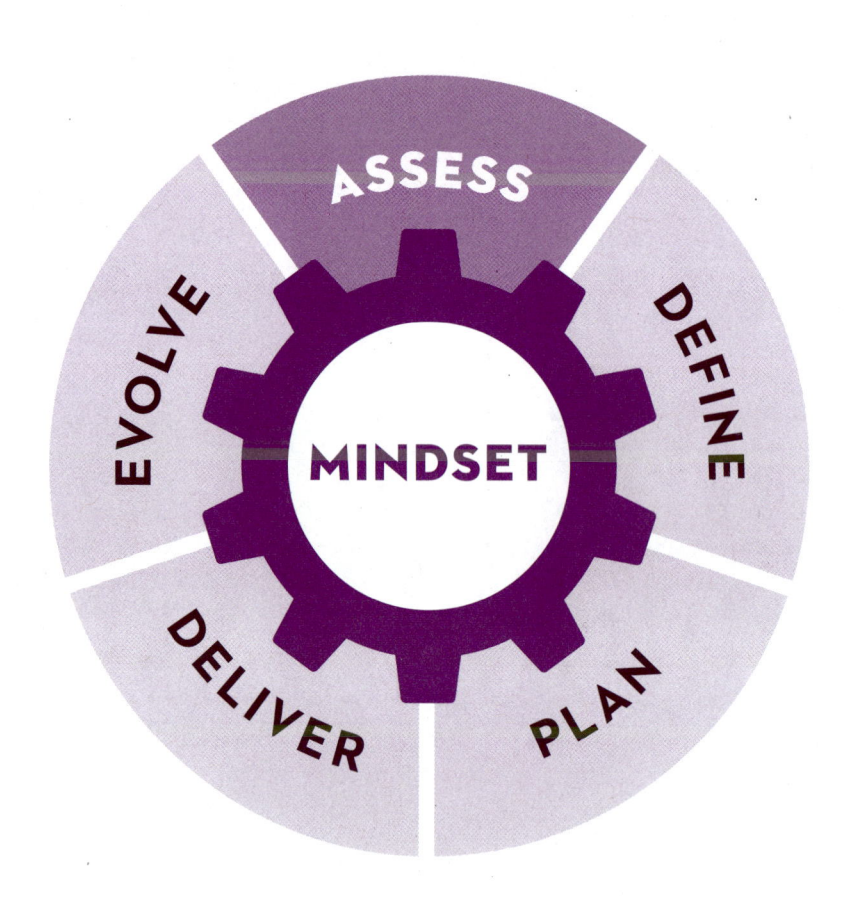

- ASSESS
- DEFINE
- PLAN
- DELIVER
- EVOLVE

Now that you have the big picture of what you'll do, why, and how you're going to do it, it's time to dive into your first cycle of the IMPACT Engine System.

There's no reason to go on this journey alone. Even if you're just getting started, there are many ways to get the people in your organization excited about and invested in the change you're leading. The first thing you'll do is learn our approach to building strong relationships early and how it helps people open up to you about what's really going on in your organization. You'll have a much easier time getting your stakeholders to tell you all the details about their pain points and enlisting their support to make the necessary changes if they already know, like, and trust you.

As with everything in this book, there's a good reason for the order. Once you have a handle on who your stakeholders are, you will look at how strategy delivery is currently happening in products, programs, and projects from *their* perspective. You will create a complete picture of the people, processes, and systems in place now, and pinpoint where you have opportunities to drive more value for the organization while avoiding the common mistakes that could derail your success.

And when you wrap up this stage, you'll have a prioritized list of challenges to address and invested leaders and teams who are excited about supporting you.

Let's do this!

Bring Them with You

I WALKED INTO the large conference room, ready for my first steering committee meeting as the new head of strategy delivery. Meera, one of the program managers, was setting up her laptop and notes at the end of the long table.

"Good morning, Meera!" I said, extending my hand. "Great to see you again! I'm looking forward to seeing one of these steering committee meetings in action."

Meera shook my hand with a weak smile. "Nice to see you, Laura. I'll do my best to give you a sense of how these go."

I could tell from Meera's tense body language that she felt apprehensive about the meeting. I guessed that my presence as an observer put additional pressure on her. I'd been told by the executive sponsor that none of the program managers on my team were "any good," and I was guessing Meera thought I was there to evaluate her performance.

Over the next 15 minutes, various executives strolled into the room, most at least five minutes late. They grabbed coffee and chatted among themselves, barely glancing at Meera.

When the last executive took his seat, Meera began her presentation. She summarized progress and challenges for each project clearly, but she was obviously nervous.

The executives looked up from their phones to interrupt her repeatedly, demanding to know why certain deliverables were delayed. Though Meera explained her mitigation strategies, the executives continued to grill her. None of them liked seeing red alerts all over the dashboard, and they used it as evidence to prove she was failing instead of seeing it as a call for help.

I cringed internally, seeing how they put Meera on the defensive. She was doing her best under the circumstances, but lacked support from these sponsors who took no ownership.

After the painful hour-long meeting ended, I pulled Meera aside. "Thanks for letting me observe," I said. "I appreciate you tolerating an additional pressure with me here. But it helped me see exactly what's going on."

"This was an easy one! Mark has had much more difficult meetings because he's running the program where Julian is a sponsor."

"*That* was an easy one? Wow. Why don't the sponsors ever ask how they can help?"

Meera shrugged. "They never do! They just yell at us when things go wrong, but it takes us weeks to get on their calendars when we need a decision or to get their team members to turn in deliverables."

"But that's not right. You're doing this work *for* them. They aren't taking any ownership." I explained my vision for clarifying roles and responsibilities between the program managers and the steering committee. It was clear that no one had taught these business leaders how to be good sponsors. And Meera's role was to be the navigator—to show them the way as *they* drove the delivery of their strategy.

Meera's eyes lit up for the first time. "That would help a lot, Laura. They think all of us program managers are to blame for everything." She went on to tell me more about the dysfunctions she perceived.

Over the next few weeks, I held a series of one-on-one meetings with the sponsors and then working sessions with the sponsors and program managers together. We had open dialogues where each side could express their pain points without judgment.

I reflected to them the pain points they'd told me using their exact words, so they felt heard and understood while helping them see they had to be part of the solution.

Then I stood in front of a large room full of steering committee members and told them, "These are *your* programs the program managers are running. If they fail, you fail. You are responsible for their success."

I showed them their pain points, the solutions we could put in place, and how those solutions would drive the better outcomes they were looking for.

The dots were starting to connect for the executives. They could more clearly see the role they weren't playing that was leading to this ripple effect of challenges for the programs. Teaching them how to be good sponsors and then holding them accountable for playing that role was the only way the portfolio of programs was going to get back on track.

Now, with a team of eager program managers and sponsors seeing the root causes, we collaboratively designed new governance processes that delineated clear responsibilities.

Within a few months, our steering committee meetings transformed into productive collaborations. Meera, and the rest of the program managers, gained confidence in reporting progress and raising issues early. The executives stepped up to remove roadblocks and provide guidance. Everyone was impressed with how fast the programs and people on them all got into flow.

The secret to our success in such a short time was bringing our stakeholders with us through the change process, after connecting their pain to the solution we could create and the success it would drive for them personally. I knew right away what was going on, but if I had shown them the solution too early or without connecting it to their pain, we would have hit a wall of resistance. Instead, none of them felt like the change was being done *to* them and everyone was invested because we were going to fix what mattered to them most.

In this stage of the process, leaders often make two big mistakes:

1 They underestimate the importance of developing meaningful relationships with stakeholders early and leveraging those relationships to help drive change.

2. They rush to solutions they think are needed before truly understanding the stakeholders' challenges, so they end up with services that no one wants.

These mistakes underlie most change resistance and will stop you from making the progress you need to build credibility fast.

But you won't make these mistakes. Can you see what would have happened if I had made either of the two mistakes above?

If I had not brought the program managers and sponsors with me through the change process and had simply skipped ahead to building a governance structure, every one of the sponsors would have resisted because they wouldn't have understood why it mattered or their role in driving success. Even some of the program managers would have complained about the "extra work" I was asking them to do.

If I had simply replaced all the program managers, like a few of the sponsors suggested, the problem would have remained because the root cause wouldn't have been addressed. The root cause was that sponsors weren't properly trained or engaged in the delivery of their own programs, not that the program managers were bad at their jobs.

We fixed the right problems in the right order by properly engaging stakeholders, documenting their pain points in their own words, and then leading them on a journey of solving the right problems. Everyone was on board. In fact, this made the work flow with ease.

Often, people want to rush this process, but trust me, addressing the right root causes instead of chasing a million vague symptoms will make things flow much faster, not slow you down. But to get to the right solutions, you must first build relationships with your stakeholders so that they trust you enough to give you the time of day and let you uncover the truth about what's happening from their perspective.

In this chapter, we'll prevent the first mistake by making sure you build the right strong relationships, and in the next chapter, you'll learn how to avoid the second mistake, so you have a good picture of what pain points your solutions will address.

As you develop these important relationships, be intentional about determining your stakeholders' readiness to support the change journey, which you'll learn more about later in this chapter.

Your executives want to see that you are leveling up.

Remember, you may think you know where you should focus first, but the obvious problems you uncover during your assessments may only be symptoms of underlying root causes. You'll learn how to figure out if you're at the root cause in Chapter 6. Stay with this process and you'll see what I mean.

You'll also be on the lookout for that key champion—your sponsor—to partner with on this journey through change. You may already know who this person is because they nominated you for this role, or they might simply be your direct boss who is invested in your success. Once you know who this person is, it's important to evaluate if your sponsor is prepared to support you effectively and understands their role in removing roadblocks and guiding you toward success.

You're About to Level Up

A very interesting pattern has developed through the years that we've been running the IMPACT Engine System implementation program and IMPACT Accelerator Mastermind coaching program. Many of our program participants pay for the program out of pocket because they know they need it to support them through this process and a lot of companies no longer pay for these types of programs. However, by the time they get to the end of Stage Two, most of them ask for and get reimbursement from their companies. At first, I thought it was an interesting coincidence that it always seemed to be at the end of this stage. However, after digging into it, I could clearly see why.

For the first time, both the delivery leader and the executives see a brighter future and how they can get there faster together. The delivery leader starts speaking the language of the business instead of waiting for their project management speak to be understood by the executives. The executives notice a change in the conversations they are having with the delivery leader and how the focus has shifted to solving business problems, not project problems. Even at this early stage, the executives see what's possible and trust that this leader will help them achieve their goals because they have a clear strategy for doing so. And the icing on the cake is that these delivery leaders didn't wait for permission to invest in themselves so they could help the organization achieve its strategic goals. They are leveling up and being recognized for it.

And that's exactly what your executives want to see: that you are leveling up and helping the organization do the same.

As you do the work I'm going to guide you through in this book, keep that IMPACT Driver Mindset front and center in your thinking. Pay close attention to *how* I suggest you apply the techniques in this book. Look for the places I'm encouraging you to bring people with you through change using what you say, how you say it, and when you say it. Each step you take has been planned intentionally, knowing what will get you seen as the trusted business partner your executives want by their side to help them achieve their goals. Trust in yourself that you can do what I'm teaching you. I bet you'll be surprised at how well it works and how naturally it comes with a little practice.

When this shift happens, you'll start to notice your stakeholders are talking to you differently, seeing you through a new lens, and engaging with you in a whole new way. You are building the organization that they *want*, which shows them you hear them loud and clear on what matters to them most. That's the fastest way to gain a colleague's trust—knowing and acting on their WIIFM (pronounced "wiff-um"—What's in it for me?).

Identify Stakeholders and Build Trust

"I don't get it. It seems impossible to get anything done here," I said with frustration.

David nodded knowingly. "It can be frustrating at first. This company values relationships over task completion. It's a different pace."

I was confiding in my very unlikely advocate. Everyone was afraid of David. He was the executive sponsor for the portfolio of programs my project management office was delivering. Even his own team seemed to cower when he came into the room. It had taken me a long time to earn his trust, but he saw that my goals and his were aligned.

"But why does it take so long for decisions to get made?" I pressed. "We could move twice as fast if people would just make up their minds." I favored progress over relationships—this was work after all, not my personal life—and I was struggling to navigate the politics in this organization.

David smiled. "Patience, my friend. These relationships are the foundation that will allow our changes to stick. If we try to rush too fast, we'll meet resistance at every turn. But if we bring others along with us, convince them of the vision, we'll gain advocates to propel our initiatives forward."

I sighed, taking in his advice. He was right—my impatience was slowing me down. Without partnerships across the organization, I was spinning my wheels.

We worked in a very relationship-based company with a clear cultural message: relationships matter more than progress—which explained the 16 separate interviews with stakeholders I'd had just to get the job. If I was going to be successful, I would have to realize that by building these relationships first, I was going to get a lot more done over time than trying to push changes through on my own. I needed to learn to play the long game.

Over the years, I've come to realize that to become an IMPACT Driver, it's worth it to invest time in building strong partnerships with the people who will be involved in your changes. You will need their support every step of the way. The IMPACT Engine System approach weaves strong stakeholder engagement throughout the entire process; it is key to your success. No matter how tempted you are to fast-forward to the Define or Deliver stages to start getting things done, resist that temptation—for your own career's sake.

Your success will depend on the people you have around you, so you must identify who will help you determine your initial areas of focus so that you can deliver that minimum viable product. Usually, that includes the executives who put you into the role. After all, they are paying the bills. They want a return on their investment, and they have the power to move you out of the role if they don't have confidence that you can deliver results.

To help your organization deliver the strategy with the highest possible ROI as quickly as possible, you must answer an important question: Why? The people who can answer this for you best are the executives responsible for defining the strategy. You must get clear on what the executives want and why they want it so that you can ensure all the work that happens is done in alignment with that "why." Once you've talked to the executives, you can expand the circle to include more stakeholders as you intentionally focus on building strong partnerships more broadly.

When I use the word "stakeholder," who comes to mind for you? Although you should interview your boss and executive team first, keep the broader organization in mind as well. There are people throughout the organization who will greatly influence your success in driving meaningful and sustainable change. Expand the definition of stakeholder to be inclusive of people in the organization who can help you effect change. Your new definition of stakeholder is anyone who can positively or negatively affect the outcome of your initiative, believes they can, or believes they will be affected by the outcome of your work.

Beyond the key executives you serve, you may realize you should include the teams working on projects, the project managers, the business owners, and the end customer expecting the outcomes of this work. Those are the typical groups people think of when they hear the word "stakeholder," but I want to broaden that definition even more so that you don't miss people who can influence the outcomes of the work you're doing. You don't want to miss someone who can derail your changes or who may have the potential to support you as you are implementing change throughout your organization.

I know seeing a long list of people to include might feel overwhelming, but don't worry, I've got you. Although it's critical to eventually talk to a wide range of people across the organization, don't feel pressure to talk to everyone at once. As with everything you're learning in this book, doing things in the right sequence matters.

In the first cycle where you are building your MVP, start with the executives, because they are making this investment in you and your team (if you have one) and they need to see a return for that investment quickly. Then expand your circle to include other players by paying attention to what the executives tell you. They will hint or directly tell you where to look next. With the MVP cycle, you will choose one primary service for your first round of value delivery, but only after you have worked with the executives to prioritize the pain points and have then done your Root Cause Analysis to ensure that solution is addressing the root cause and not just symptoms. (That Root Cause Analysis will happen in Stage Three: Define.)

Once you have talked to the executives and have heard the challenges and opportunities from their viewpoint, you can talk to the project managers, other delivery leaders, functional managers, product owners, any other business leaders, and customers. If your conversations with the executives didn't leave you with a strong sense of where you should focus next, I suggest a sampling of each group. Usually, however, you will start to see patterns from the first conversations that will guide you on the right path of who to talk to next. Just remember, stakeholder conversations will be ongoing, so just get started and go far enough to find a clear MVP and then keep those conversations going as you work through the stages.

Your Organization's Change Culture

Every organization has its own unique way that changes get implemented. In fact, you can have many different subcultures in a single company with their own unique sets of political challenges and ways of working. You need to be aware of both the official organizational chart as well as "how change really happens"; they are usually not the same thing.

I like to create a cultural change map that overlays an org chart to see how all the people are connected. Who plays golf together on the weekends? Who goes to lunch together? Where do I see informal conversations happening? Who tends to back who up in meetings? This will take you some time to learn, but it's well worth the effort.

Those with the power and influence in your cultural change map are important pieces on the chessboard that you'll need, both to implement the road map of changes you're creating through your services and to navigate the delivery of the organization's strategy. Invest the time to learn these dynamics and add them to your Stakeholder Engagement Plan, which we will review in the next section.

While you're doing this, be on the lookout for clues as to the appetite for change within your organization. Every organization adopts change in different ways and at a different pace. The pace also depends on how much change is currently under way. If there are a lot of transformational changes happening organization-wide, you'll need to manage the number of changes you create and try to roll out at the same time. Change fatigue is real, and any changes you deliver amid an already swirling body of other changes may face an uphill battle for adoption.

One way to avoid creating change fatigue in your organization is to incorporate the changes into the overall initiative portfolio at the enterprise level. This can help you get greater visibility and support for your changes and help leaders see the totality of change taking place in the organization at one time. Remember my favorite CEO, Joel, from Chapter 3? This is exactly what he did. In fact, he made the work he was doing to build strategy delivery capability in his organization the top business priority in their strategic portfolio. He said, "If we don't do this right, none of our other strategic priorities will be successful." He was right and they were wildly successful as a result.

Consider these questions to guide your thinking on timing of the changes you're bringing to the organization:

- How open is your organization to change in general?
- Are there signs of resistance to changes taking place?
- How much change is this organization undergoing?

The answers to these questions will help you determine the pace of change you must set: you need to go just fast enough to build

Not everyone needs to be your change champion on day one.

serious momentum while not overwhelming people with more change than they can absorb.

Evaluate Your Stakeholders

As you meet with the influencers and decision-makers, you want to look for their current level of support. Are they excited to support you? If not, don't worry, you'll get them there. For now, capture in writing what you notice about how they support you. Here are some benchmarks to look for:

- **Educated stakeholders** will reinforce a consistent message about how you are creating an IMPACT together.

- **Engaged stakeholders** will eagerly participate in helping you create solutions (and will often be the early adopters of your new solutions).

- **Resistant stakeholders**, on the other hand, could come in many forms—agreement in the meeting and then doing the complete opposite, or the more direct form of simply ignoring you. No matter how the resistance shows up, you need to look for alignment of their actions with their words and invest the time in discovering the root cause of any resistance so that you can move these stakeholders to educated and engaged.

During the assessment process you'll follow in the next chapter to discover the challenges and opportunities your team can address, make a note of where each person is currently and where they need to be to support the change you're driving. Executives need to be on board but may not be when you first engage them. You might even have trouble getting on their calendar, or you might have to repeatedly remind them "what this meeting is about." Stick with it. Not everyone needs to be your change champion on day one. Just find the key stakeholders who are excited about the work you are doing and who can see how they will benefit, and get started making a difference with them. In Stage Five: Deliver, I will show you how to use the early wins from your key champions to showcase the value you're driving in the organization and create a desire from others to achieve the same benefits by working with your team.

Here's what you should address in your Stakeholder Engagement Plan:

1. Name, role, place in the organization
2. Current level of support
3. Key interests, issues, expectations
4. Engagement plan

Right now, you're doing step one above to identify the key players and step two to gauge their current level of support for you and the solutions you are charged with creating. In Chapter 5, we'll look at what to ask them to answer step three: their key interests, issues, and expectations in their own words. Then, in Stage Four, you'll develop your engagement plan.

Lovers, Haters, and Just Don't Cares

Here's a fun way to think about your stakeholders and where they are now, as well as recommendations on how to engage people in each of these categories.

Lovers

- **Description:** These stakeholders are already supportive and enthusiastic about your work. They are "cheerleaders" who want to see you succeed.

- **How to recognize them:** Eager to be involved, offer help proactively, advocate for you in meetings, willing to commit resources.

- **How to engage them:** Appreciate your lovers! Keep them involved by asking them to pilot your solutions, and showcase their successes to help influence others to join the party.

Haters

- **Description:** These stakeholders are opposed to or resistant to the change you're driving. They may actively try to derail your efforts.

- **How to recognize them:** Critical of ideas, focus on obstacles/risks, communicate negativity about the changes, the team, or you, and avoid involvement or committing resources.

- **How to engage them:** Understand the root cause of resistance, address concerns, and provide additional education/clarity. Hug your haters! You might be resistant to engaging with them since they aren't on your side, but I see that as a missed opportunity. The good thing about this group is that you know who they are because they are telling you what they think. Instead of avoiding them, bring them into the fold. They may know something you don't about why your plans may fail. For example, they may tell you about why your predecessor failed, which will prevent you from making the same mistakes. *Really listen* to them talk about their concerns, and then ask them what they would do if they were in your shoes and why. Then find a way to implement an idea of theirs, and, the best part, give them all the credit! This pulls them into the fold as an advocate and gives them a sense of ownership of outcomes. Make sure their idea is successful and keep engaging them to share their next "brilliant idea" with you so you can keep that positive engagement going. Haters can quickly become lovers because most people love their own ideas.

Just Don't Cares

- **Description:** These stakeholders are neutral or apathetic. They neither love nor hate the changes you're creating. It's not a priority for them.

- **How to recognize them:** Lukewarm or disinterested reactions, avoid meetings, don't engage unless directly asked.

- **How to engage them:** Do not underestimate the importance of engaging this group! If they should care and don't, they could derail your progress. They might be building competing capabilities instead of partnering with you, or simply acting like your team doesn't exist, showing that you are not valuable to them and possibly to others in the organization. Spend time learning what they do care about, and ask good questions to identify the business challenges they are facing or where the opportunities are for them to be even more successful.

As you map out your stakeholders, track their level of support over time. Prioritize focusing on haters and just don't cares based on their ability to influence your team's success. The more critical the stakeholder, the more important to focus on moving them to supportive, as you move forward.

Who Is Your Sponsor?

As you do the Chapter 5 assessments, you'll learn what people care about and how to tie what you're doing to those priorities. This approach will help you gain support from more than just one key stakeholder. I encourage you to have an advisory board of key people who care about your success and stand to benefit from it. However, there should be one key person in your circle of support who is as invested as you are in the success of this endeavor. That's your sponsor. While a team or department doesn't usually have a sponsor, the change you are leading to create a values-driven business function does need an extra level of support.

Your sponsor is the person who cares the most about what you are building and/or has the most to gain from your success. They may be your direct boss or not. They might be a key customer in the business area that you provide support for, like David was for my program team, or it could be someone in the C-suite, which is ideal. The more you engage with the person identified as your sponsor, the more you'll confirm if they have truly bought in to the change you're leading. If they haven't really bought in yet, you can seek out others to fill that gap for now, which can be especially helpful if your current sponsor doesn't have a lot of internal influence anyway.

You might be surprised to find champions for your change in unlikely places, and while you need only one sponsor, you can use all the support you can get from everyone you can recruit. Those change champions can be the early adopters for your services, act as vocal supporters of your team, and even sit on that advisory board to guide your team's direction over time. They may also feed you important information to help you succeed.

If you do not have someone in a sponsorship role, it can create a huge risk to your success. So can having the wrong person in the role.

An uneducated sponsor won't know how to support you when you ask for help. A disengaged sponsor won't be able to get you necessary resources (time, money, people, access, information, etc.) and remove roadblocks when needed, which slows down progress. A poor change leader or an ineffective influencer may make your job harder. Take the time to identify your sponsor (and all your change champions) and then give them everything they need to be by your side every step of the way. Even your sponsor might need to be guided through the change process in a way that makes their WIIFM clear to them. Knowing what they care about is just as important as it is with all of your other stakeholders.

Once you've identified your critical sponsor, it's time to develop a clear agreement on how your partnership will work. Many sponsors, especially first-timers, don't understand what is expected of them. Sponsors are not born, they are made. So it is important to help your sponsor be the best they can be by building a partnership agreement describing how to ensure the change is successful. Take the time to educate them about the process you are going through (they might even enjoy receiving their own copy of this book) and where and how you'll require their support. You don't need to bog them down in all the details, but you do have to identify the critical places where you will need their help. Then give them the information they need to know and the talking points they may want to say to remove barriers, negotiate on your behalf, champion change, and help you navigate the organization.

Ensure that you update your sponsor at regular intervals, so when you bring a problem to them with proposed solutions, they will be familiar with the scenario and can help you determine the right path and quickly remove barriers to progress for you. This is why it's helpful for you to have a sponsor with influence in the organization. At some point, you will rely on that relationship to help you implement change and enlist support from other areas in the organization.

Evaluate Your Team

There's one last stakeholder group you will want to take a close look at, and that's your team.

If you don't yet have a team, you can use this evaluation process to do two things: 1) identify the people you will need in the future to deliver the services that your stakeholders are going to want, and 2) identify people in other parts of the organization who are already doing this strategy delivery work, such as product or project managers. Even if they don't report to you, you can think of them as part of your team—or your extended network—if they are interested in helping you define your services. They will likely benefit once you deliver them. This dual role of providing input into the process and benefiting from the service can be a great way to build a sense of community.

If you do have a team today, consider how that team is organized and whether you have who you need by your side to deliver on the brighter future you are all building together. The makeup of your team should match the services you are delivering, and may need to evolve to meet future demands. There's a reason so many companies go through organizational changes where boxes on the org chart are shifted every few years—the company is evolving and the way you organize the people needs to evolve with it. The same might be true for your team. It doesn't have to mean job cuts, but it does mean you need to evaluate who you have and ensure that you build a team that supports how you intend to serve the broader organization in the future.

Do you have the right roles defined? Do you have any gaps on your team? Are your team members set up for success now, and if not, where will you need to make changes? You will need the right team, with the right mix of strengths, and the right organizational structure to support their success over time. If you find that you need to make organizational changes, you could consider developing a job rotation program to bring in new talent from other parts of the organization and allow people on your team to explore other opportunities. For now, just assess where you are today. When you determine the services you will put in place to address the root causes of the stakeholder pain points in Stage Three: Define, you'll look at how to organize your team to best serve the broader organization.

While you're doing this team assessment work, take time to reflect on your own leadership as well. Regardless of whether you manage a team or work independently today, evaluating your change readiness and leadership skills is critical to positioning you for success in the future. This self-assessment will highlight areas to develop as you guide your team's transformation into an IMPACT Engine. Leading change requires preparation—take stock of your own capabilities in embracing change and rallying others to drive this journey forward. The transformation you must drive starts with your own leadership growth and change readiness.

This is a great time to look back at your IMPACT Driver Mindset Worksheet and reflect on the places you may need to develop skills or adjust your own thinking to lead the changes that are coming. Everyone has strengths and weaknesses, and true leaders are honest with themselves about where they stand and then put a plan of action in place to achieve the desired state. Fortunately, leaders don't need to be perfect; no one is. Effective leaders know how to inspire others to achieve a better future, and you'll learn how to do this throughout this book. One aspect of that inspiration is learning how to bring others along on the journey of change.

People are not resistant to change. They are resistant to having change done *to* them.

The Change Resistance Myth

It's a commonly held belief that people are just naturally resistant to change and that this resistance is what is preventing them from delivering the right organizational changes in their companies. Maybe you have even had this thought yourself.

But it is simply not true. It's not that people in your organization are particularly resistant to change. What they are resistant to is having change done *to* them.

When you hit change resistance, it's because there isn't enough investment in building strong stakeholder relationships. The stakeholders feel like the change is something that they don't want or think they need, and it is being forced upon them.

Don't believe me?

Consider some of the biggest changes people can make in their lives—marriage, having children, moving, getting a pet. People all over the world do these things willingly every day. Even the people in your organization! They take on hobbies, sign up for classes, change jobs, strive for more in their careers, and make all kinds of changes in their lives. Every day.

People want autonomy, freedom, and the ability to make their own decisions with a sense of control over their destiny. When they believe someone is forcing change on them that they don't understand, they push back, just like you would if someone grabbed your hand and started pulling you in a direction that you didn't want to go. Even if the place they were taking you was "for your own good." Likely you wouldn't go with them if you didn't want to or know why it was good for you.

If you are facing change resistance in your organization, that's on you, not them. They are just being human. You must change how you engage them so that they want to be a part of this change. Will you get everyone on board? No, not at first. But you'll get a lot more than you might think if you follow the guidance in this book and are able to show the results they're seeking.

The bottom line is that you will only be successful if you build strong relationships with your stakeholders and become a trusted partner on this change journey.

Just remember: People are not resistant to change. They are resistant to having change done *to* them.

Trust yourself. Trust the process. It's time to make an IMPACT.

MAKE AN IMPACT

Think: How will you proactively engage stakeholders to bring them with you through the change process?

Do: Download the Organizational Change Assessment to evaluate your organization's change culture.

5

Give Them What They Want

"I'M JUST hitting so much resistance when I try to roll services out to our stakeholders," Diane shared with the Mastermind group. "They don't seem to want anything that we're creating, even though we know it's exactly what they need."

When Diane first joined the IMPACT Engine System implementation program, I noticed that she was flying through the online steps. I messaged her then saying that she was going too fast and there was no way she'd had the conversations required to properly engage stakeholders to bring them through the change process. A few months later, she shared concerns about her lack of progress in our Mastermind coaching session. I wasn't surprised. I asked, "Do you remember when I reached out because you were going too fast through the program? You told me not to worry because you just wanted to see what was to come and then you'd go back and do all the steps. I bet you skipped something important, and I can tell you exactly what it was. Do you want my guess?"

Diane begged, "Yes, please! I'm stuck."

"I am willing to bet you went straight to implementing the solutions you thought were best without going through the steps to engage stakeholders in this process, like you learned in the Assess stage."

"Ugh! You're right. I did," she said sheepishly. "But we had to get things done quickly or we would lose credibility. I didn't have time to wait on a bunch of interviews. My team had been in place for months and we hadn't delivered any services yet. Plus, I already knew what they needed."

"Right, but now you're even further behind because you are trying to implement changes and you don't have anyone interested in engaging with you. You have to go back and build those relationships to earn your stakeholders' trust. But the way you do it is by solving the challenges that they *want* solved instead of what you think they *need*." Many of her peers in the Mastermind began nodding, having learned this lesson themselves—her challenge, though completely avoidable, was not uncommon.

Diane had made the big mistake we see happen all the time. The delivery leaders think they know best and start implementing solutions that the stakeholders don't want. Don't do this. This entire stage in the process is designed to bring them with you, and when you do, you'll get all the buy-in and support you need for your changes.

Diane did eventually get back on track, but it took her a lot longer to build buy-in and earn credibility than if she had followed these steps in order. You cannot skip ahead here; you must take each of these steps seriously and do the work to see the results. If you fly through this and think "I'll come back to it later," you won't. The busyness of the day-to-day sets in and then you will hit a wall of resistance that will stop you in your tracks. The right level of engagement here will help you build champions for the change you're implementing and speed you up, not slow you down.

The delivery capability you are building doesn't belong to you. It's there to support the organization in delivering on the strategy more effectively. This means you need to partner with the people who will benefit from these services to truly understand what is working for them and what is not, even if you don't yet have their full support.

Do your stakeholders see you as a trusted adviser and business partner? Is it clear to your stakeholders how your team helps them drive business value faster? If you ask different stakeholders in your organization what you do and how they value it, will you get similar answers? And will those answers be positive or negative?

You will only be effective if you learn how to build a coalition of support while exploring all the opportunities for delivering business value in your organization. You're going to learn exactly how to engage your executives, project teams, and other key stakeholders in a way that gets their attention and keeps them on board throughout the process. The IMPACT Engine System is all about bringing people with you through change. And yes, a thread of organizational change management runs throughout the entire program—it's why our clients and students are incredibly successful.

But what happens if they don't want to talk to you? When Diane first reached out to a couple of stakeholders, she was met with resistance. People didn't know much about what she was doing or why they should care. It felt easier to just figure it out on her own instead of dealing with the repeated rejection she was sure she would face if she kept asking questions and "bothering" her stakeholders. She just wasn't up for being a door-to-door salesperson.

You may have stakeholders who give you the cold shoulder when you're just starting out. That's OK. Keep going. This resistance is likely tied to fear that you will make things harder for them or expose gaps in how they are accomplishing work today. And the truth is that at some point, you could expose gaps in delivery. That's why you're there, but it's not necessarily the place to start. It's crucial that you start by focusing on what they already *know* they want to improve, the problems they already see. The pain they are experiencing today. You may have to do some detective work to find the pain, but they all have it. Listen and ask good questions. Pay attention to what your stakeholders *aren't* saying.

Shifting your approach to focus on what matters most to your key stakeholders goes a long way to building trust, earning credibility, and getting that critical buy-in you'll need for the long term. And this can all be earned before you've ever delivered anything, by engaging with them early and in the right way. You build credibility just by listening to your stakeholders and involving them in the solution.

Now that you know who all your stakeholders are from the work you did in the last chapter, we'll turn our attention to uncovering their challenges and the opportunities to elevate strategy delivery for your organization. Later in this chapter, you will engage your stakeholders in a prioritization process to evaluate the information you've gathered from them and let them help you determine where you should focus first.

These steps will help you build stakeholder engagement and buy-in early so that, together, you can move faster and with less resistance.

Don't Give Them What They Need

When delivery leaders are asked to start solving for the pain points they either see or have heard in the form of complaints from others, it can be incredibly tempting to start giving stakeholders the medicine they need to take. These leaders get busy "fixing" projects by creating templates, implementing tools, and building methodology; hiring project managers; and putting everyone through certification training. They may even make the case to consolidate project people who are working in different parts of the organization to create their delivery empire. Unfortunately, the most important step in this process is missing. They have failed to have the right conversations with stakeholders to learn what the real pain points are in the stakeholders' words, which means the solutions they are putting in place might not resonate with stakeholders.

In the meantime, while their team is focused on building out a methodology, creating templates, implementing tools, and investing in process, their stakeholders see no positive changes in their experience, only people busy doing things that aren't important to them. These well-intentioned delivery leaders are giving the stakeholders the medicine they think they need to take instead of directly addressing what the stakeholders said they want. This gives stakeholders the impression that what is happening "isn't for them," and

Give them what they *want* before you give them what they *need*.

it drives a wedge between the changes they see and what they care about. The damage caused by this approach can be extremely detrimental to building the strong stakeholder partnerships needed to be successful. Don't let that happen to you; you don't have time to waste.

Here's the kicker: even if you are right about what they need to be successful, you're still wrong because you won't be successful in the long run if they don't feel like what you are building is really for them. It's not about being right. It's about getting results.

The answer?

Give them what they *want* before you give them what they *need*. And how do you know what they want? Ask. Here's how.

How to Gather Meaningful Input

Here are some of the many ways you can gather input from stakeholders.

1 **One-on-one interviews:** In-depth discussion with each stakeholder to understand their needs, concerns, and perspectives.

2 **Focus groups:** Collaborative guided discussions with small groups of stakeholders that can uncover valuable insights.

3 **Questionnaires and surveys:** Well-designed surveys distributed to stakeholders that can gather input from a large group. It is best to include both quantitative ratings and open-ended qualitative responses and to make the input anonymous, so you are more likely to get the truth from them.

4 **Interactive workshops:** Collaborative sessions focused on a specific topic that allow stakeholders to share insights through hands-on activities and reconvene to provide continued input in later stages. They can include activities such as Root Cause Analysis, value mapping, and brainstorming.

5   **Review/audit of existing process and projects:** Observing stakeholders in their environment to reveal challenges and opportunities that the other information-gathering methods did not uncover.

Stakeholder	Interviews	Focus Groups	Surveys	Workshops	Project Audits
Executives	✓			✓	
Project Managers	✓	✓	✓	✓	✓
Functional Managers	✓	✓			
Team Members			✓		
Customers			✓		✓

EXAMPLE

No matter what assessment approaches you use, your goal is to answer these four questions:

1   **Start:** What should we start? What isn't happening that could drive better strategy delivery?

2   **Stop:** What should we stop? What is getting in the way of successful strategy delivery?

3   **Shift:** What should we shift? What is in place now that could change to drive successful strategy delivery?

4   **Save:** What should we save? What is working well that should not be changed?

The information you gather here should be focused on the perspective of the stakeholders you are talking to: What is *their* experience?

Don't get into the solutions you believe should be in place. Your job at this point is to listen, learn, and document findings.

My favorite method for executives is one-on-one interviews. I know you might be thinking, "Who has time to talk to everyone one-on-one?" Trust me, it's worth the time. When my company works with clients, one of our senior team members always has one-on-one conversations with the executives. This approach speeds up our assessment process and points us to where to look next.

You will find out things you would never find out in a survey. You can read facial expressions, tone, and body language. You can have an "off the record" conversation about something that's really bothering them. They will share things you'd never hear them repeat elsewhere. And doing this helps them begin to build trust with you.

To become a trusted adviser with a seat at the table, it is critical to earn your stakeholders' trust, and that trust will disappear completely if you tell anyone else what they told you off the record. You must keep things they tell you in confidence. You'd better believe executives talk to each other, so they'll hear if you've repeated something they've told you in confidence, and they won't make that mistake again. They might even be testing you. You can keep the specifics of conversations to yourself while still using what you learned to influence your other conversations, the questions you ask, and the places you look to provide value.

Start by scheduling meetings with the executives that your team supports, both the ones in your reporting chain and the ones who use or will use your services. If you are providing an enterprise solution, talk to all the C-suite executives.

The questions to ask the executives are intentionally simple. You want to know what they are worried about, what their experience is with the delivery process, where they see challenges, and where there are uncaptured opportunities.

What do you do if they won't make time for you? I'd go back to Chapter 4 and apply the stakeholder engagement techniques you learned there. Find the executives who are willing to talk to you, and when you schedule time with them, make sure it's clear that you are not taking them through a bunch of processes. Your goal is to help them solve their business pain points, and to do that, you need to know what those pain points are.

Here's one way you can phrase the request: "I would like to schedule a brief meeting with you next week so that I can better understand your top business priorities and pain points. This will help me identify the most important areas of focus for my team as we build capability to help accelerate strategy delivery. Your perspective will ensure we are aligned right from the start on delivering the highest-value outcomes for the business."

The key is to make it clear what's in it for them—how their time investment will help ensure the work you are doing meets their needs and delivers business value. The "so that" statement focuses on the benefits to them rather than just asking to take up their precious time. People make time for what is important to them.

Although the specific questions you ask may vary for each specific person, here are several that we have seen work well. Based on the language your organization is using now to talk about the work you're doing, you could ask about "project" or "strategy delivery" or "product lifecycle," for example—whatever you think will resonate best with your audience. My preference is usually "strategy delivery" because what you'll need to fix is usually beyond the start-to-finish of a project. Send the executives these questions in advance so that they have time to consider their answers. You want to ask the questions one-on-one, but as you expand your interviews to people in the rest of the organization, you can use the same questions with a small group of people who are on the same team. To keep your stakeholders engaged in the process, make sure you write down their words so you can repeat those words when you come back with your findings.

Here are some example questions to get you started:

1 What role(s) do you usually play in strategy delivery (projects)?

2 What role(s) do people on your team usually play?

3 What do you see working well today?

4   Where are the opportunities for improvement?

5   Could you please describe what success looks like in your eyes?

6   What do you think might stand in our way of achieving successful strategy delivery?

7   Is there anything else we should know?

8   Who else should we talk to?

This last question does a lot more than simply give you a list of names—you'll learn a little about the organizational dynamics and who talks to whom. Every time I have one of these conversations, I'm looking for the names of other people that I should talk to next. It will likely come up in conversation, but if it doesn't, you can ask this open-ended question and they will mention someone (from their team, from their peers, from their customers) who can provide either a different perspective or validate what they are telling you. This might give you a hint who they consider to be trusted peers or team members.

In the rare cases that the person you're talking to does not have anyone else to recommend even after you ask them directly, that might be a red flag. When people want to help, they usually offer suggestions of where to look next. If they don't offer that, pay close attention to the rest of their answers and behavior because they might not be engaged or truly supporting your success. People who want you to succeed will find ways to help you do so.

A word of caution: Watch out for "lack of" responses to your interview questions. When used in describing a pain point, the term "lack of" often suggests a desired solution rather than an experienced issue. For example, "The reason we don't have accountability is lack of a proper software tool." In this case, the interviewee assumes that the solution to accountability is a tool. While software can provide more visibility, it's not going to address a core leadership issue: leaders not feeling or being held accountable for business outcomes. Dig deeper and keep them focused on the real core pain—lack of accountability and ownership in driving the intended business outcomes. We'll get to root causes later.

Once you've met with the executives, you will have a clear sense of which data-gathering techniques you should use next to gather the rest of the inputs in the assessment process. The executives will have left clues about where to focus first. Now you can start engaging the project sponsors, project managers, functional managers, and project team members that you will support to gather perspectives from the people who are closer to the action.

As you broaden the group of stakeholders you talk to across different parts of the organization, you may be surprised by what you hear. What initially appears to be a big problem might be something that affects only one department or might just be frustration from a squeaky wheel that isn't shared by all the other stakeholders. Don't worry, you won't be the one deciding what to work on first, that's the job of the executives (more on this at the end of the chapter).

When you conduct these interviews, you'll hear about a lot of things that may seem easy to fix. But resist the temptation to start immediately fixing issues based on initial interviews. Unless the solution is a straightforward action that only takes a few minutes, such as making a call, sending an email, or providing existing resources, prematurely chasing every problem you hear about can divert your focus from setting projects up for long-term success—and you'll probably waste time putting bandages on symptoms instead of addressing root causes. You want to keep moving, but you don't want to jump to answers too early before you've done the work to be sure you're looking at the bigger picture.

Remember that you are following an iterative process. You don't need to talk to every stakeholder on every team in the first round. The two weeks recommended for the Assess stage is to begin conversations with the critical stakeholders. Over time, talking to people about the work you're doing should simply become a part of your routine, so there will be plenty of opportunities in the coming weeks and months for additional conversations. For now, you just want to cover the top-priority stakeholders who will influence the outcomes of your initial success. You can start talking to other stakeholders after those first two weeks and in a focused process in the next cycle. You are not trying to check a task off a list. You are trying to build long-lasting relationships to drive huge success in your organization. That takes time and should be done over time.

Don't Say No, But Don't Just Say Yes

"Yes" seemed like such an innocent word, but it got me in a lot of trouble. I was asked to build an enterprise-level PMO (EPMO) to support the entire organization after successfully building and running a department-level PMO. I had built several delivery teams at this point and had a clear picture of what it would take to be successful. I knew I needed to talk to the executives first, and so I met with each department head to learn about their challenges with the delivery process and explore opportunities to drive more value. Thanks to my time running that department PMO, I knew all too well that we had some resisters in these ranks, so I was eager to please and to show that we could provide support.

As I scheduled the meetings with department heads, there was one executive that I dreaded meeting with the most. Mona was a tough cookie, and it would not be easy to convince her to use our EPMO for services she was currently managing within her team. She had a command-and-control management style and, although the C-suite led with a different approach, they didn't stand in her way because she got results.

I met with Mona first, which was probably my first mistake because she was very resistant to letting go of control, but things did get off to a great start. I asked questions and listened to Mona talk about her pain points and challenges. She shared a mix of things she wanted to see change in her department, as well as her thoughts on what other departments should be doing better. I was so grateful she was confiding in me and wanted to be sure she not only liked me but could count on me to help her. But that eagerness to please got me in trouble.

As she rattled off the things she wanted to see changed, she would ask, "Is this something you can help with?" and in my exuberant state, I said, "Yes, of course we can!" to *every single one* of them. The problem was, as I met with other business leaders, I said the same thing. Before I knew it, I had met with every department head and said yes to everything they were hoping to address. I could clearly see ways that we could help, and I wasn't wrong. We could address these challenges. The problem was *when*. Because I had said yes to every business leader along the way, they all expected their most important priority to be addressed first.

My big mistake in these conversations? I didn't manage expectations that it would take time to deliver on all these promises, or tell the department heads that my team, although decently sized, was not going to be able to do everything at once. I felt an overwhelming sense of responsibility to please everyone quickly for the sake of my team's reputation, and this created undue pressure that made it harder to get even one thing done.

The next few months were rough, as the team and I tried to move quickly to make good on my promises. We started to burn out, and through the grapevine I began to hear that the executives, especially Mona, were running out of patience. Word got back to me that she was working on a solution like the one she had asked me to create for her. My team was already two months into working on our solution for her, but because we were doing too many things at once, progress was slow. I was out of time.

When everything is important, nothing is important.

You won't move quickly on anything if you're trying to do everything at once. I said yes to everything to earn credibility, but instead I hurt my credibility and had to dig myself out of a hole.

At that point, I needed a different approach. If I lost Mona's support and buy-in, other leaders would be quick to follow. I quickly pulled the executives into a meeting to reset expectations and prioritize. My team and I worked through the steps I'm going to cover in the next section to present the findings of our assessment work across all the departments, and we put the responsibility back into the executives' hands so they could prioritize what we would work on.

When everything is important, nothing is important.

Remember, instead of saying yes to everything, even if you're agreeing to things you know your team can do, help your stakeholders understand that the important work of prioritization is yet to come and, most importantly, that they will be involved in the process. This doesn't mean saying no to requests; that can shut down conversation and forward momentum. It means telling them what will be needed to accomplish the yes. As you'll discover in Chapter 10, it means saying "Yes, and here's what it will take..."

As you wrap up your conversations, you can say, "Great! The next steps are to finish our first round of interviews and then combine all the feedback for you and the other executives to review and prioritize the areas of focus together. Then we will create a clear plan for moving forward into the stage of determining root causes and developing the right solutions over time to address those root causes. You'll be with us every step of the way so we can be sure what matters most to the organization as a whole, and to you specifically, is addressed. If you think of anything else you'd like to share in the meantime, please reach out to me."

Later, I discovered that Mona was testing me and pulling a move you need to watch out for. My boss found out that Mona had no intention of turning over program management of her strategic initiatives to the EPMO, which is why she was building her own solution at the same time. She knew if she asked for the moon and the stars, she would overwhelm me with so much work that I wouldn't notice she was moving ahead with her own solutions to the same problems.

This is an important lesson to learn, and I'd rather you learn it from me instead of learning it the hard way. Not everyone will be by your side every step of the way, but don't give up. If you try to do everything at once on your own, without bringing your stakeholders through the process, you will be left with too much work and no support. This can lead, as we've seen many times, to a lot of duplicate effort, with teams in different parts of the organization working on the same things in different ways. By including your stakeholders in the assessment process and keeping that engagement strong throughout the coming stages, you are ensuring they will remain with you as you develop and deliver solutions together.

Use Their Words and Listen for the WIIFM

Make sure you write down the answers to your questions that your stakeholders give *in their words*. Capture what they say, how they say it, and what emotion they carry when they say it. Don't paraphrase or reword it based on what you think they mean. You will use their exact words when you come back to talk to them about how the solutions you are developing will address their specific pain points. This technique has proven to be incredibly effective in building stakeholder buy-in because they see themselves reflected in the pain points and they see that you understand deeply what they are going through. Then, when you offer the solution, they are more invested in that solution. In Chapter 8, you'll learn about the communication framework that connects the input you are gathering now with the solutions you propose and the IMPACT they will have on the organization. The critical first step in that framework is using the exact words your stakeholders give you in these interviews.

You may remember that I used the popular acronym WIIFM in Chapter 4. That's the question your stakeholders are asking, whether they say it out loud or not: "What's in it for me?" When you are having conversations with stakeholders, you're also looking for what they care about personally. Keep listening for their WIIFM because it usually comes out in conversations, whether they say it directly or you can sense it by what they choose to share with you. It could be something personal like a promotion, looking good in front of their boss or the board, more reasonable work hours, or spending less time in the details. Whatever it is, make a note of it, because you can weave that information into conversations later, which shows you care about what matters most *to them*.

In my experience, everyone has a WIIFM for the organization and another WIIFM that's personal and underlies most of their decision-making. Your job is to find them both.

Don't Ask What Your Team Should Do

A word of caution: Do not ask your executives or other stakeholders what your delivery team "should do." You don't want the answer to that question. They aren't the experts in the delivery space; you are, even if you're just getting started. The stakeholders' job is to run their part of the business, and yours is to help ensure a brighter future by enabling the delivery of the organization's strategy.

If your stakeholders set the tone and tell you what your team should do, you'll end up with different viewpoints from each one of them. And frankly, most of them will be making it up as they go along. They may know what they've seen work elsewhere, but they probably don't know exactly what it took to make it work. Or if they're asked, they could simply be thrown off by the question and not want to look foolish by not having an answer, so they might make something up. Very likely, they will answer from their own point of view and address what they feel will help their group most, rather than from the enterprise view.

When each stakeholder has their own view of what your team should do and how you should do it and they voice that view, they set expectations that they feel you must live up to. If you ask this question of different stakeholders, you will find yourself in a constant battle of managing conflicting expectations. What they think your team should do will be varied (and sometimes even just a bad idea).

Instead, simply ask the same questions you are asking the executives that allow you to get a clear picture of stakeholders' experience being a part of the strategy and project delivery process. Then you can come back once you've gathered all your input and enlist their support in prioritizing their challenges and desires alongside all the other executives. For many of them, this will be the first time they've had to prioritize anything related to enabling high-powered strategy delivery.

Your stakeholders may push you to skip the interview questions and jump straight into talking about solutions. This is common in teams that are solution focused, like the IT department, for example. Stand firm. Remind them that your first step is to listen and understand their current experiences so that the right solutions are put in place to solve the right root causes. Gathering their input is crucial to prioritizing what will move the needle fastest and will support the work you're going to do next in Stage Three: Define. In the Define stage, you will use *their words* about *their experience* as the starting point for the conversations about the services your team will deliver, and the input from these interviews is necessary to do the Root Cause Analysis.

I'll show you how to help stakeholders prioritize at the end of this chapter. Then in Chapter 6, you'll learn how to get to the root of their challenges and design the services that target them.

Assess Your Current Capabilities

Once you have collected the input from your stakeholders and evaluated how projects are currently delivered in your organization, you can turn your attention to your own team. The information you've collected about what is working and what isn't will feed nicely into your evaluation of how your team is serving the organization and give you a more holistic picture than if you had started at this step. When you understand how and where project and strategy delivery are happening within your organization, within and beyond your immediate responsibility, you gain a comprehensive overview of the entire strategy lifecycle and the opportunities to provide value.

While I recommend starting with your own department that you're working in, wherever there is strategy and project delivery happening across the organization outside of your purview, it's helpful to explore those places as well. You may find opportunities to collaborate with your peers and leverage what already exists.

For example, if you are creating a department-level PMO and there are PMOs supporting other departments, you will want to learn more about what they are doing and how they are doing it.

Meet with the leaders of those teams, learn about their processes, pay attention to how their stakeholders talk about the services they provide. What are they doing that is working well, and where are their opportunities for improvement? What challenges do they talk about? These are all clues that can shape your strategy.

And if you're setting up an enterprise-level function to support different delivery teams in different departments, those delivery teams are part of your core stakeholder group. Learn everything you can about the services they provide and the capabilities they've built. You want to know what works well that could be expanded to work for the whole organization and what might need improving. Make it clear to these teams that you want to be careful not to break what is already working well—this will help them let their guard down a little so that you can partner more effectively. People can be very territorial about what they've built, and while they may have a different view than you do about what works, you don't want to miss goodness that can be expanded to serve others. This collaborative approach also helps them see your engagement as a partnership, not a takeover.

If you feel they would react positively, you could even gift them a copy of this book as a friendly, alliance-building gesture, and invite them into the assessment process you are going through. Combining forces to solve problems and grow together not only makes it easier to work together, but it also looks good to the executives when they see how well their teams are collaborating. These other teams that provide similar services are an opportunity for collaboration that can make the entire organization stronger, and you will have facilitated that improvement. We often suggest setting up a collaboration group that you could call a community of practice (CoP) or center of excellence (CoE) to give the delivery teams an opportunity to connect, learn and grow together, and be a part of influencing a future where everyone works together to deliver on the organization's strategy.

The Bigger-Picture SWOT Analysis

The SWOT Analysis is an evaluation of strengths, weaknesses, opportunities, and threats. This assessment is done in two parts.

First, you look inward at your own team and the services you are providing today, if you have an existing delivery function, and where the opportunities are to improve the entire strategy lifecycle. Then you evaluate what services exist throughout the organization to see where opportunities for improvement and collaboration exist. The inputs to this process will include the challenges, opportunities, and stakeholder evaluation work you've done so far in this stage.

When you've completed both parts of the assessment, you'll have the full picture that your executives are seeing, you'll have a more holistic view of what your team can do to help elevate the entire strategy delivery process, and you'll be able to find economies of scale by leveraging what is working elsewhere.

For example, if you're building an enterprise team and supporting other product or project delivery teams, where they have weaknesses, you could offer a service that supports all the delivery teams across the enterprise. Their weaknesses become your opportunities, and their strengths become places you don't need to worry about right now. The services these delivery teams are doing well also offer an opportunity for collaboration among the teams that you can facilitate, such as the community of practice mentioned above. We will explore these types of services more in the next stage, the Define stage.

The timing of this assessment is important. Once you've talked to the key stakeholders in this first round of assessment work, you'll have a different lens to look at your own team and better understand your strengths, weaknesses, opportunities, and threats through your stakeholders' eyes. They will provide new insight and perspective into what they value, what they don't, where they want support, and where they have yet to be convinced that you can help them. Your perspective is valuable, and certainly you are going to see things they don't, but remember, this organization does not belong to you. It belongs to the stakeholders because it delivers services to support those stakeholders all working to deliver the organization's strategy. Conduct the SWOT Analysis with your stakeholders' input in mind.

Don't worry if you are currently a team of one and just getting started. Remember, when you look at the full strategy lifecycle and at everyone who is working on delivering projects across the organization, your team is bigger than just you. Look at all the places where project delivery work is happening now in the organization and apply the four SWOT viewpoints. Someone is doing projects and some aspects of the delivery process are working well, so you don't want to break them. Given that you're reading this book, I suspect there are other aspects that stakeholders want fixed fast. As you will not be able to accomplish anything significant entirely on your own, you will need to do some relationship building, investigating, and exploring of what work is happening today and where to support each phase of the strategy lifecycle to provide value.

The SWOT Analysis with Your Team

The SWOT Analysis exercise is a great way to engage your existing team or a core group of project people in the process of evaluating the current state and starting to think about what is possible for an even brighter future. Your team is an important stakeholder group that needs to be included in this process, and they are probably hungry to be part of designing better solutions to their own pain points. Including them in the stakeholder interviews and SWOT Analysis will go a long way toward building their engagement in the process and their desire to drive better outcomes. Remember, the services you must create or elevate to achieve those better outcomes are *for* your stakeholders—including your team members who will deliver those solutions.

For example, if you have a team of project managers working with you (or sprinkled throughout the organization) to deliver projects, they will have tons of ideas on ways to improve the project delivery process. Note, however, that their perspective might still be focused on addressing symptoms, not root causes. They will likely say there aren't enough resources to do the projects, and as you'll learn in Chapter 6, that is usually a symptom of problems with the strategy definition phase. Collect their input on all of their pain points like you are doing for every other stakeholder group, and then complete the SWOT Analysis together. It will be an input you'll use throughout the Define stage.

As you conduct the SWOT Analysis, remember that you are looking across all aspects of the strategy lifecycle that you learned about in Chapter 1. For example, is there an opportunity for you to set projects up for success before they start, or do you have any critical business areas where you need to build stronger relationships? Keep an open mind and look for new opportunities to provide value to the organization even beyond project execution.

Here's a list of questions to help you facilitate your SWOT Analysis.

Strengths

1. What do stakeholders most value?
2. What do stakeholders perceive is working well now?
3. What does the broader organization do well today?
4. What parts of the organization are currently being supported?
5. Which project functions have the best support?
6. What are the most requested existing services?
7. What skills and expertise do we currently have as a team?

Weaknesses

1. What do stakeholders value least in the strategy delivery process?
2. Where is strategy delivery currently falling short?
3. Which business areas don't have support today? (This is also an opportunity.)
4. Which parts of the project delivery process have the least support?
5. What are the common complaints about project delivery?
6. What are the gaps in skills or resources within your team?

Opportunities

1. How can you align with the organization's strategy objecyives?
2. What new support requests are coming in that you don't support yet?
3. Which business areas need the most additional support?
4. Which services are dropped due to insufficient resources?
5. Which services have the most room for improvement?
6. Where could you support other parts of the strategy lifecycle?
7. How might you accelerate, streamline, and optimize project and strategy delivery?

Threats

1. Which services are also provided by other departments?
2. Which business areas have reduced reliance on services?
3. Which goals/objectives have been consistently missed?
4. Has funding declined relative to other business areas, and if so, where have cuts been made?
5. What are the largest frustrations of your stakeholders?
6. Are there conflicting organizational objectives that are not aligned with the desired outcomes?

Consider organizing the SWOT Analysis by the strategy lifecycle phases—strategy definition, execution, and realization—so you always keep the full picture of different places in the strategy process you can support front and center in your thinking.

After you complete the SWOT Analysis, you have done all the assessment work needed in Stage Two to prepare a presentation for your executives to keep them engaged in this process. You will need their input and support to guide your areas of focus in the rest of the stages.

SWOT ANALYSIS BY STRATEGY LIFECYCLE PHASE

STRENGTHS	WEAKNESSES
Strategy Definition:	Strategy Definition:
Strategy Execution:	Strategy Execution:
Strategy Realization:	Strategy Realization:

OPPORTUNITIES	THREATS
Strategy Definition:	Strategy Definition:
Strategy Execution:	Strategy Execution:
Strategy Realization:	Strategy Realization:

The Assessment Findings Presentation

It seemed like we were all on the same page. We were meeting with the top executives for a client to report the challenges we'd discovered in our assessment process. We walked the two top executives through our assessment findings, root causes (that you'll learn how to uncover in the Define stage), and top-level recommendations. Nina was nodding along and asking clarifying questions, but George did most of the talking. He said, "None of this is surprising and I see how it's holding us back. We need to make changes now if we're going to set ourselves up for a stronger year next year." With George's approval to proceed, we helped the team work on getting the first solution in place.

But things weren't moving as quickly as they normally do. Something was up.

My team reported that work kept getting stalled. It turned out that Nina had reservations that she chose not to voice in that meeting and, instead, quietly redirected her staff away from our recommendations, telling her team that she was "not convinced" it was the right path.

This required us to go back to the beginning of the stakeholder engagement process with Nina and dig deeper to find her WIIFM until we found out what she was truly afraid of—that she would lose control over the work she had her team doing. Nina was afraid that if the way she was allocating her resources to projects was exposed, it might uncover some gaps in her management approach. Her key trusted team members often hijacked other projects to steal resources for their priorities. It was leading to chaos, but Nina didn't see any other way to get her team's priorities done. What she didn't realize was that there was a much simpler way. Our recommendations were going to bring transparency, but they were also going to bring a lot less chaos and give Nina greater control. The work we had to do to set her at ease took a lot longer than it would have if we had initially done more digging to find that fear and had then shown her exactly how we would alleviate it. Sometimes stakeholders just won't share their concerns, so you have to pay attention to what they are doing, not just what they are saying.

Just like Diane experienced at the beginning of this chapter, you will have to invest the time at some point in this process, and it's a lot easier to do it earlier in the process than having to add relationship repair steps later.

The next week I found myself in the exact same situation with another client, and this time, I very intentionally guided the leaders to take their time, even when they wanted to "jump to the recommendations" and skip the critical step of getting everyone on the same page. After the meeting, I pulled the COO aside. "I know you want to get to the good stuff, but what would have happened if we had started talking about our recommendations and Linda didn't agree with the collected pain points or the root causes driving the need for change? Your transformation won't succeed unless we bring everyone with us through the change process." We would be in trouble if we didn't take the time to get on the same page now—especially since Linda, the CFO, had the ear of the president and had not fully bought in to the approach.

In the following weeks, we saw a shift with Linda. Not only had she bought in, because we'd taken the time to bring her through the process, but she started to speak up a lot more in meetings and showed a strong desire to take ownership of working together to get to the better business outcomes. Linda now has a robust strategy delivery office reporting to her, and the company has been able to deliver three times as many projects in a year that are all directly aligned with helping the company scale and expand their service offerings much faster than they had predicted in their five-year plan.

The work you do to present your findings and get feedback will make or break your success in the long run, so take your time here to ensure your executives are invested in the process before you proceed. You'll benefit from having them by your side every step of the way.

In this final step in Stage Two: Assess, you walk your executives through the findings of your assessment process, engage them by asking for feedback (e.g., Anything missing? Any surprises? Anything you disagree with?), and enlist their help in prioritizing where you will focus your energy first. You will certainly find more challenges and opportunities than you can possibly address all at once, so remember to prioritize rather than trying to boil the ocean and fix everything at once. Your goal with this presentation is to educate the executives on what you have discovered and get them to identify priorities where your team will focus first, second, and third.

Don't be surprised if, like George, they say they are already aware of the challenges and respond with, "Well of course, that's why we hired you!" Many leaders know that there are challenges, but they might be shocked by some of the details you share about what the ripple effect of the challenges they see is doing to the productivity and morale in the organization. Every time I've done this—when I was in your shoes, and now with our client executives—we've shone a light on challenges they didn't realize were happening. Reassure them that this is normal. They couldn't possibly be expected to know everything that's happening in the organization or they wouldn't be able to do their jobs at the executive level. They're lucky to have you to give them visibility into how things are working now and how they can partner with you to build a better future together.

For example, many times, staff are not comfortable telling the unvarnished truth about what's really going on in their department. That could be because the executives haven't created a culture of transparency and have failed to celebrate honesty when things aren't working well—like when someone uses red on a status report to indicate the project is off track. In some organizations, there is a culture of fear around being honest about how work is progressing. Or it could be that staff don't realize that it's safe to tell the truth about where projects are and that the executives actually want them to do so. Executives are always telling me, "I can't make decisions because I don't even have a clear picture of what's going on in the organization." They don't need to know it all, but they have to know enough to help you and the rest of the teams responsible for delivery. This process is aimed at uncovering the holistic picture of what is really happening, including in the hearts and minds of their hardworking project people. If you hide the truth, the executives can't help you or take ownership of the outcomes.

It's also quite possible that the executives just don't know what they don't know. Maybe they aren't asking good questions, or maybe it's simply that no one person can know how everything is going across the whole organization, especially as the organization grows and becomes more departmentalized. Silos often prevent full transparency and cross-collaboration; if that's the case in your organization, it's OK to identify this dynamic and share it with everyone. This is an opportunity for your team to create transparency and open communication where it doesn't exist today. An organizational weakness becomes an opportunity for a service you create, and this kind of help for your executives is a fast way to earn their trust and respect.

You will also be asking your executives to prioritize the challenges and opportunities you've gathered so you can figure out where your team spends time in the first and each subsequent IMPACT Delivery

Cycle. And if they have not been the best at setting priorities (as you may have discovered in the assessment process), this is your chance to role-model prioritization. You will specifically guide them through a process of prioritizing your findings, which will demonstrate the power of prioritization and focus to drive fast results. The entire IMPACT Engine System is geared toward high-value fast results.

You must focus on prioritization, specifically, with your executives because every executive I've ever met (including me) wants to do more and do it faster than their team could possibly handle. Prioritization is also a powerful skill that every executive needs in order to effectively deliver their strategy. By asking them to set priorities, you will build buy-in and create accountability with your business leaders, who are part of both the problem (because they can't unsee the truth when you show it to them) and the solution (because they will now be asked to help you determine what to address when). Your presentation of the assessment findings will help your stakeholders prioritize their pain points so you can get to work to solve them in order of priority.

Your presentation positions you to shift the focus from outputs to better business outcomes. By connecting the pain points, opportunities, and insights gathered during the assessment, you will facilitate the prioritization of specific areas that need focus so you can begin solving problems in the next stage, all with the support of your stakeholders. Although you will avoid discussing solutions during this conversation, your prioritized list of the pain points is the key input to the Root Cause Analysis you'll go on to do in Chapter 6.

And remember, even if you think you already know what to fix and are anxious to get to the fixing part, hold off for a little bit longer. This presentation is a critical step in creating transparency around the real challenges that are happening through the eyes of those delivering the strategy, and earning that early buy-in will prevent change resistance later. You'll need your executives to tell you where to focus first. Since you might come back to them later to ask for funding or resources, they need to *feel* the pain that's happening in their organization. That will motivate them to help you fix it.

Shift the focus from outputs to better business outcomes.

The goal of the assessment findings presentation is to create space for everyone to get on the same page regarding the organization's challenges and opportunities. During this exercise, participants have a chance to hear about what is working and what is not working for their peers, to see themselves and their teams reflected in your findings, and to feel the pain the organization has been going through.

So, what should this assessment presentation look like? Here are the components of the presentation and tips on facilitating the conversation with your executives.

1 **Executive summary:** This page should answer the question "Why are we here?" Give the presentation participants context for the task you've been assigned to solve. Make sure you include information about their expectations and the fact that they will be asked to prioritize your team's areas of focus.

2 **Assessment approach:** Walk the participants through a summary of the steps you took, the stakeholders you talked to or the groups that were represented, and the assessments you completed. Help them understand how comprehensive the assessment is and the critical role this holistic input plays in finding the right path forward. Pro tip: Share a list of everyone engaged in this process to acknowledge their effort, as well as to ensure that your executives can see who is supporting this process and who might be missing.

3 **What's working well:** It can help put your participants at ease if you can point out a few things you discovered that are working well in the strategy delivery process today. You can organize them into themes that emerged when interviewing stakeholders. For example, certain departments might have good processes or resources that can be shared to accelerate improvements in other areas of the organization.

4 **Assessment findings:** Provide a summary of the key learnings from your assessment work. Organize the feedback, observations, and any measurable results that illustrate what is working and not working today so participants can start to understand and relate

to the improvement opportunities. It's best to have only a few key data points per page of your presentation so your participants can focus on and process what you are telling them. Allow space for them to find and talk about what they care about from your list so that everyone has those insights in mind when they prioritize. Remember to focus on current state reflections instead of allowing the conversation to veer toward solutions. You'll see why in Chapter 6.

5 **Challenges:** Present the key findings you discovered through your interviews so your executives start to feel a sense of urgency around solving the problems that interfere with achieving their desired business results. You can use the strategy lifecycle to show where the problems usually start. This will get them thinking about the possible root causes and areas of focus.

6 **Opportunities:** Show the places that you and the stakeholders have discovered opportunities for improvement (to address pain points) and expansion of services (to support new areas). You can use the SWOT Analysis findings and the business challenges and pain points that your stakeholders shared, as well as any opportunities for improvement.

7 **Industry perspective:** If this is helpful to your leaders, show them the data that supports their desire for improved strategy delivery outcomes and the challenges facing organizations broadly. You can use this book and any of the statistics it references, and the industry status of the IMPACT Engine System, to help you build credibility in your approach.

8 **Prioritize challenges and opportunities:** With the findings in hand, you can now guide the participants through a prioritization process. This is not a detailed plan of solutions, only a ranking of the challenges and opportunities identified. Facilitate an exercise to prioritize the order in which these challenges and opportunities are addressed. The good news here is that because you are only prioritizing symptoms, you'll likely be able to fix several of these priorities with one solution to their root cause.

9. **Next steps:** Tell them what you'll do next. First you will conduct a Root Cause Analysis to uncover the underlying problems that result in the symptoms they now see. Then you will develop solutions to address those root causes. After that, you will define an IMPACT Delivery Model to show them what business problems your team will solve, in priority order. Let them know that you'll be back at the end of the Plan stage to walk through the root causes, recommended solutions, and the road map to get there.

In many organizations, socializing your draft presentation can go a long way to building the pre-meeting support that will translate to the necessary buy-in in the room. No one likes to be blindsided, especially since some of your findings could be interpreted as management shortcomings. Follow the cultural norms of your organization to pull in key supporters early to help you draft the content and even do the necessary wordsmithing. At the very least, you will want to be in lockstep with your sponsor, and they may even want to put their stamp of approval on it before the big meeting.

Remember, this journey is not about superficial temporary fixes to symptoms or implementing generic solutions. It is about developing a nuanced understanding of your organization and addressing its unique challenges in a way that drives meaningful and lasting IMPACT. With a comprehensive assessment process, you can lay the foundation for success and pave the way for effective delivery practices within your organization.

If you don't have people on your team yet, this can be a great place to ask to add team members to help you address the assessment findings, determine the root causes, and work with you to design and build solutions to those root causes. Once your stakeholders see how focused you are on solving what matters most to them and begin to feel shared pain, they will be more likely to want to invest in helping you get there.

You will need the work from this stage to proceed to the next, so if you haven't completed it, go do that work now. Start with the executive in your department and see what that conversation uncovers for you. Remember, having good stakeholder conversations is not a one-time thing. You will have these conversations continually. You just need to have enough to give you a sense of what's happening, and each conversation will point you to where you need to look next.

Trust yourself. Trust the process. It's time to make an IMPACT.

MAKE AN IMPACT

Think: Do you have a clear picture of your stakeholders' challenges and opportunities?

Do: Download the Stakeholder Engagement Plan and complete the Challenges and Opportunities section. When that's complete, create your assessment findings presentation and schedule the meeting with your key stakeholders.

STAGE 3

DEFINE HIGH-IMPACT SERVICES

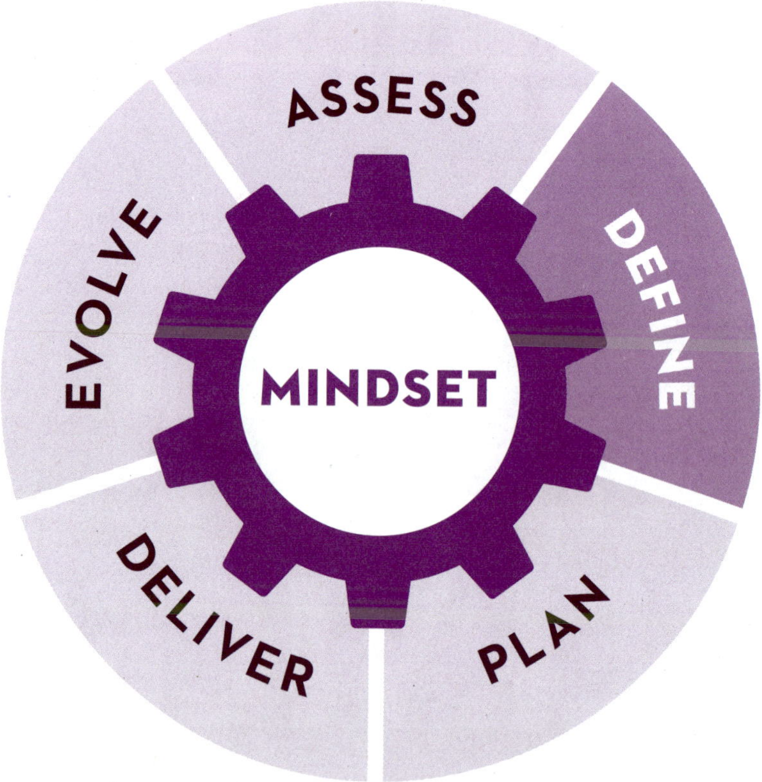
ASSESS
DEFINE
PLAN
DELIVER
EVOLVE
MINDSET

This stage is about defining the IMPACT delivery services and capability you will create for the organization.

In the Assess stage, you partnered with your business leaders to create a prioritized list of challenges and opportunities to address. You will now conduct a Root Cause Analysis to determine what's driving those challenges, so you solve the right problems and make space for the new opportunities to be realized. Then you will know what services you need to build in order to address the root causes discovered.

Your goal is acceleration of IMPACT. Delivery leaders often create services that feel like they are just slowing everyone down and then wonder why they hit a wall of resistance. You'll learn what services to put in place, and in what order, to have your stakeholders begging for more and feeling like it's *their* idea!

It's important to remember that you will be iterating your way to IMPACT, meaning you will go through each of these cycles again and again, making incremental changes that let you show value fast while keeping the changes manageable and digestible by the organization. In your MVP cycle, your aim is to gain a comprehensive understanding of the challenges, opportunities, root causes, and solutions—but not to implement everything in that first cycle. In Stage Four: Plan, you'll then use the prioritization you already did with executives to help you figure out which service you'll introduce for your MVP cycle and in subsequent cycles.

Let's do this!

Solve the Right Problems

JACK WAS the CEO of a Fortune 500 company that had been in business for many years, but they were facing a significant challenge: successfully executing the company's strategy to position themselves as a market leader. Jack was super frustrated by the time he reached out to my organization for help.

As we embarked on this journey with Jack and his team, we discovered a glaring gap between those who defined the strategy and those who were responsible for implementing it. This gap had plagued the company for years, hindering their progress and causing widespread frustration. Projects faltered and the desired outcomes remained elusive. Something had to change. Feeling confident that the business strategy was sound, Jack's leadership team had asked us to "fix broken projects" so they could get the better business outcomes the strategy promised. Our team dove in quickly to learn what might be leading to slow delivery.

When the leadership would toss the strategy into the laps of the delivery team, their strategy execution office would ask one important question: "How important is this compared to everything else you want us to do?" And how did the leadership team respond? "Well, it's really important, like everything else." Because they didn't feel empowered to challenge this mandate, the delivery teams got busy dividing up the team across everything. The result? Teams ended up with 1/16th of a critical resource on their project. How can anyone get anything done with 1/16th of a person?

They were learning a tough lesson—when everything is important, nothing is important.

The slow progress stressed out all the team managers, who would tell their people to fill any open moments with work, which usually ended up being busywork or pet projects that were not aligned to the strategy. This caused the progress on the most important projects to slow down even more. Jack's team spent all day working frantically on everything they thought was important, switching from task to task based on who or what was squeaking most loudly, and without clearly aligned priorities. Everyone looked busy, but no one was getting to the critical business outcomes. Busy does not equal productive. Busy gets in the way of productive.

In response, the delivery teams started to complain that they didn't have enough resources to do the work on their plates, but every request for additional budget or resources was denied because the executives didn't want to invest more money until they started seeing results—they didn't believe that people were working hard enough anyway. And so the gap between the strategy and execution widened. Every "closing the gap" technique Jack was told to try made things worse. His business strategy was slipping through his fingers.

All the team wanted was to make the leadership happy. But here's the worst part: they didn't know how to do that because they didn't know what Jack wanted.

When I asked Jack's managers about their workload, they were clearly proud of how "busy" everyone was, even though they struggled to explain why they were doing the work they were doing. I talked to them about aligning their priorities to the company strategy, and almost every single middle manager said the same thing: "What strategy?"

How could Jack's managers not know what the company's strategy was when Jack's leadership team seemed so clear? When I asked Jack how he'd shared that strategy with the organization, it turned out that he had spent nine months perfecting that strategy with his

Solve business problems, not just project problems.

leaders. But then he spent only 60 minutes laying it out for the delivery team in a town hall meeting, believing that was sufficient.

What Jack's team failed to realize is that simply telling the organization what the strategy is in a one-way meeting does not embed that strategy into the minds, behaviors, and culture of the organization. The delivery teams were left to draw their own conclusions about where they fit into this overall strategy. The executives may have seen the big picture, but they failed to turn that into a meaningful set of priorities that the delivery teams could embrace and execute.

To fix this, the delivery team was going to need to stop trying to fix projects and start looking at the business problems standing in the way of success.

Your job is to solve business problems, not just project problems. So you must use what you learned about the business problems in your organization as your stakeholders see them (Stage Two: Assess) so that you can get to the root causes. If you jump to addressing those symptoms without getting to the root causes first, you will almost certainly waste time putting a bandage on a problem that requires surgery.

The beauty of addressing root causes instead of only symptoms is that often you can solve many pain points at once. One of the things we needed to do to get Jack's organization back on track was a Root Cause Analysis. Now let me take you through the technique we used to do that.

Find Root Cause with the Five Whys Technique

Although there are many techniques for doing a Root Cause Analysis, my favorite is the Five Whys technique developed by Sakichi Toyoda, the founder of Toyota Industries, to improve Toyota's manufacturing process. It's easy to use and doesn't require a lot of explanation. In fact, many parents already have experience with this technique thanks to inquisitive toddlers wanting to know more about the way the world works—although for them it's more like 50 Whys.

When we conducted a Root Cause Analysis in Jack's organization, we used the Five Whys to ensure the solutions we put in place would address what was really going on. It is a simple technique that allowed us to engage in meaningful conversations with stakeholders, which was part of our strategy to keep them going with us through the entire process.

You start this technique by identifying a problem, which is the work you did in the Assess stage. Pick one of the pain points you heard about in the assessment process. Then simply ask why that problem is happening.

When you get the answer to that "why," you then ask why *that* is happening, and keep asking until you are comfortable that you have reached the root cause (which is not always exactly five times, the name of the technique notwithstanding). Likely multiple pain points will present themselves in this process (just like you will hear multiple pain points from your stakeholders in the assessment process), but keep asking and try not to get distracted by symptoms or jump to solutions. You know you've arrived at the root cause when you've uncovered a fundamental reason that, if addressed, would prevent the problem from occurring again. The root cause often creates a ripple effect of symptoms.

In my experience, you just know when you get to the root cause. It's the problem you must fix first so you can create the ripple effect of improvement through several other pain points.

Here are some of the indicators that you have located the root cause.

1 **Collaboration:** The Five Whys technique is often conducted as a team so you can unlock the root causes together. When the team members agree that they have identified the underlying cause that, if resolved, would eliminate the problem, you may have found the root cause.

    Key question: Who needs to be in this conversation to answer the why questions?

2 **Logical progression:** As you ask why repeatedly, you should be able to establish an orderly sequence of cause-and-effect relationships. Each new "why" should build upon the previous answer, until you reach a point where you can clearly see that asking more why questions isn't necessary. Even better, you should see a pattern in which many of the symptoms start to converge on a small set of possible root causes.

Key question: Has the logical progression narrowed the candidate root causes to a select few?

3 **Necessity and sufficiency:** If you can narrow the candidate root causes down to a simple one, it must necessarily have a direct and significant influence on the problem, without any other contributing factors playing a major role. If, however, a single candidate root cause by itself is not sufficient to cause the downstream pain points, then bundle more of the "select few" in until the combination is sufficient. When you can name a root cause that would eliminate the problem(s), you have likely found it.

Key question: Will addressing the identified root cause create the desired ripple effect that addresses the major pain points?

That root cause can be used to build a strong story that makes it nearly impossible to resist taking action. You do this by showing not only the symptom and root cause, but the consequences of inaction. In your Root Cause Analysis Worksheet, you can document each of these talking points to facilitate that discussion.

- **Symptom:** The description of the challenge in their words.
- **Root cause:** What's really driving the symptom you see.
- **Outcome:** The positive benefit they want to see.
- **Consequences:** The implications if the root cause is not addressed. This should outline what risks, costs, or other negative effects they are experiencing or could face if they don't act.

While ultimately we'll be talking in terms of positive IMPACT across your organization when the root cause is addressed, it can be helpful to also make the consequences of inaction clear. Make a compelling case for why doing nothing is in fact deciding to continue with the same negative consequences your stakeholders have been complaining about. Not doing anything is still making a decision—a decision to accept that the negative consequences will continue. The decision-makers need to see that and own it.

While the Five Whys technique is not foolproof, it can guide you in the right direction. Use it as a starting point and complement it with other problem-solving techniques as needed. For example, in prior project management or business process improvement training, you may have learned about Ishikawa (or fishbone) diagrams, Pareto Analysis, causal factor trees, or scatterplots. Each of these techniques can be useful, but don't you dare start trying to use them all! That's a recipe for analysis paralysis and a growing list of impatient stakeholders. If your organization is already using a specific root cause technique effectively, by all means use it. If not, give the Five Whys a try. The goal is to keep it simple and know that the more you do this exercise, the faster you'll see the root causes. If you are struggling to get to the root cause, then you may not have the right people in the conversation. In that case, now is the time to expand your circle of participants. You'll get to the root cause faster together and, as a bonus, more people will become invested in the process and in supporting the solution.

In my company, we do this work for our clients all the time and we have so much fun with the exercise. Because we've seen a lot of clients across industries struggle with similar problems, we can usually draft the Root Cause Analysis in our heads quickly after conducting a set of stakeholder interviews with executives and key resources who are engaged in the full strategy lifecycle. But do you know what we don't do, even as experts? Jump to any conclusions.

There are two reasons for that. First, our instincts might tell us we have the answers early, but we still need to be sure, so we have to go through this whole process. Second, we must bring the stakeholders with us on this journey. If we immediately start giving them the answers without first helping them see the truth for themselves, then they may not believe us and they will certainly take more convincing when we propose the solutions.

Connecting the assessment findings discussed in Chapter 5 with the root causes work described here prepares executives to have the "aha" moments you need them to have to support the services you're going to recommend next.

The Five Whys in Action

When we used the Five Whys with Jack's company, we were responding to their chief complaint that projects were taking too long and costing too much. Business leaders blamed the delivery teams and the managers leading the projects. Typically, this is where delivery leaders will be lured into a false sense that they have the answer and assume that better project management training will fix the issue. We heard, "If only the project managers were better at managing projects, we would have projects meeting the time and budget requirements."

So we met with the project managers to learn why projects were routinely off track. Every project manager explained that they were doing their best to keep things moving, but that project team members were always behind on their deliverables. Why? Their functional managers regularly added new work to their plates after they had made commitments on their deliverables and deadlines.

The functional team members said that what started as reasonable timelines went out the window the minute that their boss added one of their own pet projects to the team's plate. They didn't feel empowered to question the additional workload or ask leaders to help prioritize their time, so they just kept trying to keep all the work moving ahead.

Even the project managers who were best at managing scope found they had little control over the disruptive shifts in priority and associated resource assignments, and their attempts to communicate the consequences came across as complaining—or worse, as "project manager geek speak." The project managers were begging leaders for more resources to handle the additional workload, but no one had a clear picture of all the work happening.

When executives looked at each project individually, the volume of work seemed reasonable. Similarly, the functional managers viewed the workload they were assigning as appropriate in size.

While the workload might have appeared manageable when viewed through independent lenses, collectively there was likely too much on everyone's plates. The individual project and functional managers were working in silos, without an understanding of the organization's total workload.

When we asked why the functional managers were doubling up on work, we learned that each department was measured by the work in their departments and not by the outcomes of the larger cross-functional initiatives. It turned out that the strategy was being defined at the executive level, and projects were being defined and budgeted through a separate process. To make matters worse, the strategy was not an input to the annual planning process for projects or performance plans for the staff. There was no connection between strategy for the organization, work being done by teams, and how performance was being measured. We also discovered that no one was looking at the big picture of all of the work collectively across the organization.

Finally, we got to the root cause and identified something they could fix. Jack's organization was missing clear alignment between the strategy, holistic prioritization for the projects managed across departments, and visibility into the work being managed in the departments in alignment with that strategy. This led to extremely slow progress, exhausted staff, and a lot of waste.

If we had started fixing the symptoms as the team saw them, we'd have trained project managers and added more templates, processes, and tools to manage the schedule and budget. We would have called attention to the perceived resource shortages and suggested hiring

FIND ROOT CAUSE BY ASKING "WHY?"

SYMPTOM

Projects take too long and cost too much

WHY?

Project managers not managing projects well

WHY?

Project team members always behind

WHY?

Projects keep getting added to the plate

WHY?

More projects than staff to do them

WHY?

Shifting and unclear priorities

SOLUTION

Visibility, prioritization, and strategic alignment

EXAMPLE

more people. However, these actions would have done nothing to address the fact that the business leaders were not prioritizing work for the teams or allowing them time to do it. Adding more people to the project delivery process would have masked the problem somewhat, but without addressing the root cause, it would have perpetuated the problem rather than solving it. In fact, adding more people to a chaotic process might have slowed projects down even more.

Instead, we helped the leaders clarify and communicate their strategy, created a governance model to drive cohesive decision-making, and implemented a project portfolio prioritization framework that helped everyone see what work was happening. This helped business leaders work together to create clear priorities for all work being done by staff, and showed the business leaders where the team needed them to accelerate getting to business outcomes, instead of unintentionally slowing things down.

Once we had a prioritized list of projects, we staggered the work throughout the year so that the teams had more time to work on the highest-priority projects first. Only when they were finished with those high-priority projects did they start the next group of projects. By the end of that first year, the teams completed three times as many projects in a single year as they had with a similar-sized portfolio the year before. This is the power of prioritization and focused teams.

And here's the best part: individual performance and employee retention both went up significantly during this time. Teams were empowered to get their projects done faster. Everyone felt great and they got three times the work done. When you fix the root cause, a positive ripple effect happens.

The Five Whys approach is simple and encourages curiosity, engagement, and relationship building, all the things you want to do with your stakeholders and teams. It doesn't require any special tools or extra work to set up, and it is easy for everyone to understand. After you demonstrate the power of "why," it can easily become a part of your everyday conversations moving forward.

When you fix the root cause, a positive ripple effect happens.

As you're having these collaborative conversations, you may notice that certain stakeholders will have "aha" moments as they realize some of the root causes. Excellent work! This is part of bringing them with you through the change process. You are the navigator of the Root Cause Analysis, and you want to allow your stakeholders to have a sense of ownership by being in the driver's seat exploring issues and determining root causes. The more they feel like it's their idea, the more they will buy into the entire process.

Once you complete the Root Cause Analysis, you will know what services you need to put in place to address those root causes across the entire strategy lifecycle. The next chapter will guide you through the process of identifying the right services to support your organization in accelerating strategy delivery.

Trust yourself. Trust the process. It's time to make an IMPACT.

MAKE AN IMPACT

Think: What is the best way to lead the organization to identify the root causes of the challenges and opportunities your stakeholders identified? Who are the right people to engage in this process?

Do: Download the Root Cause Analysis Worksheet to get to the underlying business challenges you must address.

Create Solutions Across the Strategy Lifecycle

YOU ARE now ready to determine solutions to address the root causes you discovered in the last chapter—and there's a reason you are halfway through this book before I talk about how to develop solutions. It's a lot easier and faster when you're solving the right problems.

Although this stage explores the ways that you can deliver services and capabilities for your organization, you don't want to start delivering those services just yet. This stage is about *defining*, not delivering. Your goal for now is to determine what services will support your organization to get the right people delivering the right projects the right way at the right time. And that right time is what we'll address next.

Sequence Matters

When Priya joined as the new Strategy Director, she inherited a team frustrated by unclear direction and haphazardly defined and prioritized projects. Initiatives were constantly delayed or descoped midstream as priorities abruptly shifted.

Priya worked with her stakeholders to determine the root causes: no formal intake process, ineffective governance, unclear business cases for projects, and everything feeling like it was a number one priority.

She approached the CTO, Jeff, about addressing these foundational issues first before implementing any new systems. But Jeff dismissed Priya's concerns and forged ahead with his pet project—a new enterprise project management system. "This system will solve all our problems if we just get it in place," he insisted. "It will impose the governance we need through its configurable workflows and auto-prioritize projects based on data."

Priya pushed back. "But if everything is still entering through informal channels, and we don't have our decision-making processes clear, won't we just end up with garbage data in a shiny new system?"

Jeff waved his hand. "Once the system is implemented, people will be forced to use it properly. Do I need to escalate this to the CEO and let her know you are obstructing progress?"

Intimidated, Priya reluctantly agreed to implement the new system. As predicted, problems emerged immediately. Since intake and prioritization remained broken, scrapped projects and priorities littered the system. Everything was still a number one priority and most of the users "forced" to use the system had never even logged in because they were too busy putting heroic effort into getting their projects done. Priya's team spent more time trying to clean things up and chase people for their project status updates than using the system properly.

Angry project managers stormed into Priya's office. "This system is useless; it doesn't reflect reality! I'm sticking with my spreadsheets," one complained. The business stakeholders wouldn't even engage and they kept blaming the IT department for pushing their technology on the rest of the organization.

Priya tried to address their concerns and provide more training, but no one was interested. They had lost faith in the system and in Priya's leadership.

After 12 frustrating months, the CEO finally intervened. She admonished Jeff, "This expensive system has only made things worse!" She called us and it didn't take long to figure out that everything was a mess and no amount of technology was going to fix that. "At best, this system will help you do the wrong things faster," I told her.

We guided her whole leadership team through what was happening and why. We put the expansion of the software on hold and guided Priya through the process of setting a stronger foundation for the software to sit upon.

Within six months, priorities were aligned, resources were freed up, and projects were moving smoothly again. The strategy office finally had credibility to get people to adopt the system, and their expansion of the platform was now welcomed instead of resisted. Priya knew they needed the right foundation first before implementing any tools, but she hadn't invested enough time in Stage Two—building the relationship with Jeff and other executives. She wished she had trusted her instincts from the beginning or had known what to say to get Jeff on board so they could have avoided this painful process.

If you find yourself in a similar situation, go back to the stakeholder engagement techniques from Stage Two and invest time in building relationships with the influencers who are attempting to steamroll you. Assume positive intent and truly listen to their pain points, pressures, challenges, and fears. You're sure to find common ground you both believe in. And that foundation will give you a trusted platform to build upon so you can start working together to solve the problems you are facing instead of battling it out or getting bullied by someone with a bigger title in your organization.

Avoid the Software-First Trap

If your stakeholders ask you to start by adding software first, be careful about following through on this direction—it's going to make it much harder for you to get the results you need quickly. You might implement the wrong software for your organization or, as Priya experienced, automate a bad process and make the situation worse. You may spend a lot of time to deliver something that does not address your stakeholders' most obvious challenges. Remember, you are looking for root causes, not symptoms. If a tool is difficult to use, that is even worse. You need good process, and people in place to execute that process, before you automate it. Automating bad process just digs a hole that is harder to get out of.

You'll know if you are in the software trap if people think the tool will solve all the problems or conversely complain the software is hard to use, if they don't use it at all, if the real data is sitting on people's computers outside of the software, or if you are duplicating effort. If any of these situations are happening right now for your organization, hit the pause button. Check out the services you can implement using our framework in the next section and revisit the software once you have the right foundational layers in place. This is a great example of where sequence matters.

Even if you have already purchased software or are about to, my advice would be to hold off on implementing it until you get through Stage Four: Plan. It's about timing and getting things done in the right order in the right way to achieve ultimate success. You want to use technology to automate and accelerate the right process with the right people working on the right priorities. Otherwise, you will just have people doing bad process faster—making the situation worse.

When the Leader Is the Problem

Steve hired my company to help him build a project management office. He said his mix of client projects and internal projects were taking too long and the company was losing too much of the potential profit on client engagements. It didn't take me long to see what was going on. In fact, it was obvious after the first few meetings. I couldn't get Steve to focus. We would meet with him to give him updates on the work that needed his leadership team's attention, and he would spend much of the meeting reading emails on his tablet.

This lack of focus permeated his organization. No one was focused and it was costing the organization millions. The leadership team's desire to be everywhere at once led to a cascading series of meetings, each triggering another, and ultimately contributing to a slowdown in organizational processes. There was no organized method for getting the leadership team's attention when there were issues, and sometimes it would take weeks to get on the executives' calendars when a decision needed to be made. The leaders didn't realize that because nothing had their focus for long, they were the ones slowing projects down by taking so long to make decisions. Nothing else we were going to do to "fix project management" would have mattered at all if we couldn't create focus. Remember, step one in the IMPACT Driver Mindset is Instill Focus. That's where we had to start, but how do you tell the boss that they need to change first?

You may have experienced a leader like this and not have known how to address it. It's hard to say "You're the problem" to your business leaders. Admittedly, it's much easier for a consultant to say what needs to be said because that's why they've hired us, and we aren't at risk of losing our job for upsetting the executive with the truth. But don't forget: your expertise is also why they've hired you. You are the expert, and as you discover these root causes, it's important that you find a way to change the behaviors at the executive level that are contributing to the problems you are seeing.

Here's how I handled the problem of focus when I was in your shoes. For a short time, I had a manager who seemed overwhelmed by the responsibilities of her role. She couldn't figure out what to focus on and was constantly trying to "multitask" by reading emails or doing things on her computer when I had a one-on-one meeting with her. Her brain couldn't really process what I was saying while she was reading and responding to emails, so I usually felt like I was talking to myself. She didn't seem to notice that this made me and the rest of her team feel unimportant and our work low priority. To address her lack of attention, I would simply say, "I will come back at another time. This topic is too important to not have your full attention. When is a better time for you?" That's usually enough to get someone to realize what they are doing, and it gives them the opportunity to tell you if there really is something more important that they must address at that moment.

I used that same technique with Steve to get him to refocus on the conversations we were having with him. I also added, in that case, that the meeting was for him and that we would be asking him to make some decisions based on what we were telling him, so we needed his full attention. He put his device aside and engaged fully with us.

Once we addressed the focus problem, we could start fixing the other challenges in the strategy lifecycle.

Organize the Solutions Across the Strategy Lifecycle

Before you develop any solutions, it can be helpful to organize the root causes by the three phases of the strategy lifecycle. You may find root causes in problems that are happening before projects start in your organization (strategy definition). If you fix those first, it's likely that projects are better set up for success before they start and that the perceived challenges happening in the strategy execution phase "magically" disappear because people are better enabled to do good work.

For the rest of this chapter, I am going to explore some categories of services and capabilities that you can deliver, with the goal of identifying areas where you can make the greatest IMPACT. This is not an all-inclusive list, just enough to get you thinking about what you could do to solve the business problems your organization has and expose you to some ways you can rethink some typical services you may see in the industry.

Here's what you must remember: you are creating services that are uniquely designed to serve your organization and solve the specific root causes you have already determined. They must be a fit for what most easily solves your organization's business problems. That means no generic list derived without the inputs of your assessment

Fix root causes, not symptoms.

process is going to be adequate. You must do the work to figure out what will be best for your organization.

These services are organized by the three phases of the strategy lifecycle (Chapter 1) so that you understand what kinds of solutions to root causes you can deliver to set the strategy up for success, to accelerate execution of that strategy, and to realize the intended measurable business value faster. Remember, when you fix problems in the right order, you can often address several symptoms at once. That means we start at the front end of the strategy lifecycle with services that set delivery teams up for success before the projects ever start.

Strategy Definition

When you set up your organization's business strategy for success, the projects to deliver that strategy are also set up for success. If you establish right-sized governance mechanisms and implement effective portfolio management practices, your organization can allocate resources better, enhance decision-making processes, and make sure strategy and execution are aligned. A strong leadership team is essential for making informed decisions, prioritizing work, and aligning teams with organizational goals; you are the one who will put right-sized governance and portfolio management in place to support your leaders in making the necessary decisions to keep the strategy moving forward.

If you are tempted to skip ahead to the strategy execution phase to start fixing things, stop. You must make sure the strategy execution phase is built on top of the strong foundation of a well-supported strategy definition phase. Otherwise, you're setting the organization up to do the wrong work better.

For example, if you have every project start the first day of the fiscal year, your resources will be spread so thinly that everything might start, but none of the projects will move very quickly. Instead, you might stagger the projects to start when you have the team members available to do the work, and you'll find that, with a focused team, projects can gain some serious momentum in the strategy execution phase and finish much faster. You'll also see a much higher return on investment for the project in strategy realization because it won't cost so much time and money to get that work done. Everyone will be in flow.

However, nothing you do will make much of a difference if all the projects are labeled as a number one priority, or if the projects have no clear alignment with the organization's business strategy. When thinking about services you could create, the first places I usually recommend checking are governance, portfolio management, and prioritization—all solutions that you would implement in the strategy definition phase.

As you consider potential service offerings, ask yourself these three questions:

1 Do you have a strong leadership team that is making educated and informed decisions about projects?

2 Is the leadership team prioritizing work so that it can happen in the order of most value for the organization?

3 Are delivery teams well aligned with the organizational goals so they can deliver quickly while driving the greatest ROI?

If the answer to any of these three questions is no, this is likely where you will want to start with defining solutions. Starting in the right place, you can benefit from the ripple effect that comes from setting the whole strategy delivery lifecycle up for success.

If these elements are already in place now, great! Read through each of the following services to evaluate the effectiveness of the solution and consider, with your root causes in mind, if there are any changes that you should make now. You might find opportunities to elevate delivery of your current services.

OK, keeping your root causes in hand, let's look at some ways you can address them.

Strategy Governance Framework

A governance framework provides the overarching structure, policies, processes, and roles for managing initiatives and projects across the enterprise. It establishes decision-making authority, stage gates, and governance bodies and defines the high-level processes for executing work from idea through benefits realization.

Why it matters: If a root cause of the pain points is that your business leaders cannot make decisions because they don't have a model for effective decision-making, this solution can help. A solid governance framework is crucial for making sure an organization's strategy is supported and delivered successfully at all phases of the strategy lifecycle. It lays out clear, structured processes to guide the entire journey of strategy delivery, ensuring the right decisions are being made by the right people at the right time.

A governance framework creates shared understanding among all parties involved about their specific roles in supporting the strategy at each phase. This understanding fosters collaboration, minimizes confusion, and prevents redundant efforts, which can be a common challenge. It enables the organization to work toward strategic objectives as a unified leadership team.

A strong governance framework also emphasizes prioritizing high-value initiatives and allocating resources to those initiatives to accelerate progress on the organization's most important goals. By streamlining decision-making through an effective governance process, organizations can achieve objectives efficiently, maximize value, and drive higher-IMPACT outcomes with clarity and transparency. For governance to work well, you will need an effective portfolio management model, which we'll cover next.

Portfolio Management Model

A portfolio management model focuses specifically on managing a portfolio of initiatives in an organization. It encompasses prioritization, capacity planning, resource optimization, balancing, and monitoring, and enables governance of the body of work. A portfolio management model gives a view of the full scope of projects and enables strategic decision-making by the governance function defined above to maximize the value of the portfolio.

Why it matters: Many executives will complain that they know how to make decisions and are more than happy to do so, but they don't have the information they need to make them. A portfolio management model can address this root cause. Implementing an effective portfolio management model is crucial for optimizing an organization's strategy execution and driving better results. This approach aligns all key decision-makers and makes priorities visible to the delivery teams doing the work, so the organization can steer straight toward strategic goals.

A portfolio perspective enables objective analysis to determine which projects will deliver the highest returns, ensuring resources flow to the initiatives that drive the most value. It also allows for mixing high-risk, high-reward projects with safer bets to manage risk exposure, balancing risk vs. reward.

The portfolio view lets you see resource utilization across the enterprise. This allows for better allocation and capacity-planning decisions. It also facilitates regular reviews to reprioritize or cancel lagging projects as business needs evolve.

By taking a strategic portfolio approach, you become a key player in optimizing strategy rather than just driving tactical project execution. This elevated role also increases your influence and ability to add value by giving executives much-needed insight into all the work.

Portfolio Prioritization Framework

Project portfolio prioritization focuses on ranking and sequencing initiatives within an organization's portfolio. It uses specific frameworks and techniques to rank priorities based on criteria such as ROI, required resources, strategic alignment, and risk. Methods like weighted scoring, analytic hierarchy process (AHP), and priority matrices help determine relative priority. Portfolio prioritization is a key input that feeds into the broader portfolio management process.

Why it matters: An effective portfolio prioritization framework is essential to guide focused strategy execution. It could be a great solution to the "everything is a number one priority" root cause. This systematic approach helps you focus on continuously executing the right work with optimized resources, managed risks, and adaptability to market dynamics. It lets you see the path to achieve strategic goals.

Portfolio prioritization maximizes IMPACT by optimizing resource utilization on key initiatives and reducing losses through smart sequencing decisions. It also allows for quick realignment as business conditions evolve.

My friend Stuart Easton taught me to use the analytic hierarchy process to reduce decision bias and build consensus between stakeholders. This prevents the "squeaky wheel" or the top leader's "gut feel" from driving choices.

Intake Processes and Business Cases

Robust intake processes and detailed business cases enable rigorous evaluation of proposed initiatives before approval. Intake processes define a structured system for submitting new project requests, including proposal requirements, templates, and approval workflow. Business cases outline the rationale for undertaking a project or initiative by defining objectives, costs, timelines, resources required, risks, and expected business benefits tied to strategic goals. Together, solid intake processes and business cases arm decision-makers with the necessary information.

Why it matters: Many of the symptoms of project delivery challenges can be tied back to projects being poorly defined before they start. Clear intake processes and business cases are essential for aligning strategy execution through informed decision-making. They prevent disjointed efforts by enabling executives to set priorities based on defined costs, benefits, and alignment to strategy. Predefined objectives build in accountability and allow tracking of benefits realization and ultimate business value and ROI. Strong intake processes and business cases drive performance by enabling proposal owners to detail how their project will achieve strategic goals within a defined timeframe and budget. The projects are positioned for success with baked-in accountability on the proposal owner to achieve the success criteria laid out in the business case.

Strategy Execution

Once you have determined the strategy definition services and you know that your organization has the governance, portfolio, prioritization, and intake processes to ensure the right projects are being delivered, you can switch gears to look at the strategy execution services to help the organization execute projects better. Just keep in mind that your goal here is using these solutions to accelerate value delivery, not slow it down.

Let's first look at your team. Even if you don't have a team right now, that's OK. You'll learn how to expand your reach to enlist the support of others to help you deliver services in Stage Five: Deliver. Then, with the right organizational structure in place for your strategy delivery function, you can finally start looking at building right-sized methodology, process, templates, and tools.

Talent Requirements

Your goal here is to ensure that the right people are doing the right work, at the right times, the right way. That means you are going to identify and build the right team of people, enable them to get work done quickly, and help them understand why the work they are doing matters so they can keep an eye on the outcomes they are driving through this work, instead of focusing solely on the outputs.

Why it matters: You may realize that you don't have enough of the right people. Throwing more people at the projects won't solve the root cause if the people you have are not the right people for the job. Defining talent needs up front ensures your team is clear about what skills and capacities are required to drive the outcomes executives are

Your goal is the right people doing the right work, at the right times, the right way.

looking for. "We need more people" isn't usually compelling enough to get them to act. However, if you can be clear about specific roles, responsibilities, and capabilities needed to solve the root causes you've identified and link them to their pain points, you're more likely to get your executives' attention. Your job is to show them that the solution to their challenges is directly tied to the people you will bring in to solve those challenges. Having justifiable requirements also makes it easy to identify places you can ask for assistance or temporary support from other parts of the organization.

Project Delivery Framework

A project delivery framework is the methodology, templates, processes, tools, and metrics implemented to execute projects and accelerate achieving intended business outcomes. It provides structure and guidance tailored to an organization's needs to get results faster. An effective project delivery framework aligns the approach for delivering projects with the business objectives those projects are meant to achieve.

Why it matters: If the project delivery experience varies greatly from project to project or department to department, you may be able to solve it by giving people a common framework to use each time a project is started. Implementing a solid project delivery framework designed to accelerate outcomes provides valuable structure and guidance to get good results faster. It's essential to have an effective methodology deployment that aligns to business needs, rather than forcing a rigid one-size-fits-all process. This enables focus on the right activities to drive success for each unique project type.

Tools and Resources

Defining the right tools and resources to support the project delivery framework means identifying the systems, templates, training, staffing, and other assets required to support effective project delivery. It involves selecting, designing, and providing tools and resources that will enhance value, efficiency, scalability, and consistency of project work.

Why it matters: Once you've put a lot of the foundational layers in place, you can use software and other resources to accelerate progress. Well-designed tools and resources, when implemented at the right time, enhance value delivery, efficiency, scalability, and consistency of project work. The key is to add just enough structure through tools to speed work up, rather than slowing things down with rigid or overly complex systems that try to account for every possible project variation.

Taking the time to intentionally identify and provide the proper tools and resources eliminates roadblocks for project teams and enables them to focus their efforts on delivering outcomes. Equipped with the right assets, teams can execute work more seamlessly.

Community of Practice

A community of practice is a formal or informal group of people doing delivery work in your organization. It deliberately cuts across formal organizational reporting structure to create a cohesive team of peers who are working together to create a better strategy delivery experience for the entire organization. The members of this group are the people closest to the work taking place, so they can provide valuable insight into the challenges and help you find those root causes, as well as help you develop solutions and be early adopters of the services you are creating.

Why it matters: This approach can help to create a sense of community and shared mission among the project people in your organization. Instead of trying to go it alone, you can do more to accelerate project and value delivery together. Creating a community of practice is a great way to bring people with you through change: build your coalition of support by engaging the people who do project delivery work now in your organization. If you have a small team, engaging other people in the organization who do similar work can be a way to multiply the size of your team fast.

Strategy Realization

Much work in the project management industry has centered on benefits management. But you should know that there's a difference between benefits and value. Benefits are the expected return for the project being delivered, but those benefits come at a cost, and you must measure whether the cost was worth the benefits. The question to ask here is: Did your business leaders get the return on their investment in this project that was defined in the business case and expected when the project was approved?

Although you absolutely can and should measure the triple constraint of time, scope, and cost for projects, make sure that people understand that only tells them how you're progressing, not the results you'll achieve. The triple constraint shows only that you are creating the outputs that were expected, but not if those outputs will achieve the intended business outcomes. You need to go beyond the triple constraint to the "worth it factor."

What matters most is to maximize ROI at the project level, while informing trade-off decisions to maximize ROI across the portfolio. The moment your projects start to fail on this prime objective, you need to seriously consider restructuring the project so that the ultimate goals can be achieved, if it's even still possible. After all, your business leaders need to know that the projects are achieving their business goals in a way that maximizes the return on their investments, and not just for one project but for all of them. While leaders do care about individual project performance, especially for the department-level projects, the top executives are responsible for ROI across the entire project portfolio.

The best place to look for the right metrics for the projects are the strategic goals your organization has defined for those initiatives and the business case success criteria for each project. If you don't have measurable success criteria for projects yet, start here. A strong business case does not have to be complicated, but it does need to make clear why the project is happening, the business problem it must solve, and what success looks like. And success should be a set of measurable criteria that clearly shows that the goals of the project are achieved. The business case should define the measurements that will show the IMPACT these projects will make.

Business leaders see projects as investments, and when your organization starts moving from tracking the benefits that the project created to ensuring that those benefits were worth achieving in the first place, you get closer to your business leaders seeing you as a strategic partner on their journey to deliver strategy. They are thinking about ROI, even if they don't take the time to truly measure it, so you need to be too—and your project metrics must reflect this.

Now, usually when I start talking about ROI in a keynote or workshop, I hear the "Yeah, but..." monster crawl up on the shoulders of the audience members as they start explaining all the reasons that ROI doesn't work in *their* organization. I'll hear, "Yeah, but we are in a nonprofit organization, so we're focused on mission, not ROI," or "Yeah, but we're in the government so we don't measure ROI."

First, as a tax-paying citizen it makes me sad to hear people in government say this. Second, all good executives think in terms of return on their investment in energy, time, money, resources, and focus to achieve their business goals. Every CEO that I've ever talked to across commercial, government, and nonprofit organizations has used the term "ROI" when telling me what matters most to them. Well, except for one.

Peter was the CEO of a small community-based organization that was focused on making the world a better place. However, the organization was struggling to achieve its goals. His team had a lot of work on their plates, but because they were not properly organized, they were failing to meet deadlines and were at risk of losing future projects.

Peter hired my company to help him improve the organization's ability to deliver on the client projects. It didn't take long to identify the root of the problem: the team was not properly connected to why it was important to get these projects done in a timely manner, with high quality, and with as little waste as possible. They didn't understand the importance to the company's bottom line of meeting deadlines or ensuring a high ROI.

When I talked to Peter about connecting his team to ROI, he immediately bristled. Although he was running a for-profit company, he was passionate about changing the world for the better with his mission-focused organization and didn't want to be thought of as a money-hungry consulting firm focused on dollars. "That's not the culture we've built here," he said.

"But if you lose money on these projects or just break even," I told him, "you won't be able to grow. You're going to limit your company's ability to serve the broader community."

Peter wasn't convinced, and I realized I would need to show him instead of telling him.

The team was desperate to get more help to deliver their consulting services to their clients, but the budget couldn't support it. Projects were taking too long and costing the organization too much money, and no amount of process was going to fix that until everyone was working optimally.

We worked with Peter and his leadership team to establish a PMO that would be responsible for aligning the delivery teams in a way that helped them accelerate service delivery for their clients while costing Peter's organization less in staff cost. First, we helped them develop a new set of goals and objectives to get projects completed more efficiently by keeping people focused. We also created a system for tracking progress and measuring results tied to the performance of their projects. This helped the team to see the direct effect of their work and gave them a sense of ownership over the projects. Once they increased efficiency of the client engagements, they now had more room in the budget to hire staff that they desperately needed so they could bid on some of the bigger projects they wanted to take on.

As a result of these changes, the organization's efficiency improved dramatically. They were able to meet deadlines, increase their ROI, and take on more customer projects. The organization was able to achieve their financial goals, they had very happy customers, *and* they were making a real difference in the world. It turns out ROI did matter to Peter.

If your organization struggles to use the term "ROI," try calling it the "worth it factor." Tell your stakeholders that your job is to ensure that all the projects the organization invests in achieve the business goals in a way that makes them worth doing in the first place so that the organization can thrive.

There are two types of metrics to look at here:

1. Metrics that show the ROI (or what we call the "worth it factor") for the projects that are delivering the organization's strategy.

2. Metrics that show how the services your delivery team creates are driving value for the organization.

We'll cover the strategy realization metrics momentarily, and we'll look at how to measure and talk about the IMPACT of your services in the next chapter.

Benefits Tracking

Benefits tracking measures that projects and programs deliver the intended business goals defined in the business case. It involves identifying the specific business outcomes and objectives that an initiative aims to achieve, and then systematically measuring progress against those goals over time.

Why it matters: Benefits tracking enables organizations to demonstrate the concrete and strategic results of major initiatives. By setting up metrics and criteria to track these results from the outset, organizations can foster accountability and provide tangible data that leadership can use for informed decision-making about which projects could yield the best business results. However, this is only part of the equation. Business leaders also need to understand the cost to achieve these benefits and the opportunity cost of one project over another. Consistent tracking and reporting of benefits realization rates over time further improves planning and estimation for future initiatives, but there's more to do when it comes to measurement—we have to see the total value equation.

IMPACT Metrics

Don't settle for measuring project benefits or performance alone; it's only part of the puzzle. To truly demonstrate the overall value your strategy brings, you need metrics that prove your projects were worth every penny of investment and every hour of effort. And be sure to ask, "Did the benefits outweigh the cost so that this project was genuinely worth the investment in the first place?" Your executives need to know the answer to this question even if they haven't been asking. This not only focuses efforts on what matters most to the business, but also helps optimize the ROI of project portfolios by showcasing the real-world business value being achieved.

To demonstrate value, we use metrics like ROI or the "worth it factor" data. The sweet spot for the right metrics is the strategic goals and the success criteria laid out in your business case for each project. If you're lacking in either area, it's time to fix that. Crafting a robust business case doesn't mean drowning in complexity; it means crystal-clear explanations of why the project exists, the business problem it's tackling, and what success looks like. Success, of course, should be a set of measurable criteria proving you hit your project goals.

Hand leaders measurements that scream IMPACT. Business leaders don't see projects as just projects—they're investments. Shift from just tracking benefits to ensuring those benefits were worth chasing in the first place. This is how you transition from a project leader to a strategic partner on the road to delivering strategy. Leaders are crunching numbers, thinking ROI. You should be too.

Plus, it feels great to deliver and celebrate real, measurable results! This becomes the gift that keeps on giving: as people gain confidence, get recognized, and feel the satisfaction of delivering meaningful results, they become more motivated to do it again and again. Dig into the benefits and outcomes that are expected from initiatives. Set up criteria, gather data, and keep a close eye on progress to ensure you're reaping the intended benefits. Go beyond the basics—share reports and insights that showcase the real IMPACT of your organization's strategy.

In addition to traditional project management metrics (time, scope, and budget), here are some metrics to use to assess the total business value of projects.

1 Return on Investment (ROI)

Metric: ROI = (Net Benefits ÷ Cost) × 100

Description: Measures the financial return generated by a project in relation to its cost. Net benefits can include revenue generation, cost savings, or other financial gains.

2 Cost-Benefit Ratio (CBR)

Metric: CBR = Net Benefits ÷ Cost

Description: Similar to ROI, CBR represents the relationship between the project's net benefits and its cost. It helps in evaluating the cost-effectiveness of the project.

3 Business Value Realization

Metric: Percentage of Business Value Realization

Description: Compares the actual business value realized from the project to its expected or planned business value. It reflects how well the project delivers on its intended outcomes. This is especially helpful when business value needs to be driven over a relatively long period of time to reach breakeven, for example.

4 Strategic Alignment Index

Metric: Strategic Alignment Index = (Degree of Alignment ÷ Total Possible Alignment) × 100

Description: Measures the extent to which the project aligns with the organization's strategic objectives. Degree of alignment is assessed through KPIs tied to strategic goals.

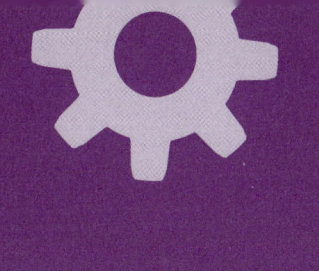

Go beyond the triple constraint to the "worth it factor."

5 Customer Satisfaction Index

Metric: Customer Satisfaction Score (CSAT)

Description: Collects feedback from project stakeholders, including end users and customers, to gauge their satisfaction with the project's deliverables and outcomes.

6 Time to Market

Metric: Time to Market = Project Completion Date – Project Start Date

Description: Measures the time it takes to deliver a project from initiation to completion. Faster time to market is often associated with increased business value, because the faster the project delivers its product, service, or result, the sooner the organization can start seeing the benefits.

7 Innovation IMPACT

Metric: Number of Innovative Features or Processes Implemented

Description: Quantifies the level of innovation introduced by the project, such as new features, technologies, or processes that contribute to the organization's competitive advantage.

8 Risk Management Effectiveness

Metric: Percentage of Identified Risks Managed

Description: Assesses how effectively the project team identifies and proactively manages risks, which can affect the project's success and long-term business value.

9 Staff Productivity Improvement

Metric: Percentage Increase in Productivity

Description: Measures the IMPACT of the project on the productivity of the workforce. This can include improvements in efficiency, reduced manual effort, or streamlined processes.

10 Adoption Rate

Metric: Percentage of Stakeholders Adopting Project Outputs

Description: Evaluates how well the project outputs are adopted by end users or stakeholders, indicating the practical utility and acceptance of the delivered solutions. As the percentage increases, you are more likely to achieve the business outcomes and enjoy a higher return on the project's investment.

When implementing any metrics, it's important to tailor them to the specific goals and characteristics of each project. Regularly collecting and analyzing the right metrics throughout the project lifecycle allows leaders to make data-driven decisions and continuously optimize project and portfolio performance.

Performance Management and Reporting

Performance management and reporting involves establishing key performance indicators (KPIs) that directly tie into an organization's strategic objectives. It entails monitoring the progress of projects and initiatives against those KPIs on an ongoing basis. This goes beyond simply tracking milestone completion—it means taking a holistic view of performance to spot any emerging risks or obstacles that could impede strategy delivery. The goal is to enable data-driven decisions through regular performance updates that provide leadership and stakeholders visibility into what is driving outcomes.

Why it matters: Performance management and reporting is critical for ensuring strategic success because it links projects and programs to overarching business goals. By monitoring the right KPIs, organizations can understand what is working well and what needs adjustment in order to achieve desired outcomes. This fosters accountability and gives leadership crucial insights to course-correct as needed. Tying performance data directly to strategy also helps focus efforts on what matters most to the business. Comprehensive performance monitoring provides meaningful visibility and diagnostic capability to optimize implementation and maximize the value of strategic investments. In essence, it is the foundation for data-driven decision-making that advances an organization's most important objectives. It's not just about hitting milestones; it's about understanding progress and spotting any hiccups or risks that might throw your strategy off course. Nail down performance management by tying KPIs directly to strategic objectives. Keep a watchful eye on project and initiative performance, delivering regular updates to stakeholders and leadership.

Change Management and Adoption

Change management and adoption involves equipping organizations to successfully transition to new processes, systems, organizational structures, or strategies. It includes developing comprehensive plans to guide transitions, educate stakeholders, and foster user adoption. Tactics may involve communication strategies, training programs, coaching, and reinforcement interventions. The goal is to cultivate change leadership capabilities across the organization, not just within a single department.

Why it matters: Without effective change management, organizations risk low adoption rates, resistance, and implementation failures that compromise intended outcomes. By taking an inclusive approach and building organization-wide change competencies, companies can smoothly guide stakeholders through transitions. This drives strategy adoption and maximizes the benefits realized. Change management also focuses on the human dimensions of change, providing the tools and support people need to thrive during periods of transition, maintaining engagement and productivity. With strong change management and broad involvement in facilitating adoption, organizations can operationalize new initiatives successfully and sustain stakeholder commitment. In essence, change management is a vital ingredient for activating strategy and improving the odds of realizing targeted business results.

Organizational change management doesn't belong buried in a single department of the company. It's everyone's responsibility to help the organization change for the better, but you can provide services such as change plans, communication strategies, and training programs to create an inclusive environment of change leadership and competency development across the organization and increase adoption of the changes your team is driving.

Continuous Improvement

Continuous improvement involves systematically capturing lessons learned from past projects and experiences in order to optimize future initiatives. It entails facilitating knowledge sharing to identify best practices as well as mistakes to avoid. Continuous improvement also means conducting post-implementation reviews of projects to gather feedback and recommendations that can be incorporated into the next iteration of strategy execution. The goal is to break the cycle of repeated mistakes and ensure that each initiative benefits from past wins and failures.

Why it matters: Continuous improvement enables organizations to optimize the value of project investments over time by learning from experience. However, without processes to capture and apply lessons across teams, organizations risk repeating mistakes and flawed strategies, and duplication of effort. Teams that facilitate knowledge sharing, identify best practices, and incorporate learnings through post-implementation reviews position themselves for greater efficiency, innovation, and strategic agility.

Too often, organizations fail to learn from past mistakes and successes because they don't have a meaningful lessons learned process. Ensure projects continue benefiting from experience by supporting effective capture and integration of learnings into new initiatives.

Conduct reviews to provide feedback for ongoing refinements. With continuous improvement embedded, teams can build on successes rather than reinventing the wheel each time. This fosters collaboration through shared knowledge across functions instead of siloed activities.

Benefits Sustainability and Handover

Benefits sustainability and handover involves establishing processes to transition responsibility for maintaining project outcomes to operational teams once implementation is complete. This means identifying business owners who will be accountable for sustaining benefits over the long term and equipping them to optimize results. Structured handover procedures are created to formally transfer knowledge, resources, and control to operational leaders and their staff.

Why it matters: While a handover strategy should be built into the project delivery framework, it is often missing, which leads to gaps in support or unhappy end users. Without effective handover planning during the project, operational teams may lack the capacity, knowledge, or resources to maintain outcomes, putting benefits at risk. Weak transitions can also lead to continued reliance on project teams, which distracts them from delivering new initiatives and slows down future strategy delivery.

As the strategy is realized, you can help ensure benefits are achieved sustainably by putting processes in place to effectively transition responsibility for maintaining outcomes to business owners. Create a clear and structured handoff process that enables operational teams to fully own optimizations going forward. This allows project managers to focus on driving new strategic programs without distraction. Ultimately, strong sustainability and handover processes allow organizations to optimize return on project investments by maintaining benefits over the long term.

And remember, all of the solutions you create are designed to accelerate the IMPACT your organization can make for the strategy. More won't always be better.

Now that you know the categories of services that you can create, it's time to determine which services you can deliver to address each of the root causes you've established. Complete the IMPACT Services Register to address the root causes you identified for the challenges and opportunities defined by your stakeholders.

MAKE AN IMPACT

Think: What services could you deliver to help your organization address the root causes identified?

Do: Download the IMPACT Services Register to document the solutions you will create to address the root causes you discovered in Chapter 6.

Determine Your "Worth It Factor"

IN THE last chapter, we reviewed metrics for the projects themselves, but you can't stop there. Your executives also need to see how the team you are running is moving the organizational needle. They want to know that the investments they are making in time, money, energy, resources, and focus are going to pay off—that the investments are worth making. What is your team's "worth it factor"?

Your team is not a cost center. It's an IMPACT Engine that drives measurable business value. Most delivery leaders brag about the size of their project portfolio measured in terms of the budget for their projects—"We're managing a $1 billion portfolio of projects"—but that's just showing the cost side of the equation. What's more meaningful is showing how the work you are doing is creating a return on that investment—"We're driving $5 billion in profit for this organization." Of course, there are other ways to show the "worth it factor" your team is creating for the broader organization, which is why it's important for you to understand your organization's strategy and how they define success broadly. When you shift your thinking about the work you do to focus on the outcomes, not the inputs and outputs, you are more closely aligned with how your business leaders measure results—and one step closer to securing a seat at the table.

This shift in focus requires a perspective that goes beyond the project lifecycle to the bigger-picture portfolio of products, programs, and projects and how your team is ensuring all of them are aligned with and in service of delivering that strategy. One example of the often-overlooked services that a delivery team like yours can create is measuring the effectiveness of the strategy across the full lifecycle from ideas through to measurable business success criteria to ensure it is achieving the intended business goals. Project people are usually handed the project when it is ready to start, and then they move on to the next project as soon as it's delivered. And while product teams are around beyond the lifecycle of a single project, those teams are generally focused on that one product, not the effectiveness of the entire strategy to achieve the intended business goals. This is where your team comes in. Because you are running a sustainable business function, not a project or product team, you will be around long after the project ends. You can measure the outcomes each completed project creates, not just the outputs it delivered.

Make sure you have at least one metric you can use for the hallway conversations when you, your team, your sponsor, and other stakeholders talk about the value your team drives holistically for the organization. Most organizations have a small subset of key "bragging rights" they use to talk about how their company is changing the world. Whether it's profitability for a publicly traded company, effectiveness of services delivered by a government agency, or the way a nonprofit is changing lives, there's always something the leaders in the organization talk about as a key performance metric. Know what that is and then ask yourself, "How does my team align to that measure of success?" The answer should be easy if the services you're providing are tied to realizing the organization's strategy.

Tie Services to Value

Beyond a "worth it factor" metric for projects, you'll need to measure the "worth it factor" for your team. For example, the services you create in the strategy definition phase around portfolio management, prioritization, and governance can ensure that projects are aligned with the strategy right from the start, that they are prioritized and organized around maximizing throughput to achieve that ROI, and that the leaders in the organization are given the information they need to make educated and informed decisions to drive that throughput in the best way. This is exactly what we did for Peter's project management office, which you learned about in the last chapter. The PMO was measuring performance and ROI for projects, as well as the IMPACT of the services they created to help drive higher ROI across the whole portfolio of client projects.

For now, your only job is to define the types of metrics you will track for each service you create. Later in this chapter you'll learn more about how to communicate that value. Remember, what gets measured gets done. Defining the metrics will help you focus your attention and the efforts of the team on what matters most.

Your metrics don't have to be perfect. Just start with something that feels right and then keep iterating your way to IMPACT. The metrics that you create will depend on what your organizational leaders care about and what you really need to know to drive success, not just for the projects but for the strategy. You want metrics to show the business leaders the needle is moving, both for the services you're creating and for the way you're supporting strategy delivery.

Just like for an individual project, not all benefits will be financial. Some of our clients have developed what they call an IMPACT metric, which can work well for nonprofit organizations and other mission-focused institutions (where ROI or other financial metrics may not be as compelling) or can simply be a welcome addition to the hard numbers. Consider the work the organization does to achieve the mission and how you know that your organization's work is making a difference. If you don't already have a single metric at

Your team is not a cost center. It's an IMPACT Engine that drives measurable business value.

the highest level that shows how your organization is making an IMPACT in the world, you can help them develop that metric and call it an IMPACT metric.

You don't need to define these metrics on your own. Remember the pain points you collected from your stakeholders? You not only asked them about challenges and opportunities, but you also asked them what success looked like. That's your metric. If it's not something quite measurable, brainstorm with them until you get a clear picture of how you'll know the needle is moving for each service. You can simply ask, "How will we know this service is working?" You will use these metrics as the last piece to the five-step IMPACT Communication Framework you will learn about next.

When we implemented a new governance and portfolio management process for a recent Fortune 500 client, the executives told us success would look like better visibility into all projects happening across the organization, increased alignment of projects to strategic priorities, and more efficient allocation of resources on the most important initiatives.

To track the success of the new process, we defined three key metrics:

1 Percentage of projects tied directly to a strategic priority.

   Target: 75 percent.

2 Project resource utilization rate on strategic priorities.

   Target: 85 percent.

3 Projects achieving all intended business outcomes.

   Target: 90 percent.

On a quarterly basis, the strategy delivery office we established for them reports these metrics to the executives. In the first year after implementing the new governance and portfolio management process, we have seen the project strategic alignment metric improve from 24 percent to 68 percent, strategically aligned resource utilization go from 36 percent to 81 percent, and achieving all intended business outcomes rise from 18 percent to 75 percent.

That was just the first year. Notice the massive increases across the board by creating the right focus and measuring what mattered to the executives. Did they hit their high marks in the first year? Nope. But were the executives happy? No, they were ecstatic! They appreciated that this was an evolutionary process and were thrilled that they saw huge jumps in focus, productivity, and measurable business IMPACT in a relatively short period of time. This was the result of simply putting the right services in place to help the organization align and focus on these priorities.

By defining clear success metrics up front and reviewing progress regularly, we have been able to demonstrate the value these services provided. The executives now have the visibility they wanted into the project portfolio, are confident resources are being used wisely, and see that more projects are hitting their targets. This has increased buy-in for the strategy delivery office and fueled further investment in continuous improvement of even more services the office is creating to make an even bigger IMPACT.

Consider how you felt about the targets that you read above. If you were implementing them for your organization, do they feel too low, too high, or just right? This client was very nervous and thought that they were unattainable. We recommended that this client develop high numbers with their goal metrics anyway. After collaborating with their leadership team, together we agreed to aim high so that the teams could feel the seriousness of this shift and challenge themselves to think differently and work together to achieve those big numbers. If you aim low, you might make it, but so what? If you aim high and you get close, you'll have moved the needle, and the executives and the teams doing the work will feel the difference you're all making together.

If you do try this approach to aim high, make sure your executives are in on it with you, so that they celebrate and reward getting close to those stretch goals to keep the momentum going with the teams. During our assessment work, we discovered that this client was fortunate to have executives who would support this approach, but not every organization is so lucky, which is why the stakeholder assessment work in Stage Two is so important. Regardless of your organization's culture, the key is to work together with your executives to define success.

Next you'll use the metrics you just defined to support your communication with stakeholders. You'll use their own words (from your stakeholder assessment notes) to link their pain points to the metrics, and to ensure a common understanding of how success will be measured. You'll learn how to do this using our IMPACT Communication Framework, which has five simple steps.

The IMPACT Communication Framework

Now that you know how you will measure that your services are delivering the value they should, you need to make sure that you know how to talk about these services in a way that keeps stakeholders interested. Remember, you're still bringing people with you through the change process, so you must make sure they see your solutions as the antidote to their pain. Your stakeholders are buying the solutions to their problems.

When delivery leaders start talking about how they will solve business challenges, they often lose stakeholders quickly by geeking out on their cool solutions. Instead of going on about the "what," you want to focus mostly on the "why."

The "why" for your solutions goes right back to the challenges and opportunities your stakeholders told you about in the Assess stage: what they care about. That is all you need to talk about. So don't waste time trying to sell your services.

Your stakeholders aren't interested in your deliverables or process; they are interested and willing to invest in the outcomes you will create for them—the answers to their top-priority problems. And sometimes you will have different definitions of success for different stakeholders.

In Jack's company from Chapter 6, it was clear that the executives were frustrated that the teams weren't moving fast enough, while the functional managers were feeling pressure to meet different goals for their departments, and project teams were being pulled in different directions. The solutions we recommended after doing our Root Cause Analysis had a positive ripple effect on the entire organization once implemented, but how we talked about them to each of these groups varied.

To get to this win-win situation, we had to truly understand the challenges and opportunities of each stakeholder group and find a shared solution that we could communicate in a way that addressed what each of them cared about most. You can apply this same approach using the IMPACT Communication Framework that we'll unpack next. It's designed to support all your conversations with stakeholders from this point forward. You now know what services you will deliver to address the root causes of their pain points, the outcomes those services will drive and the IMPACT they will have on the organization, as well as the way you'll measure that it's all working as planned. In Stage Four: Plan, you'll also use this framework when you head into conversations with your business leaders about your IMPACT Delivery Model that combines all of the work from the Assess, Define, and Plan stages.

This framework will help you have the right conversations with your stakeholders so that when it comes to what you and your team do, everyone knows the answer to the question "So what?" Your success depends on your stakeholders understanding and connecting what they care about to the value you're driving—and being able to talk about it.

In Stage Four, you will add this to your comprehensive communications plan that highlights not only progress but also the IMPACT you're making based on the established metrics and the IMPACT Delivery Model. Here are the five components of this framework.

IMPACT COMMUNICATION FRAMEWORK

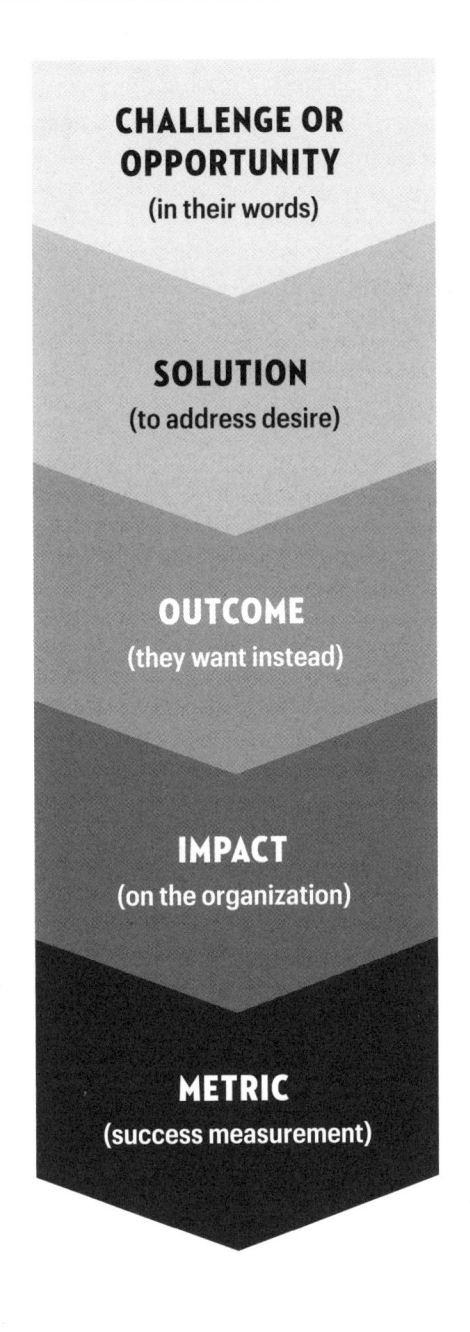

CHALLENGE OR OPPORTUNITY
(in their words)

SOLUTION
(to address desire)

OUTCOME
(they want instead)

IMPACT
(on the organization)

METRIC
(success measurement)

1. **Challenge or Opportunity:** This is the exact words your stakeholders used to explain their experience, pain points, desires, and expectations to describe the challenge or opportunity you collected in Stage Two: Assess. By using their words, you will create an immediate connection to what comes next because you've made it about them.

2. **Solution:** This is the service or capability that you will put in place to address their challenge or opportunity. Be simple and straightforward and don't geek out on all the cool features and functions of the solution—they only care if the solution is going to address what they are looking for.

3. **Outcome:** This is the result that they desire once your solution is in place and is usually the opposite of the challenge or the realization of the opportunity described in step one. Again, put the outcome in *their* words, the words you collected in answer to the question "What does success look like to you?"

4. **IMPACT:** This is the effect that the solution, once it is in place, will have on the organization or customers. These are the words your stakeholders used to describe the future state when the results of the service are realized. Reminding them of the IMPACT helps the stakeholder see the greater value the solution drives beyond the immediate pain point that is being addressed.

5. **Metric:** This is how your stakeholders will know the solution addresses the challenge or opportunity in a meaningful and measurable way. The questions to ask yourself when determining what metric(s) to use for your organization are "How will we know we were successful?" and "What do my stakeholders care about most?" Ensure that any metrics provide measurable business value, and reserve time to intentionally track and report on this value regularly.

These five steps sound simple—and they are. Don't let the simplicity mesmerize you into thinking they aren't critical. This is a case where the whole is more than the sum of its parts. By having a meaningful conversation using these five steps in this order, you are poised to make a meaningful IMPACT.

IMPACT Communication in Action

Let's look at how the five-step IMPACT Communication Framework works in action.

1 **Challenge:** Jack's executive team complained that they didn't have a clear picture of "what all of these people are working on" and were uncertain whether the most valuable work was being prioritized. What are the executives communicating? That they didn't have enough transparency into the work to ensure the most important work was happening, which would prevent them from being able to make well-informed decisions when asked.

2 **Solution:** Solutions you can put in place to create transparency include project portfolio governance, metrics/dashboards/reporting, and a communication strategy that ensures the right information is made available to business leaders to support informed decision-making.

3 **Outcome:** The outcome is simply the opposite of their current experience: you are giving them transparency and an answer to their question about "what all of these people are working on."

4 **IMPACT:** You could describe it this way: "Using a straightforward project portfolio management and governance approach, we will have greater transparency into the project work taking place so that you will have the information you need to make educated and informed decisions quickly. That will ensure that the teams are working on the highest-priority projects, while also decreasing our expenses toward lower-priority projects."

5 **Metric:** There are many different metrics that will tell you if this approach is working. Some examples could be an increase in ROI of the portfolio of projects over time, percentage of projects

aligned with strategy, percentage of staff aware of strategic objectives for projects, the time it takes to make decisions, high-priority project completions, or many others. You don't need to measure everything, just the thing that your stakeholders say will tell them the change is working. The next sentence you add to the above could look something like this: "And we will know we are successful because we expect to double our project throughput for high-priority projects in a year."

Now repeat this exercise for Jack's project managers who just wanted clear priorities and a focused team so that they could complete projects in a way that drove the right business results. The functional managers wanted to be measured by a single list of priorities that allowed them to achieve their operational goals and strategic priorities. And both groups wanted to look good in the eyes of the executives!

How will you tie each distinct stakeholder group's pain points to the same solutions identified above in a way that addresses what each of them cares about? Sometimes two little words can make all the difference.

There's another secret that I share with my Mastermind students that I've been weaving into the language I've used in this book. It's two simple words—"so that." I used it in the above example, as well. Most delivery leaders I talk to focus their conversation only on the solution. They might talk about the stakeholder's pain or a particular business challenge or opportunity, then jump to their solution and stop. However, for many stakeholders, that isn't far enough. You need to connect them to the rest of the steps, and "so that" can help you do this because what you are really answering is the question they haven't asked, "So what?" They want to know *why* they should care, and using these two little words when explaining what your team is doing can draw that connection for them. If you find yourself without the right words when you are being challenged as to why your team is doing something, just remember to use "so that" framing to answer "So what?" because that's the question they are really asking: Why should they care?

OK, now you have a much better sense of the services you need to create based on the root causes of the business challenges and opportunities identified in Stage Two: Assess, and you've determined how you will measure that those services are driving measurable business value. Remember, you should not worry about *creating* all these services just yet. Your goal in Stage Three: Define is to *identify* the list of services, be clear what they are solving and how you'll know they work. In the next stage, Plan the IMPACT Journey, you will organize these services on a timeline based on the priorities you established with your business leaders at the end of the Assess stage. As you can see, the IMPACT Engine System really does build upon itself from stage to stage.

Trust yourself. Trust the process. It's time to make an IMPACT.

MAKE AN IMPACT

Think: Now that you have your list of services, how will you show the measurable business value those services will provide?

Do: Complete the Metrics section of the IMPACT Services Register to show how you will measure the IMPACT of the services you're going to create. Then download the IMPACT Communication Framework worksheet to practice your communication scripts for different stakeholder groups.

STAGE

PLAN THE IMPACT JOURNEY

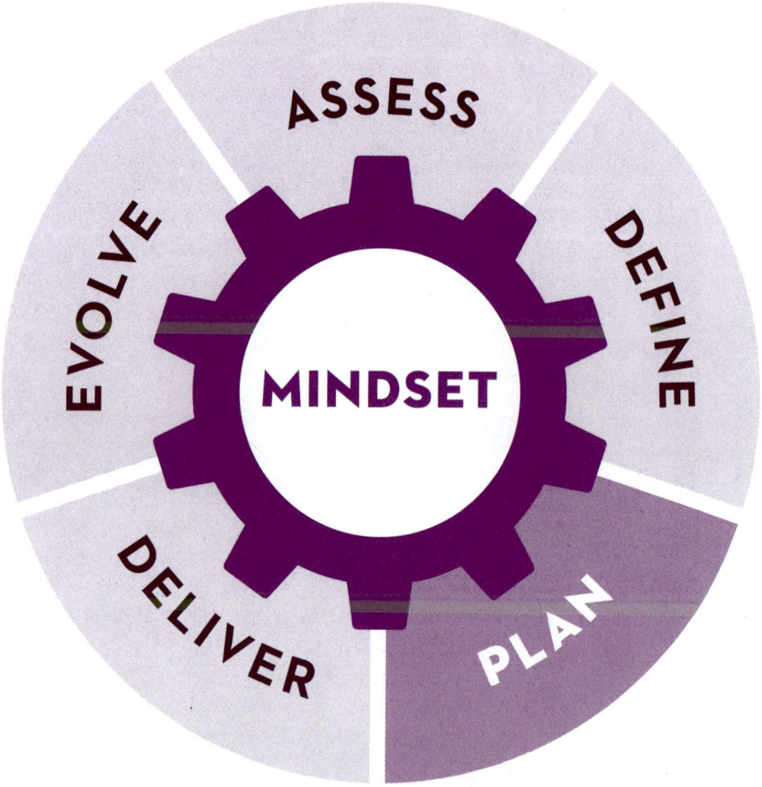
ASSESS
DEFINE
PLAN
DELIVER
EVOLVE
MINDSET

At this point in the process, I suspect you're hungry to dive into solving the root causes you now see so clearly.

You need to show value fast, and you might be tempted to skip the planning process and just start implementing.

Nope. You must do this planning work first to ensure you are creating a clear road map of value delivery for the short and long term while establishing your team as an important part of the organization's stability and growth.

I mean, aren't we always telling everyone else they must create a plan before they start executing? Well, the change required to create a sustainable business function requires even more intentional planning and stakeholder engagement than a typical project. We're playing chess here.

Stage Four gives you the planning resources you need to ensure that each new cycle of value delivery is building on the strong cycles before it, while giving you the tools you need to keep bringing your stakeholders with you through this change process. By the end of this stage, you will have done the work to start creating that pull throughout the organization for the services you're going to deliver. This work is setting you up to deliver that minimum viable product in Stage Five.

Let's do this!

9

Develop the IMPACT Delivery Framework

EVERY YEAR I host a special Thanksgiving dinner for my family. Cooking for my loved ones is a cherished tradition, so I work to make it unforgettable. Because I'm a planner and like to challenge myself to keep things interesting, I'm always thinking about the perfect assortment of delicious dishes and how to make sure everything is ready at the same time to feed a large group. Recruiting my son as the sous-chef and metrics master, he can verify that my record best time is twenty different dishes on the table within five minutes of each other!

After a few years hosting this big feast, I noticed that the plates weren't big enough to hold all the delicious food I had prepared. "We need larger plates!" I announced. Those bigger plates, only brought out on special occasions, became symbols of anticipation, promising a taste of the amazing dishes on our holiday table. The family would excitedly take a heaping spoonful of each dish and fill their plates to the brim. But as we started eating, most of us realized that, as the saying goes, our eyes were bigger than our stomachs. Larger plates just made it even harder to enjoy everything we were eating. More and bigger wasn't better. In that moment, I saw a parallel between our family feast and the challenges faced by business leaders.

Business leaders typically have an insatiable appetite for success. Fueled by ambition and the desire to impress, these leaders take on endless projects, products, and goals, thinking they can handle it all at once. But just like my family learned from our Thanksgiving feast, there is a limit to what anyone can effectively manage and achieve—without feeling sick. When leaders try to do too much all at once, it results in a lack of focus, lower-quality work, and even burnout. A more strategic and measured approach is needed.

Eventually I learned how to manage the portions on our Thanksgiving plates by cooking fewer recipes and pulling back on trying new ones, as I realized that a smaller set of new options each year allowed us to appreciate them more instead of feeling overwhelmed. Plus, I got to spend more time with family than in the kitchen, which was the whole point! Similarly, business leaders need to develop the skills of prioritization and strategic allocation of resources. This is exactly what the C-suites of our most successful clients do—limit the number of new strategic initiatives they take on each year so that the organization can effectively manage transformational change while ensuring enough resources to keep the business-as-usual activities flowing well. We all have "Thanksgiving eyes," but when leaders clearly assess the organization's true capacity, they will learn to focus on excelling in a few key areas instead of spreading themselves too thin and ultimately accomplishing less of what's most important while burning out their team.

Business leaders need to find the right balance between ambition and practicality, between aspirations and capacity. With this newfound awareness, they can create a recipe for success, ensuring that every endeavor is undertaken with purpose, focus, and the ability to enjoy the rewards. And your team is the best positioned to help them do this.

You Don't Need a Charter

Delivery leaders are frequently advised to create a charter for their team when they are creating a new delivery function. This is particularly common in the PMO space, with many downloadable templates, articles, and books relying on a project mindset to create the PMO. But I caution against doing so, and I offer a better solution that gets you more directly aligned with the business.

Charters are a necessary and extremely valuable tool to define project scope, resources, and expected results, as well as the project team's authority to deliver that project. Projects should have a charter. But you aren't creating a project. Effective strategy delivery requires you to create a sustainable functional department that delivers high-IMPACT services to help the broader organization achieve its business goals.

Do you know what other teams and departments in your company have? A business plan. That plan may vary in structure and formality, but functional service-based teams create business plans, not charters, to define how they will deliver value to the organization and customers.

Ask yourself how many of your peer business areas have created charters for their departments. Does the sales department have a charter? Does the IT department? Not likely.

Projects are temporary endeavors designed to start, end, and achieve a specific result. If you are creating a project office or team that is specific to a single project or program, create a charter designed to authorize and set that project up for success. You can still apply most of the techniques you are learning in this book, but ultimately, that team will move on to other things when the project is over. If you are creating a sustainable team or department that drives long-term strategic value, create a business plan. Sure, a charter and a business plan can contain some of the same elements, but a business plan sets you up for being a peer to other functional areas in a way that a charter can't.

You may customize this plan to meet the needs of your organization and stakeholders, but don't skip creating it. Your business plan is the main communication tool you and your team will use to help your stakeholders understand, in a way that matters to them, what you do and how you do it. You can pull the necessary pieces from this plan to create talking points for any conversation about what you and your team are doing to drive greater business value for the organization as an ROI-driving team, instead of being a cost center or administrative overhead, like so many of your peers in this space.

The business plan must accomplish these goals:

1 Clearly define the services and value your team will deliver as a value-driven business function and not simply a cost center or administrative overhead.

2 Establish your team as a strategic peer to other teams or departments in the organization.

3 Show how your team will drive measurable business value through delivery of those services instead of being seen as a cost center.

4 Set expectations for phasing services in and managing organizational capacity for change to mature over time, while acknowledging that you will be able to adapt to the organization's changing needs, as well.

Those four points build on each other logically from defining services, to positioning the team strategically, to realizing business value, to setting change expectations.

There's an IMPACT Engine Business Plan action-taking resource for you to download and complete with instructions on each section and guidance for how it can be used. To complete it, you'll want to reference your work from Stage Two (Organizational Change Assessment and Stakeholder Engagement Plan) and Stage Three (Root Cause Analysis, IMPACT Services Register, IMPACT Communication Framework). You can customize this business plan to suit your organizational needs, but be thoughtful about any sections you remove because it must continue to accomplish the above four goals.

Now you might be thinking, "How am I going to create an entire business plan for a team that I'm still defining?" Don't worry! I've got you. Even the business plan is something that you will iterate over time. And you've already done a lot of the work to answer these questions, what I call W^{5}H: why, who, what, when, where, and how.

1 You know **why** you must do this work (Stage One: Mindset and Stage Two: Assess).

2 You know **who** your stakeholders are (Stage Two: Assess).

3 You know **what** services you need to create to address the root causes of their pain points (Stage Three: Define).

4 You are about to define **when**, **where**, and **how** here in Stage Four: Plan.

Anytime you feel like something in this process is overwhelming, remember that you can "get to good enough" to start better conversations and lead people on a journey, and then on that journey you will discover more that will shape your thinking and what work you must do. This is the power of iterating. No plan is ever perfect unless someone updates it after the fact. Perfection gets in the way of progress. So just make progress.

A Unique Maturity Model

Sometimes our clients ask us to do an industry comparison of project management capability so they can see how they stack up against "the industry," and my first question is, why? Why do they need to see how they measure up with external organizations when those organizations could have different business models or approaches that are not relevant to how their business runs?

As you build out your capabilities, it can be tempting to place too much emphasis on trying to align with industry standards. The standard way an industry delivers projects may not be the goal you want to strive for—think about the average strategy delivery statistics from Chapter 1. You want to be better than the industry standard, and even more importantly, you want to help your unique organization thrive. What works for other companies may not be a right fit for your organization, so you may waste time trying to keep up with other organizations instead of focusing on driving increased business value internally based on what matters most to *your* organization.

You're better off creating your own IMPACT Maturity Model based on the services and capabilities you are going to deliver to meet the specific challenges and opportunities identified by your stakeholders. If you try to mirror what other organizations are doing or what a generic industry standard says must come at each phase of the journey, you could easily build the wrong solutions or build them in the wrong order. For example, many maturity models include building project management capabilities first, which is what gets so many organizations in trouble.

Remember, you are giving your stakeholders what they *want* before you give them what they *need*, so you must start with visible solutions that address the input you collected in Stage Two: Assess and the diagnosis of root causes you did in Stage Three: Define. For example, while your stakeholders might think the problems that they see are coming from the strategy execution phase of the strategy lifecycle, you know better. If your Root Cause Analysis told you that projects aren't set up for success before they start, you know you need to fix that first. If you heard, "What are all of these people working on?" and "Are they working on the right things?" your first level of maturity might include services like getting a full list of the projects happening in the organization, creating a simple project idea intake process, or establishing a prioritization framework for projects. The first set of services that are focused on root causes often improve the execution experience for everyone involved before the projects even start, making some strategy execution symptoms go away. So your next level of maturity can include leveling up your people and how you execute projects instead of chasing symptoms. Remember, sequence matters.

Your custom maturity model is a useful communication tool that shows how your team will be driving greater business value over time in easy-to-understand categories. The easiest way to do this might be to simply organize the services you're delivering from the IMPACT Delivery Road Map into themes. For example, you could organize the services to first ensure projects are set up for success before they are initiated, then focus on services that accelerate execution, then on services that elevate overall business value. This aligns well with the three phases of the strategy lifecycle. Here's an example.

Level 1—Initiate	Level 2—Accelerate	Level 3—Elevate
Governance Framework	Talent Development	IMPACT Metrics
Portfolio Management	Project Delivery Framework	Benefits and Value Realization
Portfolio Prioritization	Tools and Resources	Operational Handoff Support
Intake Process	Community of Practice	Lessons Learned Process
Strategic Planning and Alignment	Advisory Support	

- **Level 1—Initiate:** Setting projects up for success by establishing the fundamentals of front-end portfolio management and governance before they are started. These services align well with the strategy definition phase.
- **Level 2—Accelerate:** Accelerating business outcomes and increasing project flow. These services align well with the strategy execution phase.

- **Level 3—Elevate:** Realizing organizational IMPACT with an end-to-end focus on supporting the entire strategy lifecycle. These services align well with the strategy realization phase.

If you're anything like me, you love a good plan. So, now that we have a big picture of the long-term strategy for this function, let's go make some progress on that plan so you can see how it all comes together.

Building the IMPACT Delivery Road Map

In the planning stage, remember that iterating your way to IMPACT is both a marathon and a sprint. You need to show value quickly while giving your organization a plan for the journey and the value you will create for years to come. You need a road map that clearly communicates this journey.

Your IMPACT Delivery Road Map is the visually compelling representation of services you will deliver over the coming quarters. It shows your stakeholders where you intend to drive the desired business outcomes and value to the organization. By placing the services that you named in Stage Three: Define on a timeline, you clearly illustrate the prioritized order in which they will be completed based on the input you collected from your business leaders and stakeholders in Stage Two: Assess. This road map does not need to be complicated or fancy. Simple is best. If you have a planning tool in place already, you can build it in that tool. If not, you can download our action-taking resource IMPACT Delivery Road Map to complete this step.

At the end of Stage Four: Plan, you will review the road map with your stakeholders to validate the prioritized list of services and set expectations on which cycle will address each specific pain point. You will continue to involve your key stakeholders in this process so that you foster the buy-in that you need to be successful.

Remember, you should not attempt to deliver services for all of their challenges or opportunities at once. In your first cycle of value

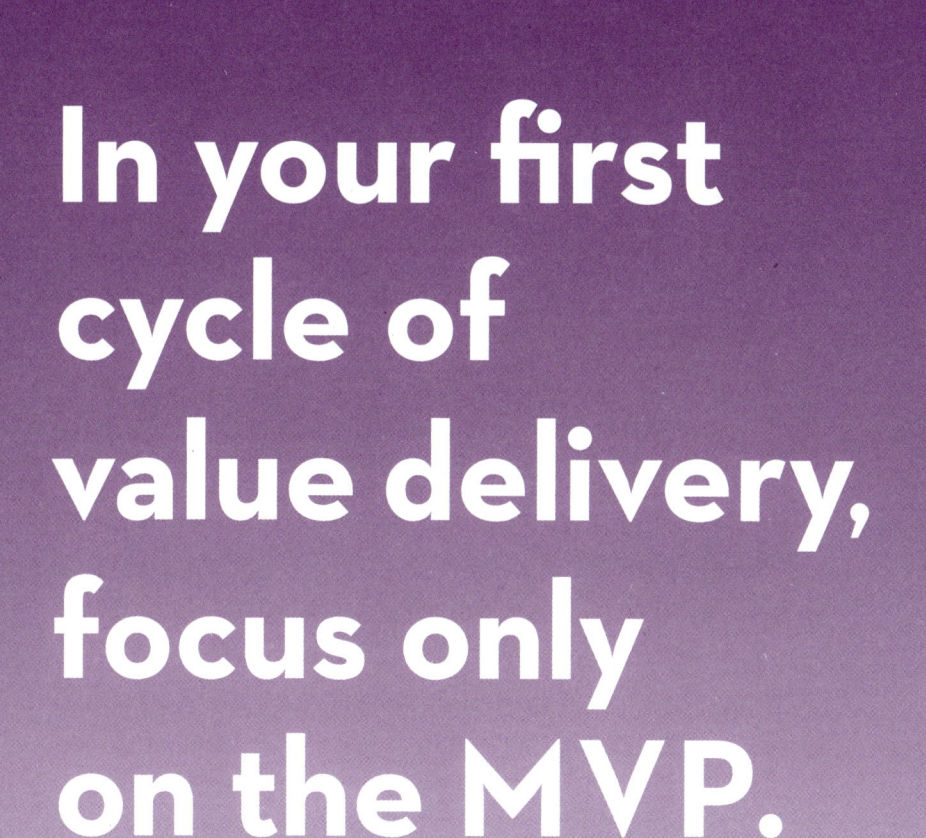

In your first cycle of value delivery, focus only on the MVP.

delivery, you focus only on your minimum viable product. However, you can lay out a road map for the next year or two to show when you will implement services in upcoming cycles. Keep in mind that it may evolve over time as you go through each cycle and get to Stage Six: Evolve, where you measure results and learn more about where you should focus next.

The components of the IMPACT Delivery Road Map are as follows:

- **Level:** The maturity level based on your unique maturity model.

- **Service:** The services you will create to address the root causes identified.

- **Challenge/Opportunity:** The challenge or opportunity this service will address.

- **Outcome:** The outcome the stakeholders can expect when the service is implemented.

- **IMPACT:** The IMPACT expected for the organization when the service is up and running.

- **Metric:** The metric you will use to track your success in achieving the business goal.

- **Timeline:** The quarterly cycles of value delivery, starting with that MVP, that are run year after year. For the timeline, we usually use symbols to denote whether something is starting, in progress, or targeted to be launched in a specific quarter. You'll see this in the legend of the downloadable IMPACT Delivery Road Map.

At a minimum, you will update your road map at the end of each quarterly cycle, as your focus and priorities evolve to respond to shifting business needs. There is no perfect plan unless you are updating it after the fact to reflect what has already happened, so expect this road map to change as you learn more, engage with stakeholders, and implement services. You will likely find new opportunities present themselves as your ripple effect of positive changes starts making waves through the organization.

30/90 Delivery and Reporting

When it comes to communicating your progress and results to business leaders, timing is everything. If you report too frequently, they won't see much change from one report to the next and it will feel like no progress is being made. If you wait too long, your stakeholders may make up their own stories about what is happening (or not), and you might lose them. You may even find that some stakeholders are creating the same services you are to fill the gap they don't feel they can wait for you to resolve, just like Mona did in Chapter 5. Keep your business leaders engaged and aware of when and how you're moving the needle. This is where 30/90 reporting comes in.

You must ensure that you're delivering services in a way that can be digested by the organization (without getting bigger plates), delivered successfully by you and your team, and showing real IMPACT quickly. The secret is iterating your way to IMPACT; essentially you are embracing an agile implementation approach to value delivery. So, how do you do that?

Deliver something new every quarter, then measure and communicate how it's going.

The Start of Each 90-Day Cycle

At the beginning of each quarter, create a project plan that shows your approach to delivering the services defined on your IMPACT Delivery Road Map for that quarter. That specific detailed plan is straightforward—the scope, the timeline, and the resources to get there. Include information for your stakeholders about where you are in the process, what services will be delivered, and when and how these changes will affect them. When you talk about the services you're delivering, use the IMPACT Communication Framework to remind stakeholders of the pain points that will be addressed, and the outcomes and IMPACT you expect to realize for each solution, so they can continue to keep that better future state in mind. The more you keep them focused on the outcomes they will experience, the more motivated they will be to see the changes through—even when it feels hard for them. Remember, you're changing how they are doing something right now, so even when it's something they want, change takes time. Your communication and reporting must prepare them for that shift, as you'll learn how to do in the next chapter.

The 30-Day Mark

Every 30 days, report to your stakeholders where you are in the process of building the services with a progress metric, and show how each of the services that are in use by your stakeholders is helping them achieve the outcomes and IMPACT they desire. Avoid using too many metrics here. One per service is sufficient, especially in the beginning. As you saw from the IMPACT Communication Framework example, there could be several different meaningful metrics, so just pick one that is easy to track and talk about for now.

The 90-Day Mark

Every quarter, report the numbers to your stakeholders—what services you delivered, the value achieved with the services, and how all that rolls up to an IMPACT metric or "worth it factor" for your whole team. Evaluate your IMPACT Delivery Road Map and determine what changes you need to make to address shifting priorities, how the current services are working, and what new information you have that informs the right next steps for your team. You will learn more about how to do this in Chapter 13.

You now have a framework to create the rest of the IMPACT Delivery Model you started in Stage Three: Define. You can create your IMPACT Engine Business Plan, IMPACT Delivery Road Map, and IMPACT Maturity Model, and you know how to report on your progress against those plans. There's a lot here, but don't stress about getting it all done and perfect. Just as the services you're going to create will go through many iterations, you will iterate your way to IMPACT with these deliverables too. Get the fundamentals in place now and keep them simple. Take full advantage of the work you've done in the prior stages to help you focus on what you need to do now.

With your planning resources in place, you can now turn your attention to bringing stakeholders with you through the change process. Your change management and communications plans are critical elements that prepare you to have meaningful conversations with your business leaders when you go back to present your full IMPACT Delivery Model to your stakeholders for approval and support. This next chapter will help you see exactly how you and your team will communicate with your stakeholders when you start delivering services in Stage Five.

Trust yourself. Trust the process. It's time to make an IMPACT.

MAKE AN IMPACT

Think: How will you deliver business value in a way that positions you as a peer to other business-focused teams?

Do: Download the IMPACT Delivery Road Map to document your services, outcomes, IMPACT, metrics, and timeline. Then download the IMPACT Engine Business Plan to communicate your plan for organizational IMPACT.

10

Become the Stakeholder Whisperer

"WHAT'S THE priority of the projects in this customer portfolio?" I asked.

The entire C-suite of the company looked at me like I had spoken to them in a foreign language. "These are our customers, all of them are important," they said in unison.

I had just joined a medium-sized company to create a PMO to manage their portfolio of customer-facing projects. This was the bread and butter of the company, and things were a hot mess. Customers were not happy with how long their projects were taking, all the change orders skyrocketed the cost, and there was no end in sight.

I looked around the room and said, "OK, do we have unlimited time, unlimited funding, and unlimited resources?"

The president stared at me as though I had three heads. What had I gotten myself into?

Wait, I thought, I love a good challenge.

Chuck, the CEO, said, "Obviously not! Just get these projects managed better and we'll be able to get them done."

I met with my team of project managers and quickly learned that staff were pulled in too many directions and were constantly fighting fires, which prevented a consistent cadence of project delivery. They begged me to talk their customers off the ledge to buy them some time to get things back on track. I ended up on the phone with several angry CEOs over the next few weeks.

At our next senior leadership meeting with all the heads of the company, I explained the root cause of the pain points I had discovered and, although it took some convincing, I got them to agree to an exercise of "organizing" the projects to create more focus.

"I know these customers are all very important to the organization," I said, "but we need a better way to organize them so the team can think differently about when and how we assign resources to them. How about we just put them into buckets: A, B, and C?"

Reluctantly, the CTO said, "OK, but how do we determine who goes in each bucket?"

"Let's start with the ones threatening lawsuits and the ones with the biggest revenue outstanding first."

After a few hours, we had organized the client work into the three buckets based on the severity of several factors, such as how far behind the projects were, money we were leaving on the table, and corporate risk to our brand from unhappy customers. The executives were exhausted from the exercise, and I realized that was as far as I was going to get them for a while.

For the next three months, we met every morning in our daily stand-up with the senior leadership team to talk about the client projects and drive greater focus on the Bucket A projects to get them flowing. Then we each had our cascading team meetings to ensure that everyone in the organization was aligned with the direction and pace set by the executives. It didn't take long for everyone at every level in the organization who was connected to the projects to start using the "bucket" language to talk about the projects and their priority.

At the same time, I created a simple portfolio report that showed each customer's projects, the status, start and end dates, and a note about where they were in the process. I posted this dashboard outside my office door and waited to see who would notice. The technical team was the first to pay attention. They normally never left their side of the building, but after a while, they'd swing by my office after getting coffee to see the latest status on the projects. Before we knew it, everyone from the support staff answering the phone to the executives had changed how they talked about and prioritized their work based on that dashboard on my wall. I would smile to myself when the executives started using the "bucket" language to refer to each of the client engagements.

At the beginning of the next quarter, I gathered the executives and showed them how many of the projects were now back on track and flowing well. I shared stories of the conversations outside my office door and the way staff were already planning their days differently, and asking better questions, so that the Bucket A projects could get done faster. They were quite proud of themselves for setting the organization up for better project delivery. As you can imagine, this also led to a lot better conversations with our customers, who were seeing progress on their projects and feeling momentum build.

And then I told the executives it was time to do the prioritization exercise again. This time, they didn't fight me quite as much in the process, but it still took a lot of convincing that more was necessary. We prioritized the Bucket A projects in numerical order. It took another couple of hours of debate, challenge, and disagreement, but we got there! I quickly realized that was as far as they were getting this month.

Another quarter went by in a flash and more bucket language could be heard in meetings. Projects that were struggling were now back on track and the delivery teams were meeting their commitments. I was building trusted relationships with our customers, and they began to believe that we could meet the commitments we were making.

Each quarter, I took the organization to another level of maturity in how they prioritized their work and engaged with the customers. Admittedly, it felt painfully slow to me to take just one baby step each quarter, but it was the only way the company was going to adopt the change and make it their own.

A year after I joined the company, I was at our annual customer conference, where I met many of these formerly angry customer

CEOs in person for the first time. I watched from the back of the room as one of the CEOs, who had been threatening legal action only a year before, now spoke about how the software had helped his company achieve their business goals. The transformation was powerful, and it never would have happened had I pushed too hard to move my company too fast. I could see the future so clearly, but I had to lead them to these outcomes at their pace. I know that I would have failed if I had let my desire for their success push them beyond the pace of change that worked for them. Years later, several of those client CEOs hired my company to help them implement strategy delivery capability because they wanted the same kind of turnaround results for their own organizations.

One of my most important lessons here was that patience was the key to my success. Although I knew there was a much faster way to get to the result, anytime I tried to move too fast for them, I hit a wall of resistance. I had to meet them where they were and take them on this transformation journey with me in a way that they could handle mentally, emotionally, and organizationally. It had to work for them if it was going to work at all.

Notice how two simple changes created a greater flow of work at every level in the organization, driving higher project throughput, less stressed team members, and happier customers—and none of it felt forced or difficult for the teams. The first change, simply exposing the project priority and status to all project team members, allowed them to prioritize their workload on their own based on simply knowing what mattered most at the enterprise level. The second change, creating a natural rhythm of communication around the projects at every level in the organization, let people create intentional focus on what mattered most in small, manageable chunks—a daily stand-up meeting. This is the power of using the IMPACT Driver Mindset to instill focus so that organizations can perform relentlessly.

No matter how simple the change is that you are trying to make, whether it's adding an intake process for projects, or simply getting the projects prioritized into buckets, you're still creating change for people. What seems so obvious and easy to you is changing the way

Resistance is often a side effect of forced change.

someone has always done something. Even if the current state is not serving them, it will take some creative influence to get your stakeholders to move away from the familiar to the unknown—even when they understand why the change is necessary.

That, my friend, is the power of organizational change management.

You must be able to implement change *with* people and *through* people, not *to* people. So many delivery leaders believe their organizations are filled with change-resistant people but, as you know by now, this is simply not true. And if you are already feeling resistance, it's fixable. Resistance is often a side effect of forced change—change that feels like it's happening to them in a way that doesn't benefit them. Delivery leaders must do a better job of bringing people with them through the process in a way that makes what matters to them clear. Proactively plan your strategy for bringing people through the changes you're creating so you can prevent or address any change resistance you experience.

You started doing change management work in the Assess stage so that you could implement your changes in alignment with the organization's culture and way of getting business done. You learned how to align your stakeholders and what they want with what you will be delivering, and you even learned how to talk about it to keep bringing them with you through the process. Now that you're in the Plan stage, you can create the Organizational Change Management Plan to lay out your approach to continuing to bring those stakeholders with you through the change process.

The Organizational Change Management Plan

Your Organizational Change Management Plan serves as a guide for documenting how you effectively share information and engage stakeholders across the organization in the change process. When you reach this point in the IMPACT Engine System, you will have a great deal of input to work with from what you've done so far in the Assess and Define stages to answer the W^5H questions.

1. **Why are the changes necessary?** Make sure you clearly explain the reasons for each change and highlight the challenges the organization currently faces to create a sense of urgency and motivate your stakeholders to embrace the changes.

2. **Who will be affected?** Name the people who will be directly impacted by the changes, such as employees, customers, or suppliers. Identify all the stakeholders who will be affected, so that they can be involved in the change process.

3. **What changes will occur?** List the specific changes that will be made, such as new processes, procedures, or technology. Be as clear and specific as possible about the changes, so that everyone understands what is happening.

4. **When will the changes take place?** Include the start and end dates for the changes, as well as any specific milestones or deadlines. Be as clear and specific as possible about the timeline, so that everyone knows what to expect.

5. **Where will the changes take place?** Identify the specific location or locations where the changes will be implemented, so that people know where to go for support or information and if the changes will affect their team.

6. **How will the changes be implemented?** Explain if it's a gradual transition or a sweeping change for the entire organization. When you clearly convey the implementation approach, individuals know what to expect and how they can support the process.

The answers to these questions will help you guide conversations and lead people through all of the changes your team is putting in place.

When you incorporate organizational change management techniques into the delivery process for your services, your adoption success increases because people don't feel like the change is being done *to* them. They feel like they're a part of the future state success.

Guiding the Transition

In Stage Two: Assess, you created a Stakeholder Engagement Plan (see Chapter 4) that supports your continuous efforts to engage stakeholders throughout the change process. This plan helps you understand what your stakeholders care about and how you keep them engaged, so that you can keep weaving what they care about into what you talk about. As you learn more about each stakeholder, update your plan accordingly. Knowing the WIIFM for all your stakeholders will be useful in the next sections as you guide them through the transition process.

Now, let's talk a little bit about the transition states that people go through when a change is happening. You'll be the navigator who guides them through this transition process.

STATES OF CHANGE

CURRENT STATE ▶ **TRANSITION PERIOD** ▶ **FUTURE STATE**

1. **Current state:** Define where stakeholders are now in terms of the W^{5}H. What's going on now in their current environment? You've done a lot of work in the assessment stage to identify the organization's strengths, weaknesses, opportunities, and threats (SWOT), to learn about your stakeholders' current pain points and where they see opportunities for growth. That's all relevant here when you're talking to stakeholders about the current state, the challenges, and the reason or impetus for making this change.

2. **Transition period:** When you're in the transition period, you're talking about getting to the future state. There are shifts that people will need to make in the way they work, the way they communicate, and the way they engage, and all of that happens in this middle-tier transition state. In the transition period, it's best to define things in terms of the processes and steps, such as, "Here's how we go from where we currently are to the future state that we all desire." In this transition period, you will walk people step by step, holding their hands, through the process to get from point A to point B.

3. **Future state:** In the future state, you want to change the language to the outcomes and IMPACT you're creating together for the organization. When you're talking about your focus, when you're talking about the direction, when you document your recommendations in your IMPACT Delivery Proposal, all those inputs go into defining things in terms of that future state outcome you're trying to create and the IMPACT that you will have.

Do you see how all the stages you've been through so far in this book connect to the three steps above? I show you the future state and what's possible with Stage One: Mindset (an important step to build buy-in), help you understand your current state in Stage Two: Assess, define the transition period in Stage Three: Define and Stage Four: Plan, and then you begin to build and iterate on the future state in Stage Five: Deliver and Stage Six: Evolve.

Remember, everything you do in change management is about bringing people from a current state to a future state and supporting that transition in a way that does the change *with* people instead of *to* people.

Now you have what you need to document your change plan to keep stakeholders engaged. You know who you will involve, how you will involve them, and the three states you will take them through. Keep it simple and iterate over time. Continually refine and adapt your Organizational Change Management Plan as you progress through the change management journey. Embrace feedback and make necessary adjustments to ensure you maintain stakeholder buy-in.

With your Organizational Change Management Plan defined, we can now transition to developing the communications plan, the often-missed secret ingredient to the success of your organizational change management efforts. The IMPACT Communications Plan will cover the specific messaging and delivery mechanisms you use at various stages of the change journey to keep those stakeholders engaged.

You're a Marketer

As you learned in the IMPACT Communication Framework in Chapter 8, you will bring your stakeholders with you through the change process by showing how the solutions you're providing help them achieve their goals.

Do you remember the bucket story from the beginning of this chapter? When I first suggested to the C-suite that we prioritize projects, they weren't interested. I could see the future state so clearly, but they couldn't. I had to help them see that the solution I was offering was the answer to their pain point. What you may not realize is that what I was doing was marketing—tying what they wanted to the solution I was offering.

Before you get weirded out thinking you aren't a salesperson so there's no way you will be doing any sales or marketing, understand that there's a huge difference between sales and marketing. You see, when sales and marketing are done well, the customer feels very much a part of the process, cared for, and that what you are doing is in their best interest and aligned with what they care about most. That's how you want your stakeholders to feel when they engage with you and your team.

The problem many delivery leaders have, and why they often hit resistance, is because they do all the pushy sales to "convince" stakeholders they are there to help, without doing any of the marketing. Do the right marketing and you won't need sales. You'll create a pull instead of a push.

The goal of marketing is simple—connect the solution you provide with the desires of your customers. With that framing, can you see how much of what you've been doing so far actually is marketing? Your stakeholders must understand how your team is going to address what they care about most. And the best news is you already know what they care about most because you asked them in the Assess stage.

The IMPACT Communications Plan is used to document how you will engage your stakeholders in meaningful ways throughout this process with clear and transparent communication, which will set you up for success in Stage Five: Deliver. The goals of this communications plan are to educate people on what you're doing and why, excite them by showing them a future that speaks to what they care about most, and fully engage stakeholders as partners in shaping the solutions to the pain points identified in the Assess stage. Here are the components.

IMPACT COMMUNICATIONS PLAN

EDUCATE
Introduce the IMPACT Engine

EXCITE
Build Excitement and Energy

ENGAGE
Create Sustainable Relationships

Educate: Explain what your delivery team is doing in terms *they* care about using your IMPACT Engine Business Plan, IMPACT Delivery Road Map, and IMPACT Maturity Model so your stakeholders understand:

- The purpose, goals, roles, and responsibilities.
- The services you will provide.
- The outcomes your services will enable.
- Details on what will change, when, and how much.
- What the services look like and how people will use them.
- How this addresses the pain they are experiencing.

Excite: Once they understand the basics, you can create stakeholder enthusiasm by:

- Sharing success stories from early adopters.
- Communicating your progress through newsletters, presentations, and internal communication platforms.
- Making it meaningful, showing how each person or team benefits.
- Addressing any implications for current roles and responsibilities.
- Encouraging engagement and asking for input when defining and delivering services.

Engage: Facilitate two-way communication, partnership, and support for your team by:

- Using an advisory board or stakeholder group to co-create solutions.
- Keeping everyone informed of progress and outcomes achieved.
- Listening extensively to gather input and ideas.
- Demonstrating potential new services and gathering feedback.
- Partnering with executives to set clear expectations that adoption is required so you can all get to the better business outcomes.
- Providing support and help throughout the transition phase.

What Happens If You Don't

Ivan was an excellent people manager. He'd built a large delivery team for a consulting organization with hundreds of project managers delivering on projects for a global enterprise. He made sure they all got the training they needed and spent a great deal of time coaching and developing his leaders. But budgets were getting tight, and the organization was looking to make cuts.

Ivan was surprised when the organization looked at reorganizing his team to cut the management structure he'd created. Ivan's team was responsible for customer project delivery and Ivan knew that his organizational structure was why they were successful. The problem, however, is that he was the only one who knew this. Ivan didn't place much value on building relationships with his peers or managing up. His peer group treated his customer delivery organization as a black box that sometimes worked and sometimes did things no one understood that slowed everyone down. His peers saw Ivan's team as administrative overhead and were happy to offer them up for sacrifice to the budget cutting committee.

Ivan's boss wasn't much help. He seemed to only be interested in his own personal gains and never shared with his leaders all the great wins and progress Ivan's team was making. Ivan found this out the hard way when that leader left, and he had his first conversation with the executive they'd both reported into. The executive had no idea of all the good work they were doing and had only heard the rumor mill about Ivan's team being too people heavy and a great place to cut costs. None of the executives realized that Ivan's team was the reason that client delivery moved as fast as it did, because Ivan's peers were taking all the credit.

Ivan scrambled to pull together reports and presentations to make up for the lack of communication about his team and the value they were driving, but it was too late. The executives had already made the decisions without his involvement, and the team was being downsized and restructured without retaining Ivan as a leader.

Sometimes, we see delivery leaders shy away from doing the marketing work necessary to own the conversation about the role their

Own the conversation about how your team solves business problems.

team is playing in helping the organization achieve its goals. This is a huge mistake. Why?

If you don't own the conversation about your value, they will.

If Ivan had invested the time to own the conversation about how his project delivery team was the linchpin to the successful delivery of client projects in a way that kept ROI high, the executives would have never even considered cutting his function. They didn't realize that Ivan's management structure was generating a large ROI for the organization.

If Ivan had invested in building relationships with his colleagues, they wouldn't have been so quick to sacrifice his team when it was time to cut expenses. Ivan saw the casual coffees and lunch get-togethers as a waste of time when he had so much work to do, but that time spent building relationships would have kept his people from being the sacrificial team.

But you can't just manage up and out, you need to ensure you own the brand of your organization in all your stakeholders' eyes.

Have you ever seen the rumor mill go wild when the executives are having secret meetings? Someone always has some farfetched opinion about what's happening. That opinion spreads and before you know it, there are various permutations of it all over the organization. This causes the executives to spend a lot of time recovering and resetting expectations with communication that is too little and too late.

I've been on the inside of those conversations when I was working in organizations and often lead them as a consultant. I immediately address the fact that the longer the teams don't know what's happening, the more dangerous their behavior will become and the harder it will be to clean up the communication mess.

In the absence of information, your stakeholders will make up their own minds about what your team should be doing, how you should be doing it, and whether they think you're successful. And while that might not seem so bad because the value you bring to the table is obvious, don't assume that. They aren't the experts. They haven't been on the IMPACT Engine System journey with you long enough to feel the positive effects of your solutions to their pain points yet. Own the conversation about how your team solves problems. Use the IMPACT Communication Framework, download the IMPACT Communications Plan template, and get that plan in place.

With your communications plan in place, you have all the pieces you need from Stage Four to go back to the executives you met with at the end of the assessment process in Stage Two and get their support to proceed with delivering that minimum viable product. It's now time to create your IMPACT Delivery Proposal to showcase your plan for addressing the root causes of their pain points through a well-planned road map of services.

Present Your IMPACT Delivery Proposal

OK! You now have your IMPACT Delivery Model—the compilation of all your work in Stages Two through Four. It's made of the deliverables you've already created.

Stage Two
- Organizational Change Assessment (Chapter 4)
- Stakeholder Engagement Plan (Chapter 5)

Stage Three
- Root Cause Analysis (Chapter 6)
- IMPACT Services Register (Chapter 7)
- IMPACT Communication Framework (Chapter 8)

Stage Four
- IMPACT Engine Business Plan (Chapter 9)
- IMPACT Delivery Road Map (Chapter 9)
- Organizational Change Management Plan (Chapter 10)
- IMPACT Communications Plan (Chapter 10)

With all the hard planning work done, you have what you need to present your plan to your executives to get the support and approval to proceed with your MVP, as well as feedback on the proposed road map that outlines how you will help your leaders achieve their business goals. You want to get their approval to proceed so they are invested in this process with you, and you may need funding, resources, or other support to deliver on everything you show them. This presentation will give them what they want—a visible path to a better future state—so you can earn their investment in getting the outcomes they desire.

The presentation should include a high-level overview of each of the components of your IMPACT Delivery Model to take them on the journey of where the organization is now (current state), where they want to go (future state), and how you are going to get them there (transition). Organize these components in your presentation using the five-step IMPACT Communication Framework you already know and love, so it tells the story of the value you intend to drive for the organization and how you'll track success. You can organize your IMPACT Delivery Proposal presentation like this.

1 **Challenge or Opportunity:** The input on stakeholders' pain points and desires from the assessment work in Stage Two, which should be familiar to them, since they prioritized these pain points and desires in your last presentation to them.

2 **Solution:** Services from Stage Three: Define organized by the root causes you uncovered.

3 **Outcome:** The changes they want to see, in their words, to move them from the current state pain collected during Stage Two to future state success.

4 **IMPACT:** The future state you are taking them to, laid out on the IMPACT Delivery Road Map.

5 **Metric:** The measurements you defined at the end of Stage Three to show how you will know the solutions are working.

And then you want to add **Next Steps**. This is where you explain how you will implement the MVP cycle of your IMPACT Delivery Road Map and that you will be back to check in with them in 30 days to report progress against that MVP, using the 30/90 protocol from Chapter 9. Note that if you're following my recommended timeline (and only creating *one* service in your MVP cycle), this lines up perfectly with when you should be moving into Stage Six: Evolve.

This presentation will garner final approval from your business leaders to proceed with building and delivering the MVP. But you'll also outline the other services and capabilities to be delivered in the upcoming quarters, as you continue iterating toward IMPACT.

When you present your proposal to your executives, be sure to stay at only the top level of information. If you bury your stakeholders in a lot of detail about your process or the solutions you're creating, you'll see their eyes glaze over. And if you lose them now, you'll have a hard time getting them back. So use the IMPACT Communication Framework to help you frame what you say and how you say it. Keep them tuned in by focusing on what they care about.

Once they are excited about your proposal, it's a good time to have a conversation about what to name your delivery team. Remember in Chapter 3 when I suggested that your executives name it? This helps with adding to the excitement and support, while also making them even more invested in its success. Just remember to keep it focused on the bigger picture, and if project management office works for everyone, great! If something like strategy delivery office resonates more with the executives, go for it!

No matter how well you plan and prepare for this important milestone in the process, it's likely that some stakeholders will not love your plan when they see that the services that matter most to them won't be delivered for a while. That's OK. Use this opportunity to remind them of the priorities that they agreed to and assure them that you will revisit priorities together as necessary. Reference the IMPACT Delivery Road Map and the order in which you are planning to deliver changes. If they need to adjust the priorities due to shifts in the business needs or otherwise, take them through that prioritization process again (see Chapter 5). And if they still aren't buying it, this is where you will use two simple words to keep them accountable for their decisions.

The Power of "Yes, And..."

It's likely that your business leaders will want it all and want it all tomorrow. That's normal. I feel the same way about changes I want to take my own company through as CEO, and I also used to when I was a business leader inside organizations. Know that this desire to have it all comes from a good place of wanting to show value and help people. But to maintain your sanity, you need a better way to keep your business leaders feeling that they are in the driver's seat when it comes to making decisions about the changes they want and how those changes are prioritized. No one can do it all at once, so they need to prioritize and make educated and informed decisions about what they are requesting.

There's a simple communication tool I teach my IMPACT Accelerator Mastermind students to use to effectively negotiate, help leaders prioritize, and put the decision-making control back in their hands. This tool requires two little words: "Yes, and..."

When your business leaders ask you if something can be done, you shouldn't say no. All that advice you've heard to "say no more often" is off base. Why? Because you don't own the decisions; the business leaders do. If you take that authority away from them, you can expect that they will disengage from the process, and you don't want that. This goes for the projects your team is responsible for and for the business function you are creating—because, remember, they're not yours. You're creating a service-based team designed to address what your stakeholders must have to do their jobs, and you want *them* to own the decisions and the solutions. You maintain buy-in by giving them what they *want* before you give them what they *need*.

When you say no, it not only creates a situation where stakeholders are hearing something they don't want to hear, but also, it's not your job to decide what your stakeholders can or cannot have. Your job isn't to make the decision for them, but to help them make educated and informed decisions. So, how do you help them make reasonable requests?

When your business leaders ask you if something can be done (even if what they are asking seems impossible), you can simply say, "Yes, and here's what it will take..." and let *them* own the decision instead of you deciding for them.

For example, let's say they ask you to crash the schedule and deliver two services in the next quarter. You know that it could be done but that it would require one more team member to do the work. So you say, "Yes, we absolutely can do that, and it will take the addition of another resource to make it happen. Would you like to proceed with adding another full-time person to this team to deliver that service in this quarter instead of next?" Sometimes, it *is* just a triple constraint (time, scope, cost/resources) conversation and you need to treat it as such.

You might be thinking, "That's great, but they are just going to tell me to do it without adding resources." Yep, I know. And this is where you need to decide if you are going to be an order taker or an IMPACT Driver. You could show them what happened last time they asked you to take on more work than the team could accomplish and a big mistake happened as a result. Bonus points if it made them look bad, because that makes it personal to them. Find the thing they care about here and use that thing to illustrate why they need to choose.

You must continue to show them how to achieve what they are looking to achieve, and make it clear that the decision to proceed happens only if the resources to do it are added.

Don't give up. Be creative: figure out how to show them the effect of their decisions, and use "Yes, and..."

Remember in Chapter 5 when I said yes to all of Mona's requests without setting expectations? What if, instead of just saying yes to everything, I had said, "*Yes*, we can help you address these challenges, *and* we will come back to all the key stakeholders to prioritize the pain points together *so that* we ensure we are focusing our limited

Use the power of "Yes, and …" to drive accountability.

resources on the highest-IMPACT services for the organization as a whole"?

Years after I discovered the power of "Yes, and..." as I was developing my craft as a professional speaker, I learned that "Yes, and..." is a rule of thumb in improvisational comedy that suggests that an improviser should accept what another improviser has stated (yes) and then expand on that line of thinking (and). The improvisers' characters may still disagree, but they keep the momentum going and create something beautiful together. Create something beautiful with your stakeholders that keeps them by your side every step of the way *while holding them accountable* for their decisions.

As an undergraduate, graduate, and fellowship student with Heroic Public Speaking—easily the best professional speaking program out there—I watched in awe as they harnessed the simple but incredibly powerful mantra "Yes, and..." to instill confidence and empowerment among speakers of all backgrounds. They made students recite a pledge, ending each verse with a resounding "Yes, and!" Every day, those words grew louder and more filled with conviction. Speakers practically yelled the affirmations by graduation, fists pumping, voices cracking. I could physically feel the vibes as we committed as one to their mission of changing the world, one speech at a time. The transformation was palpable.

I saw firsthand the motivational force of "Yes, and" thinking. Never underestimate its potential to rally a team toward change or catapult an organization forward.

And now we are moving on to Stage Five, where you will finally start delivering your first service (aka your minimum viable product). As you deliver your MVP to the organization, you'll learn how to create a delivery-focused culture with your immediate team and broader stakeholders and continue to support them through the change process.

Trust yourself. Trust the process. It's time to make an IMPACT.

MAKE AN IMPACT

Think: How will you bring people with you through this change process?

Do: Download the IMPACT Communications Plan template to document your communication strategy.

STAGE

DELIVER SUSTAINABLE VALUE

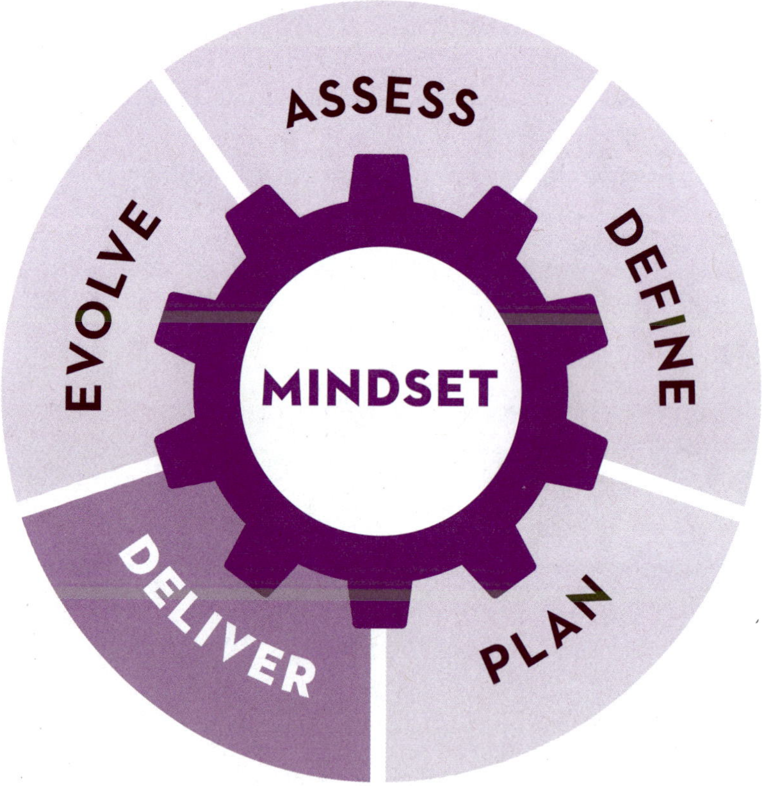
ASSESS
DEFINE
PLAN
DELIVER
EVOLVE
MINDSET

It's finally time to put that MVP service in place! In Stage Five of the IMPACT Engine System, you get to deliver sustainable value that leverages all your hard work so far.

The key here is to build your minimum viable product and ensure early wins that demonstrate undeniable organizational IMPACT for your stakeholders. Remember, simplicity is best. You don't need a long list of services to show value—just start with that one important challenge or opportunity that they want addressed first.

As you begin to build and deliver the MVP and future services, you will be far more successful if you learn how to keep those stakeholders engaged with you every step of the way. That goes for the members of your team and your own focus too. I'll look first at creating a delivery-focused culture to keep everyone engaged in getting to the critical business outcomes necessary for the organization to thrive. Then I will show you how to bring the broader stakeholder group through change while you are delivering services and creating new capabilities for the organization (and what to do if you hit change resistance), as well as how to showcase the value your IMPACT Engine is making.

Let's do this!

Create a Delivery-Focused Culture

11

I**T'S TIME** to start delivering the changes you defined for your MVP cycle. Or perhaps you are already into your next IMPACT Delivery Cycle and reviewing these steps again to remind yourself what to do, in what order, and why it matters. You have your IMPACT Delivery Model but, as with every plan, obstacles will present themselves as you start building this new service or capability. In this chapter, let's look at the bumps in the road that may slow down your progress.

It's easy to get distracted by all the things we could be doing and then not get that most important thing done. Keep your eye on the big-picture results you must drive. Know this: you have limited time to show real business value and build your credibility, so don't squander this time by trying to do too many things at once. Start by making sure all your stakeholders understand the business outcomes they are there to drive.

Focus On Outcomes, Not Outputs

Today, so many project leaders define success by the success of their projects. But that's only part of the success story—and you may not even be telling that part correctly. Often, business success is defined by how much work is happening, how much money is being spent, or how much overall progress is being made by the organization. Progress gets confused with outcomes and people assume that because they are busy, they are making progress and so they are successful. In fact, they might just be busy but not making progress or succeeding.

Progress does not equal IMPACT.

You need to redefine success in terms of the IMPACT these projects achieve. Ironically, defining success using techniques like Earned Value Management falls short because, as you discovered in Chapter 1, EVM doesn't measure value. EVM measures schedule performance and cost performance, but it doesn't tell you anything about the value and it certainly doesn't tell you anything about IMPACT. EVM doesn't measure actual outcomes and whether they were achieved as people envisioned that they should be. And therein lies the challenge.

EVM alone cannot tell your business leaders if they are going to achieve high-IMPACT business outcomes for the work that was done, only if that work will be done according to what you expect or planned from a cost and schedule perspective.

Here's a simple example. Let's say your team is running a project to implement a new system. The reason the system is being implemented (your project "why") is to create a new revenue source for the organization. Your project team diligently delivers all the defined scope, according to the originally determined timeline, and even does all the work under budget. Once the system is live, everyone expects a big bang on that new revenue, but it doesn't come. No one uses the system.

What happened? Along the way, the customer realized that the project scope needed to change. The project team said no instead of "Yes, and..." and some key features were delayed until "a future phase" instead of getting delivered when they were needed to make the project worth doing in the first place.

Was the right due diligence done up front to determine if the market really needed this system? Did the project include the proper marketing and communications planning to introduce the new system to the market? When scope decisions were made, did the team go back to the business case to determine if these changes would affect the intended outcomes? The questions are countless, but the outcome is the same.

The project did not realize the intended IMPACT.

In the eyes of the business stakeholders, this project is a failure, even if your project team did "everything right" according to EVM. This is the gap we need to close: the gap between how project people perceive success and how business stakeholders and customers do. Yes, measuring time, scope, and budget helps to measure progress toward creating the project *outputs*, but not enough to tell you if the projects are going to achieve their intended business *outcomes*.

Your project people need to know the difference between outputs and outcomes so they are focused on driving the better business outcomes that determine the business measures of success. This simple shift in thinking about and defining success for projects will go a long way toward driving a delivery-focused culture.

Remember that buckets story from Chapter 10? When I posted that simple dashboard outside my office so everyone could see the status of each of the customer projects, it changed how people organized their work. After seeing that dashboard, team members prioritized the work they had on their plates to do the work for the Bucket A projects and any work tied to a troubled project first. No one told them to do it. It just happened because they understood that these were revenue-generating projects and, without revenue, the company couldn't pay salaries. They instilled focus and performed relentlessly to achieve the intended business outcomes. The company adapted to thrive in a changing environment, I communicated with purpose to drive better actions and decisions, and the entire process transformed the mindset of how work was delivered to achieve higher ROI for our client projects. Everything goes back to that fundamental central gear of the IMPACT Driver Mindset.

You may be surprised with how easily the delivery teams will "get" the importance of shifting from perfecting outputs to driving better business outcomes if you just help them connect the work that they are responsible for to the bigger picture. Take the time to help all project team members understand the organizational strategy, the projects they are on that help to achieve the strategic goals, and how their work is supporting the delivery of those projects. People want to do work that matters, and often leaders don't take time to ensure that the people doing the work understand why it matters. This alone can go a long way to boosting your project delivery before you even implement your first services. In fact, if you don't already have a good process for developing and communicating project business cases so the "why" for your projects and the measurable success criteria are clear, this can be an excellent place to start.

Dump the Busy Badge

Ever ask someone how they are doing, and they immediately start telling you how "busy" they are? You might even have said the word "busy" when describing how you're doing. You might *feel* busy every day. We wear the busy badge of honor all the time. But the problem is that being busy is a sign of chaos, not success.

Remember, busy does not equal productive. Busy gets in the way of productive.

As Jack's leadership team learned the hard way in Chapter 6, when you focus on making sure everyone is busy, you create a lot of waste and decrease productivity. When people are busy, they tend to create more problems for themselves than the sustainable progress that the team needs. You don't have time for that waste.

Here's how busy shows up in people.

1. **Overcommitting and multitasking:** When you take on too many tasks or projects simultaneously, it can lead to a lack of focus and attention. It often results in reduced productivity and quality of work. When you are constantly busy with multiple tasks, this can prevent you from giving them your full attention, leading to mistakes and delays. Multitasking sounds good, but it's just another way of saying you're doing a lot of things at once badly.

2. **Lack of prioritization:** Being busy can sometimes make it challenging to prioritize tasks effectively. When you're constantly rushing from one task to another, it's easy to lose sight of what's truly important. Without clear priorities, you may spend valuable time on low-value tasks while neglecting critical ones, ultimately hindering your productivity.

3. **Failure to delegate or seek support:** A busy badge mindset can make it tempting to try to handle everything on your own. However, this can lead to burnout and decreased efficiency. By not delegating tasks or seeking support from colleagues or team members, you may become overwhelmed and struggle to meet deadlines or produce high-quality work.

4. **Reactive rather than proactive approach:** Being busy often means constantly reacting to incoming requests, emails, or meetings. This reactive approach can prevent you from taking the time to plan, strategize, and work on important long-term goals. Instead, you may find yourself caught up in a cycle of putting out fires and addressing immediate issues, which hampers productivity and progress.

5. **Limited time for reflection and improvement:** Busyness can leave little time for reflection, learning, and personal development. Without regular opportunities to assess your work, identify areas for improvement, and learn from your experiences, it becomes difficult to grow and enhance your productivity over time. You'll learn my framework for making space for this reflection and improvement cycle later in this chapter.

6 Increased stress and decreased well-being: A consistently busy schedule can lead to higher stress levels and decreased well-being. When you're overwhelmed and constantly rushing, it can negatively affect your mental and physical health, leading to decreased productivity in the long run.

Instead of trying to be busy, you must instill focus to keep your eye on the most important outcomes you must drive and *prioritize* just like you're asking your stakeholders to do. You can revisit the "Yes, and..." technique and use it on yourself or with your boss to help with your workload. Teach your team to do this to you too. The more effectively they manage up, the more productive you'll all be. Good leaders aren't busy. Good leaders get themselves and everyone else productive. But to be productive, you'll need to learn how to effectively narrow down your areas of focus to what matters most by picking three.

Pick Three

"Pick three!" Kendall exclaimed while holding three fingers close to my face. I didn't want to hear it. My dear friends and reciprocal business advisers Mike Hannan and Kendall Lott were sitting with me after a Washington, DC, Project Management Institute chapter dinner meeting, and I was lamenting about all the things I wanted to do in my business and how I never seemed to have enough time. It was in the early years before I had a big team, and I was trying to get a lot done with the limited resources I had. "Pick three!" he said again, as I felt the "Yeah, but..." monster climbing up onto my shoulder to tell him all the reasons that three wasn't the right number.

"You are newly married, you have a young son who needs you right now, you have a growing business, you have Project Management for Change, and you are trying to add even more big projects to your plate. No one can really handle more than three big things at once, not even you, and you're not going to do any of them well if you keep trying. You'll burn out and none of them will be important or

Whenever you get overwhelmed, remember to pick three.

you'll mess up this new marriage or the kid. You must decide what's most important and pick three. The rest will have to wait."

I didn't want to hear it. I wanted to argue with him about how *I* could handle more. I always handled more. I could do more than most people. I had a greater capacity and could figure it out. And I wasn't wrong. I *did* always figure it out. But it came at a cost. I would miss out on something in my personal life. I would not be present for an important moment. I wouldn't be able to enjoy the small moments that really were the big moments. I wouldn't be able to give each of those separate priorities my best. And I would regret that I wasn't spending more time on the things that truly mattered most.

Here's the thing, I can't stand people waiting for me. Whenever my team is waiting for me to deliver something, I always want to do that thing first. It might not be the most important thing, but it is hard for me to know someone on my team can't proceed because they are waiting for me to answer a question, review something, or make a decision. I struggled with this for years and it's why this book, a baby I've been working on for years, has taken so long to birth. I always have big projects on my plate and there are always more things I want to do than time to do it.

In my situation it was clear something had to give. I was tired. I was doing too much. And it wasn't serving me. It wasn't just about work priorities. It was about my life. All the parts. All the priorities pulling on me. I had too many number one priorities going on and it was affecting my ability to do my best work. I had to pick three.

That advice has stayed with me for a decade and will be with me for the rest of my life. When you are thinking about all the things you want to do, know that I totally get it. It's something I have to keep reminding myself about because I am on a mission to change the world and that is a lot of work. There will always be more projects I want to do than time to do them.

If you want to create a delivery-focused culture, it starts with you. Whenever you get overwhelmed, remember to pick three.

Staying focused on a smaller number of important goals helps you accelerate your leadership credibility. It gives you time to invest in building the strong relationships you will need to deliver meaningful and sustainable change. For your first cycle, you need to focus on completing that *one* MVP service, and do it faster and better than you would if you were trying to do ten at once.

Here are three things you can do to lead differently and stay focused on the things that are most important.

1 **Delegate decisions whenever you can.** You don't have to always be the one who makes every decision. Share that decision-making authority with people on your team as quickly as possible. You can't grow your team if you never let them take on more responsibility. They will make mistakes, just like you did. That's part of the growth process. Let them know you have their back, and then be patient with them as they learn what success looks like.

2 **Prioritize your time.** Take a hard look at all that is on your plate and go through the important (and painful) process of prioritizing your work and your team's work so that everyone is focused on the most important priorities for the team. I know, you must take your own medicine here and it doesn't taste the best, but prioritizing is critical to your success.

3 **Don't sweat the small stuff.** You can't be everywhere at once. You will have to get comfortable with some things needing to wait to get your attention and letting go of the small things completely. Know the difference between urgent and important, and get the important stuff done!

And whenever you feel your business leaders or team start to pile more onto your plate, don't say no, just say, "Yes, and..." to pull them into the prioritization process, take ownership of the decision to deprioritize something that's already on your plate, or delegate the responsibility to where it really belongs.

OK, now go teach your team how to do what you've just learned so they, too, can be laser-focused on delivering that MVP. And now

Busy gets in the way of productive.

that you've got your plate prioritized and your mindset focused, let's look at how to bring everyone else with you on this journey.

Manage Your Team Effectively

To lead your team through these changes, take stock of all the work on your plate and ensure you are giving yourself time to prioritize each week. Dedicate one intentionally focused hour at least once a week (or even better, once a day) to setting your intentions for delivering value. Use that hour to think and plan before you do.

Aren't we always telling our stakeholders (and even our project managers) to plan first, then do? Then why are we often caught in a vicious circle of do, do, do, with no time to plan? I know, there's just no way you can squeeze in one more hour on your calendar this week, much less add an hour per day. But you will be grateful that you did.

I remember seeing Luke sitting at his neatly organized desk every morning writing in a notebook. Not a hair out of place, dressed just like our CEO, and looking ever so calm. It was annoying. I was usually rushing into the office not long before my first meeting and then going from one meeting to the next with very little time to do any work. I'd end up staying late to get caught up on work, and Luke would walk by my office calm as ever on his way out the door—at least an hour or two before me. So annoying. I needed to figure out what he was doing differently and why he always looked so calm. His team was at least as big as mine and he had a lot of responsibilities on his plate, but he never looked as frazzled as I felt.

What was his secret? He knew that busy gets in the way of productive. His goal was being productive.

Those people who are calm all day, even under pressure, they are planning before doing. You may not see it, but they probably have a process that allows them to think and prioritize before they act. It's probably in that early hour in the morning when they are at their desk before everyone else gets in. They probably didn't leave late, frazzled and exhausted, which caused a ripple effect of activities that needed to be done late, which caused a late bedtime and a rushed morning. Sorry if that hit close to home. Sometimes we must see it to fix it, and you can't expect your team to run like clockwork if you're frazzled. Team members tend to emulate the habits of their leaders, thinking their busyness is what success looks like. It's not.

Look at your calendar now and find the first place you have an hour of time for focus, and then block that time to plan before you do. Then block the next possible spot, even if it's a few days or a week later. Then keep doing that until you are far enough out on your calendar to start doing this daily, and make it a recurring appointment with yourself. Then protect that hour of planning power like your job (and sanity) depends on it—because it does.

Can't find a full hour? That's OK. Do the first half at the end of your workday, or before you go into the office, then do the rest during the workday. Just make time to think. If you make a habit of setting aside time to focus, it will likely be the most important hour of your day. The one that tells you whether you are accomplishing your goals, keeps your team moving forward, and even offers the chance to course-correct if things aren't going as planned.

Here's how you use that power hour. You can use the One Hour Manager Worksheet download to help organize and record it.

Take 15 Minutes to Reflect

Take some time to ask yourself questions about your day to help you best prepare for the next one:

- How did it go yesterday?

- What worked?

- What didn't work?

- What roadblocks kept me from progress?

- Did I accomplish my number one important goal for the day? If not, why not? How do I learn from that and do better today?

- How does that win from yesterday help me prioritize my day today?

Take 15 Minutes to Plan

This should be obvious, but how often do we really do it? Think about your most important goals, what must get accomplished in the day, and how you are going to have the greatest IMPACT possible. Ask yourself:

- What is the most important task I can do today to have the greatest IMPACT?
- Where will I spend my energy today doing what matters?
- How many meetings do I have on my calendar, and which ones could I delegate or decline?
- Who on my team could really use some help?
- What do I need from my leadership team?
- Where am I stuck and who can help me move beyond this obstacle?
- How am I going to make time to accomplish my most important priority for the day?

Take 15 Minutes to Manage

The first 30 minutes are all about planning. The next 30 minutes are about doing.

One of the best mechanisms I've learned for keeping your team on track and headed in the right direction is the daily stand-up meeting often associated with Agile frameworks like Scrum. Here's how to use this concept to help you stay connected with your team and keep everyone in flow. Spend just 15 minutes a day of intentionally focused time (you can start doing it weekly and work up to this) with the team you manage where you ask them three questions, and only allow them to answer those three questions. Don't let them go on and on with a laundry list of everything they have on their to-do list for the day. That's not the point (and will mean you end up taking more than 15 minutes).

1. **What's your win?** It's common to want to skip to where the problems are and neglect the important step of acknowledging progress and successes. Starting with a win helps your team see and feel progress happening, which can go a long way toward building positive momentum and keeping the struggles in the context of a bigger picture. And while there are likely many accomplishments, each team member should identify the biggest one to talk about here. For example: Did you accomplish your number one priority for the day and what did it take for you to accomplish your big win? This is a chance to thank someone else who helped, shine a light on goals that are moving forward, or bring general awareness to where your priorities are impacting others. The answer should be in three sentences or less. You can ask "So what?" and coach your team to use "So that..." language to frame the information they provide.

2. **What's your priority?** Again, this should be one thing. Your goal is to get your team to talk to each other and you about their most important priority for the day. Verbalizing that priority with others creates a sense of accountability for the person and creates an opportunity for alignment (or avoiding misalignment with others' priorities). The priority should be sized so it can be accomplished in one day, or team members will just report the same thing repeatedly and you won't know if any real progress is being made toward greater goals. Again, use "So what?" and "So that..." framing.

3. **Where are you stuck?** This is a great place for your team to share with each other what is standing in the way of their progress. Again, not a laundry list, just the big thing (or person) that is standing in the way of them accomplishing their priorities. Don't be tempted to solve all the "stucks" yourself. Sometimes other members of the team can help solve the problem, while you keep others moving. Encourage your team to step in and help their teammates solve a problem or point them in the direction of the answer they seek. Sometimes, just a short response to clarify something can remove someone's perceived stuck and

get them going. Do not problem-solve in this meeting! There isn't time. Answer a question, if that can keep things moving (like "I need a yes or no decision from you on x"), but then that's it. The goal is to bring awareness in this meeting, not solve the problems. That can be for follow-up (like in the last 15-minute block of your power hour).

Now, share your own win, priority, and stuck. Many people feel like they don't understand their boss or what their boss is thinking, working on, or doing. This is your chance to help your team understand where you are headed and what matters most for you as you look out for all of them. Keep it short, clear, and focused.

Although it may not seem like much, the commitment to meeting every day will alleviate concerns that your team members aren't getting enough airtime with you, and it keeps you all in flow together. Sometimes, this might be the only time during the day that you talk to your team members—make it high-IMPACT.

Take 15 Minutes to Make Progress

Before your day gets out of control, and because I know you probably work in an environment where it's not easy to just block off all day to work on your most important priority, make these 15 minutes sacred. These are 15 minutes to focus on your most important priority for the day. It may not seem like a lot of time, but sometimes it doesn't take much to keep the momentum going for your project.

- Do you have a meeting later in the day where you are hoping to get some decisions made? Send out a quick note thanking the participants for making time for your meeting, and tell them what to expect and what you want to accomplish in the meeting.

- Is someone waiting on you for an answer, so they can proceed? Make the decision and send the email now.

- Is there something you can delegate so that progress is being made while you are in other meetings? Find someone who can do it for you and make it worth their while to do so.

I know your "Yeah, but..." monster might be saying, "I do block my calendar, but people keep scheduling meetings over it." Yes, people will do that. And you need to stay focused on what you can control and decide to either move your focus time to another slot during the day or decline the meeting. The choice is yours. Don't give someone else the authority to decide for you. At the end of the day, you need to decide what kind of leader you want to be. You can be subject to the whims of others, or you can be like Luke and be calm, clear, and focused... and getting big results.

You now have several techniques for ensuring you and your people are focused so you can deliver that MVP and all subsequent solutions in a way that drives the highest IMPACT the fastest. It will take time to make these shifts to higher productivity and outcome-focused results. It will require breaking bad habits and building new ones. I'll show you how to do that next, in Chapter 12.

Trust yourself. Trust the process. It's time to make an IMPACT.

MAKE AN IMPACT

Think: How will you create a delivery-focused culture for yourself and your team?

Do: Download the One Hour Manager Worksheet to help you optimize your management and productivity.

12

Lead the Change

NOW YOU execute your plan.

As you start delivering the services you created on your IMPACT Delivery Road Map, you will face what all the project managers you support discover at some point early in their careers: as I mentioned in Chapter 9, there's no such thing as the perfect plan unless it was updated after the project is over to reflect what really happened. Why? Because a plan is a prediction of what you think will happen in the future, not a reflection of what's already taken place.

If this is the MVP cycle, you have about four weeks to build and deliver that first service and start collecting input from your early adopters. Because you laid your plans out on a road map, you know what service you're implementing, who it serves, how it helps them, and what the outcome and IMPACT is expected to be. Now it's just a matter of execution. Go get it done.

And if you've ever managed projects before—which I'm guessing you have, even if you haven't held the title of project manager—you know the easy part is executing the plan. The harder part is ensuring all the people do what they are supposed to do on that plan. Whether you're a team of one so you know you have limited time to dedicate to this, or you're relying on other people to do the work, you have to make sure everyone is clear about the goals and knows where to focus. The last chapter was about driving a delivery-focused culture so you can create the space for this work, and this chapter is all about the change management components that are needed to ensure the people do the things to get the results. Everything else is just simple execution of your plan.

Your goal is to be sure you're doing all that you can to set your teams up for productivity, like you did in Chapter 11, and then continue to guide the people in your organization through the changes you're implementing. Remember, you are guiding them through the transition period to get to that future state *together*.

In 2014, after a Project Management Institute Washington, DC, chapter meeting, my fellow board members and I were celebrating yet another successful event. My friend Kendall, who was the chapter president at the time, jumped up on a barstool to grab everyone's attention and share his idea of elevating the project management profession through community service. He explained what he had learned about doing days of service for nonprofit organizations where business leaders could share their professional expertise to help nonprofits achieve their goals. One skill that these nonprofits found in short supply was project management.

Nonprofits always seemed to be in short supply of time, money, and other resources, and when he explained their needs to this group of project professionals, we immediately understood that this was exactly where project managers lived—in the world of delivering results with "not enough."

Inspired by this vision, I walked up to Kendall and said, "I'm going to help you make this happen." Kendall is a big ideas guy, and I am the get-it-done gal. Together we could do really big things. And we did. Between the two of us initially, and then a large group of project management volunteers, we launched the planning for the very first Project Management Day of Service on May 5, 2014. Little did we know PMDoS would become a worldwide opportunity for project leaders to use their hard-earned project management skills to make a bigger IMPACT in their communities.

The idea was simple in concept but a complex feat to pull off—bring together nonprofit organizations and project managers to scope and launch mission-critical projects for these nonprofits on a single day. With enthusiasm and determination, Kendall and I added Mike Hannan to our board, and we all started recruiting volunteers and ultimately built a team of 40 project manager volunteers forming an all-volunteer PMO. If you think you have a tough time getting your team to deliver, imagine a team of 40 volunteers all with other responsibilities and limited time—and because they were all project managers, they wanted all the answers before we started to execute. Although everyone was excited about the idea, it wasn't long before the weight of this ambitious endeavor started to create a theme of "not enough" in the volunteer PMO.

We gathered the volunteers together to start figuring out how we were going to do something that seemed impossible. I heard a chorus of "not enough" echoing around me. There wasn't enough time, with the target of Reverend Dr. Martin Luther King Jr. Day, which had been known as a national day of service, only seven months away. There was zero budget to cover the inevitable costs. And we were embarking on something that had never been done before in this way.

The team begged me to reconsider the plan and shoot for the following year because they felt there was no way we could pull this off with only seven months to plan and deliver the event, with no money and no clear path to success. The more people we talked to as we tried to gain critical support and resources to make the day happen, the more we were told that what we were attempting was impossible.

That gave me all the motivation I needed to make sure it happened. Remember my rule about not saying "can't"?

As the leader of this PMO, I had to figure out how I was going to lead a group of volunteers to create something magical with little time to show progress. I took every opportunity to speak on stage, connect with my colleagues, and get the word out that we were going to do this really cool thing that was designed to elevate the role of project management globally while helping nonprofit organizations change the world for the better one project at a time. I didn't realize it, but I was becoming the marketing engine for this new event and the PMO behind it.

And we accomplished what many felt was impossible. What made it work was that we were crystal clear why we were doing what we were doing and how we were going to use the power of project management to change the world for the better. I knew in my heart that we could do it, even when I didn't know how we'd get there.

Fast-forward to today. The event has been running every year, even during the COVID-19 pandemic, when we switched to a virtual format, with a team of volunteers that makes the seemingly impossible happen every year because they have a clear strategy and the engine to generate that IMPACT. While the goal has remained the same, the way we get there has changed for me as a leader each year. I realized that I had developed an adaptive management style to support the evolution of this PMO that would drive the changes needed to make the impossible happen. As the years went by, my approach to managing the people and the work changed.

Adaptive Management Style

Each of the stakeholders going through this transition period with you, including your team members, will adopt the changes differently. You want to make sure your team is included in the process of building and delivering these services with you, but not everyone will be 100 percent convinced that you're headed in the right direction or be certain how to get there. You must lead them. That means as the leader of this transition, you need to meet them where they are in terms of comfort with the change you are driving.

You can use an adaptive management framework to adapt your management style to bring your team through the change process, based on how familiar they are with the change you're taking them through and how clearly they know what success looks like on the other side. Here's what that looked like in my years running the fully volunteer Project Management for Change PMO.

ADAPTIVE MANAGEMENT FRAMEWORK

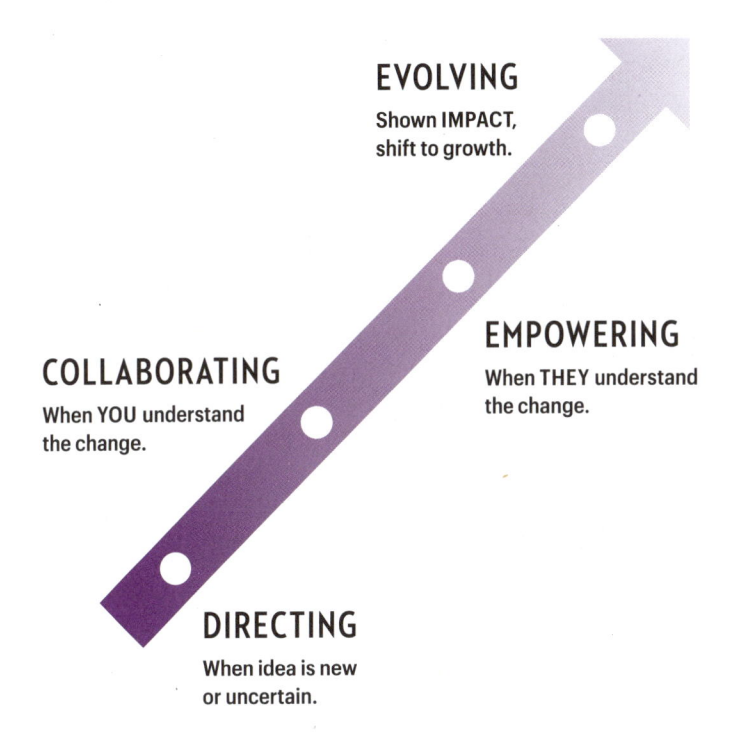

EVOLVING
Shown IMPACT, shift to growth.

EMPOWERING
When THEY understand the change.

COLLABORATING
When YOU understand the change.

DIRECTING
When idea is new or uncertain.

Directing

When introducing change, it's important to consider how you shift your management style based not only on the different ways people want to be managed, but also on how familiar they are with the change you are guiding them through. When the idea is new or uncertain and you must lead the way from the front, you need to do the directing.

In the first year, while facing the endless reasons it shouldn't happen, I had to rely heavily on trusting myself to lead this team, even when we didn't know how we were going to get there. We were building the organization from nothing, planning a groundbreaking event, and entering new territory for all of us. I was faced with endless roadblocks and had to inspire this team of volunteers while also giving them clear directions on what success looked like. I had to adopt a directing management style to lead the group through uncertain territory. Yes, we were making it up as we went along, but that was OK, if I led the way. We were iterating our way to IMPACT, and I had to trust that I could figure it out so they would come with me.

When no one is familiar with the change, even if you don't have all the answers, your team needs to have confidence in your leadership and trust that you'll find a way to achieve the desired outcomes. In a situation where the change is new to everyone, it's crucial to communicate clearly and provide specific direction to the team, especially if the vision isn't yet clear to everyone. This is particularly important when facing questions or doubts from team members who may be risk-averse or uncertain about the new change. While the goal was to empower the team to make decisions, in the beginning, we wouldn't have moved if we had waited for everyone to feel confident that what we were doing was going to work.

You may encounter resistance or hesitation from well-intentioned individuals who are supportive of the concept but feel uncomfortable with the uncertainty. It's important to recognize that not everyone will be comfortable with ambiguity. Even if some people become naysayers, you must stay focused and continue moving forward, especially when you have the necessary support from leadership.

Managing through uncertainty means accepting that you won't always have all the answers. It requires gathering information, conducting due diligence, and making decisions based on the best available information, even if some risks are involved. Doing nothing is not a viable option. It's crucial to trust your instincts and rely on your gut feeling. While there will always be what-ifs and alternative paths, indecisiveness will hinder progress. Provide direction, encourage trust in your decision-making, and keep the team moving forward.

Collaborating

The collaborating management style shows up when you as a leader understand the change and have people who have seen what success looks like.

The following year, after we had the tremendous success of year one and a long list of lessons learned to support our decisions, we were able to bring back the group of volunteers to work with Kendall and me to design the next plan and divide responsibilities differently. This time, we had a core team who had been through it before and could share their own insights and ideas about how to make it happen. While we still guided the discussion and provided most of the decision-making, the team was now more involved in figuring out how we'd get there. With a clearer sense of what success looked like, we were able to shift to a collaborating style and build the plan for the next year together.

A collaborating management style allows for greater involvement from the team, as they begin to understand the change and its implications. In this stage, you can engage the team in the strategic planning process, leveraging their insights and involving them in decision-making. Collaboration becomes more feasible as the team gains knowledge and experience with the change.

Don't forget to incorporate lessons learned into the process. After each 90-day cycle, take the time to review what worked and what didn't, and apply that feedback to the next phase. This ensures continuous improvement and maximizes the benefits of the team's input.

Empowering

When the team understands the change and can take the front seat on organizing how they want to do work, you can empower them to do it. Today many people refer to this approach as "self-organizing teams."

By year three, we had a track record of success and an even longer list of lessons learned. More team members had been through the experience. This time the team more clearly understood the change, what success looked like, and how to get there. In this third year, Kendall and I took a back seat as we handed the whiteboard marker over to the team to lead the event planning. While we were still there to guide the higher-level decision-making and ensure the project stayed on track, we could shift from a collaborating management style to an empowering management style and remain in the back seat for much of the hands-on work. The team now had an even stronger sense of ownership of the process and how to get to the desired outcomes.

An empowering approach involves delegating more decision-making authority to the team and allowing individuals to lead different aspects of the change process. At this stage, you can focus on strategic planning and leadership, while the team takes ownership of executing tasks and making higher-level decisions.

Delegation becomes essential, as it allows you to step back and empower others to contribute their expertise. By doing so, you nurture future leaders within the organization and create a collaborative environment where team members can grow and develop their skills.

Evolving

When you've shown real IMPACT and can shift to growth mode, you've reached the evolving style.

By year four, everyone knew what to do and how to get there, and had a strong desire to keep evolving the organization and the ways it would achieve the goals. We had strong leaders in place to run the event, and Kendall and I moved from hands-on to truly allowing the organization and each year's event to evolve as it needed to without direct guidance and support. We provided executive oversight, but the organization became self-directing without our regular involvement.

Today, this organization is run by a powerful team and Kendall, Mike, and I are not involved in the decisions that make the event happen. We're informed and are there for the team to provide funding and support as members of the board, but we do not get in the way of the decisions surrounding the event. PMDoS events take place in cities around the world, and the team continues to evolve what they do and how they do it to achieve the mission of changing the world one project at a time.

This organization thrives because the leaders learned how to have an adaptive management style that made room for everyone

Change resistance will derail your best-laid plans.

to be involved in the change process and provide just enough management support and guidance based on how familiar the team was with the changes we were creating. The newer your team is to the change that you are trying to create, the more you will need to be involved hands-on. As they gain experience being a part of and delivering changes and understanding what success looks like, you can move up the scale from directing to collaborating, empowering, and ultimately evolving.

Work with the Culture

Now you will learn how to use all the plans you created in Stage Four to put sustainable business solutions in place while bringing everyone with you through this change process. As you implement the MVP and subsequent cycles of value delivery, it's important to have support along the way. Real-world challenges will arise, and it's essential to bring everyone along on the journey, helping people connect to the business outcomes you are driving together.

If you are facing change resistance, it's on you. As you learned in Chapter 4, people are not resistant to change, they are resistant to having change done *to* them. So, what happens if you are already in a position where stakeholders are resistant to the changes you've been delivering or if you have some trouble spots in the organization that you need to improve? Don't fall into the trap of blaming the culture. Instead, you need to work *with* the culture to deliver change.

While it can be tempting to just work around any change resistance you're facing, this can be detrimental to your progress. Change resistance will derail your best-laid plans. You've done a lot of work to get to this point, and now that you're ready to start delivering your services, you must be sure people are not fighting you every step of the way. You will get to the outcomes faster if you have that stakeholder buy-in. You need people to help you define the changes, to help you plan out the changes, to deliver those changes, and to utilize the changes you're delivering.

When it comes to making changes in an organization and driving successful strategy delivery, there are three stages you will go through yourself and take others through: breaking habits, creating change, and making new habits. These stages play a huge role in getting everyone on board and leading to better business outcomes. A secret to preventing change from feeling too overwhelming is to focus on small, incremental shifts in behavior that steadily build new habits over time, rather than expecting major transformations right away.

CHANGE MANAGEMENT THROUGH HABITS

BREAK HABITS   **CREATE CHANGE**   **MAKE HABITS**

1. **Break habits:** First up is breaking the habits that are no longer serving the organization. Picture this: you're introducing some changes in your company, but people are stuck in their old ways. You first need to understand why they are clinging to the old ways of doing things. Then discover how these old habits are holding them back and keeping them from embracing a better way to do things. Talk openly about the damage the current habits are causing, involve everyone in the conversation, and make sure everyone understands why change is necessary. By acknowledging and addressing these habits head-on, you create an environment that embraces innovation and growth.

2. **Create change:** Next, you must instill a new way of doing things. Foster an environment where people feel encouraged to try new things and work together. Give your team the freedom to

challenge the way things have always been done and explore fresh solutions. Provide the necessary resources and support, and make sure everyone understands how the changes align with the company's strategic goals.

3   **Make habits:** Last, you must help your stakeholders learn how to turn the new ways of behaving into habits that benefit them. This is all about making those new behaviors and processes part of your organization's DNA. You want the changes to become the norm, right? So reinforce the new habits consistently. Lead by example, provide regular feedback, and celebrate the small wins along the way. When everyone sees the positive IMPACT these changes bring, the changes will become an integral part of daily operations.

Here are some additional change management strategies to help you keep resistance at bay.

1   **Engage stakeholders:** Actively involving stakeholders throughout the change process is crucial in addressing resistance. When you include stakeholders in decision-making, problem-solving, and implementation efforts, they feel valued and become part of the solution. This involvement increases their sense of ownership and commitment to the changes.

2   **Communicate the purpose and benefits:** Rather than getting caught up in the details of how the change will occur, focus on communicating the "what" and the benefits it will bring. Help stakeholders understand the purpose of the change and how it will positively IMPACT their work and the organization. Clearly articulate the advantages and outcomes to gain their support.

3   **Provide opportunities for dialogue and feedback:** Create a safe and open environment for stakeholders to express their concerns, ask questions, and give their feedback. Addressing their doubts and providing clarifications helps alleviate resistance. Actively listen to stakeholders' perspectives, acknowledge their concerns, and provide thoughtful responses to build trust and understanding.

4. **Address skepticism with evidence and testimonials:** To overcome skepticism, provide evidence and testimonials from your early adopters that demonstrate the effectiveness of the change. Share success stories from other organizations that have undergone similar changes, highlighting the positive outcomes they achieved. Additionally, use data and metrics to support the anticipated benefits and showcase the potential IMPACT of the change.

5. **Build credibility and trust:** Consistently deliver on promises and show tangible results to build credibility and trust among stakeholders. Be transparent about the progress of the change, providing regular updates and sharing milestones achieved. When you demonstrate reliability and accountability, stakeholders are more likely to accept and support the change.

6. **Provide resources and support:** Ensure that stakeholders have the necessary resources, training, and support to adapt to the change. Offer workshops, training sessions, and mentoring programs to enhance their skills and knowledge. When you create a positive and supportive environment where individuals feel empowered and capable of navigating change, it increases their confidence and reduces resistance.

7. **Address individual concerns:** Recognize that each stakeholder may have unique concerns and challenges related to the change. Take the time to understand their individual perspectives and provide personalized support. Address their specific concerns and offer solutions or alternatives that address their needs, fostering a sense of trust and cooperation.

8. **Monitor and adjust:** Continuously monitor the progress of the change initiative and assess the level of resistance. Identify any emerging issues or barriers and make necessary adjustments to the change strategy. Solicit ongoing feedback from stakeholders and be responsive to their needs throughout the process.

The Marketing Playbook

Have you ever felt pressured by a salesperson and wondered how you could get them to just stop trying to sell you? That's how your stakeholders feel when you *sell* your services to them. There's a lot of advice out there telling you that you must sell the value of your delivery function and the change you're delivering, and that you need to work harder to convince your stakeholders they need you. Stop it. It doesn't work, and it's particularly bad advice in the PMO space, where many PMOs already have a bad rap.

Ever wonder why there's so much advice out there to "sell the PMO" to your senior leaders? It goes back to the statistics in Chapter 1. There's so much selling required because leaders aren't buying it. That push is due to the templates/tools/process first focus that fills so much of the typical industry guidance. But executives don't want the typical results, and neither should you.

No one wants to be convinced or sold to. They just want to do their work and not have it be so difficult to do. What they want is their problems solved. You need to show them how what you are providing for them will solve their problems.

What you need to do is marketing, not sales. Marketing is about tying the solution you provide to the problem they have. It's that simple. So, how do you market your services to the organization? Here's a very simple model from the marketing industry that I learned from marketing influencer John Jantsch, which builds upon something you may have heard before—know, like, and trust. This model takes you the rest of the way—from awareness through to action and IMPACT. I am introducing it here so you can see how everything you've learned so far has been weaving these marketing techniques throughout. You're going to go through these stages with your stakeholders.

Know

Make yourself known. Share information from your business plan so that everyone knows about your team, what your goals are, and

THE GAME OF MARKETING

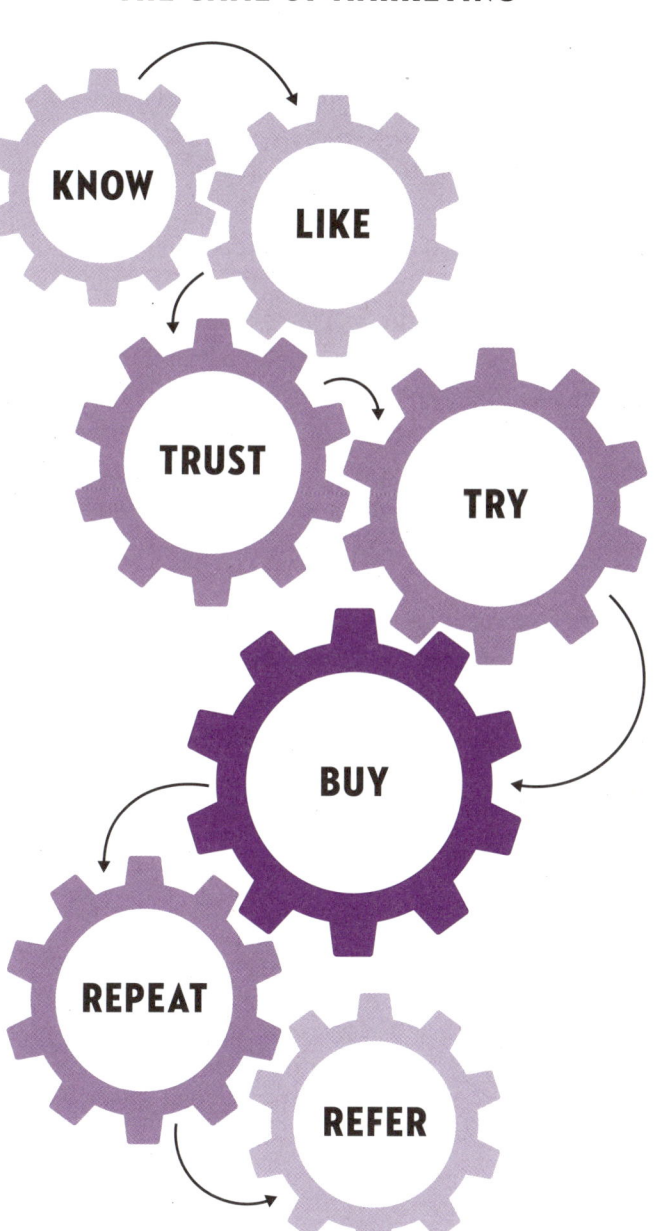

- KNOW
- LIKE
- TRUST
- TRY
- BUY
- REPEAT
- REFER

how you intend to help the organization thrive. Be visible, attend meetings, and actively participate in discussions. Show your enthusiasm and passion for delivering successful strategies. My passion is one of the key things my stakeholders love about my style and it's contagious.

Like

You have to be likable. If your stakeholders don't like you, they will find reasons not to work with you. Foster positive relationships by being approachable, friendly, and open-minded. Yes, this means you have to ask someone about their day, do the small talk, get to know them personally. You're in the people business, like it or not. And you need your stakeholders to like you if you want them to come with you. Listen actively to their needs and concerns. Make them feel heard. If you are interested in them, they will be interested in you.

Trust

Trust holds relationships together. Be transparent, share accurate and reliable information, and deliver on your promises. Establish clear governance processes to ensure accountability. By consistently demonstrating trustworthiness, you'll foster a sense of confidence in your team's ability to deliver. Share success stories and case studies to showcase the value your team brings so you can use social proof to validate how you're helping people.

Try

As you go through your iterative cycles of value delivery, you'll look to those who already know, like, and trust you to pilot your services and share their feedback. Showcase your capabilities through pilot projects or proof-of-concept initiatives. Let early success stories do the talking. By providing opportunities for early adopters to test the waters, you'll build curiosity, social proof, and generate interest in leveraging your services.

Buy
Once your stakeholders have experienced the benefits of working with you, it's time for them to buy into your services. Clearly articulate the value proposition using your IMPACT Communication Framework, showing how everything that you do is tied to helping them address their challenges and take advantage of opportunities. Provide tailored solutions and demonstrate flexibility in meeting their specific needs. When you showcase the value and outcomes, stakeholders will be more inclined to invest their resources and support you.

Repeat
You've successfully engaged your stakeholders, but the journey doesn't end there. To sustain their support, focus on delivering consistent results. Continuously communicate the IMPACT of your team's efforts, and celebrate milestones and successes. Seek feedback and actively incorporate it into your processes and service offerings. When you do this, you'll notice that your stakeholders will start to approach you with new challenges or places they think you can help. Be on the lookout for these new challenges and seek opportunities to learn, understand, and offer support.

Refer
The final stage is all about harnessing the power of word-of-mouth marketing. When stakeholders become advocates for your team, they become valuable referral sources. Encourage them to share their positive experiences with others in the organization. By creating a network of enthusiastic supporters, you'll expand the reach and influence of your team within the organization. There's nothing like FOMO (fear of missing out) to drive more engagement! Let the successes of those early adopters become your messaging. Be intentional about documenting case studies and measuring before and after (using your IMPACT metrics) so the numbers can strengthen your case.

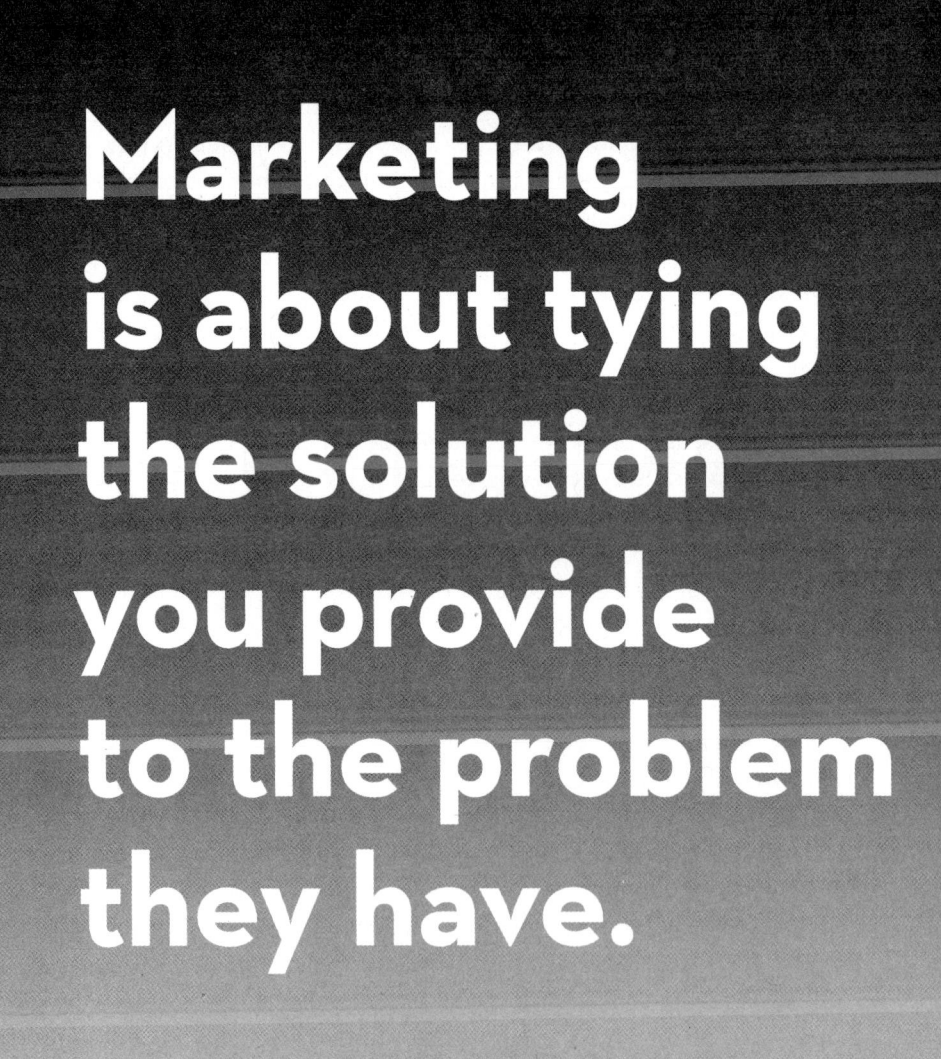

Marketing is about tying the solution you provide to the problem they have.

Remember, you don't need to convince anyone of anything. You don't need to sell, plead with, or chase anyone to get them to work with your team. When you follow the IMPACT Communication Framework you learned in Chapter 8 and apply these marketing strategies, you'll be amazed at how easy it is to get your stakeholders excited about engaging with you. Create a pull, not a push. By nurturing relationships, building trust, delivering value, and encouraging advocacy, you'll create a vibrant and successful team that drives better business outcomes and fosters a culture of collaboration and success.

As you deliver these solutions to the organization, make sure you collect early metrics and case studies to showcase how your solutions are making things easier for your stakeholders. Their early stories will help you gain momentum with other teams; when they see what's possible they will agree to come along on the journey with you. Also continue the conversation about the importance of your work within the broader organization. Use the IMPACT Communications Plan developed in Stage Four to elevate discussions happening within the organization. When you share successes and take ownership of the brand and conversation surrounding your IMPACT Engine, you enhance your role and the perception of your work.

The Power of Story

As you're rolling out your MVP and subsequent cycles of value delivery, you'll want to look for examples that show how much value you're driving for the organization. You may know that it's important to celebrate the wins you and your team are having, but you may not know how to do that in a way that doesn't make you feel uncomfortable or like you're bragging.

The answer? Stories.

Think about how the stories you've read in this book have given you new ways to think about the problems you need to solve, connected you to the work you need to do, and maybe even made you feel a little less alone. There are others going through this process too. They have found success and so can you.

What I've been doing to help you see the powerful transformation possible through story is the same experience you want to create for your stakeholders as they participate in the transformation you are leading them through. They need to feel connected to the change you are guiding them through and know that there really will be a pot of gold at the end of the rainbow. You can give that to them through storytelling, and when you do, they will be much more likely to adopt the necessary changes to help your organization grow and evolve. When you nail storytelling, it'll help strengthen your team's brand and get services adopted much faster to meet the business challenges ahead.

If the thought of having to become an inspiring storyteller feels overwhelming, don't worry, you already have a storytelling framework. You learned it in Chapter 8 when you applied the IMPACT Communication Framework to talk about how the services you were defining would create value for the organization. You can use that same framework to tell the story of success your early adopters are experiencing when they engage with your team.

First, gather a variety of stories from your early wins. Interview those stakeholders who've had positive experiences with your team to get a clear picture of the experience from their perspective. It's much more effective to have them tell you the story of the journey you guided them through instead of you creating the story for them, because they can talk about their challenges from their perspective. The juicy details are in their version of the story.

Second, collect any quantifiable results and testimonials that show the real IMPACT. The goal is to show specific examples of how your team has helped crush pain points and enabled stakeholders to achieve their goals.

When crafting these stories, focus on bringing the key details to life in a personal, vivid way. Provide the exact context of the stakeholder's situation before your team got involved (challenge or opportunity), the actions your team took to support them (solution) and give them a better future state (outcome), and the concrete results achieved (IMPACT and metric). Use descriptive language to build that story arc. Quotes from stakeholders make it feel authentic and relatable.

Then organize the story elements into the five-step IMPACT Communication Framework.

1 **Challenge or Opportunity:** Write down how your early adopters talk about the pain they experienced before your team helped them.

2 **Solution:** Briefly explain the solution you put in place with them and how you guided them through the change in a way that was simple and supportive.

3 **Outcome:** Describe the result they realized that directly addressed the pain they were experiencing, again using their words, not yours.

4 **IMPACT:** Explain the effect this result had beyond their immediate pain as they started to experience a better future state.

5 **Metric:** Include a measurable data point that affirms the better outcome and IMPACT they attained.

Here's a simple example.

I worked directly with Jamal in marketing, who was having a tough time with long delays on his team's project launches. Their campaigns were consistently missing go-live deadlines, which affected sales numbers. Jamal was understandably frustrated that completing marketing projects took so long.

When I connected with Jamal, he explained that his team's projects felt disorganized, he never knew what work was happening, and people were often pulled into other urgent work.

Our strategy delivery office implemented a standardized project management framework and trained Jamal's team on using it. We helped them establish clear project charters, a well-defined scope, and a roles and responsibilities matrix so that everyone understood who was responsible for each component of the project. We also provided coaching to help them create clear and simple project plans and showed them how to keep projects on track. We offered guidance on how to unblock delays quickly.

Within two months of partnering with us, Jamal's team launched their next campaign three weeks early. As Jamal shared, "With the strategy delivery office's help we can now plan marketing launches predictably. Our leads per month have increased 25 percent because we are finally hitting our deadlines."

With a story like that as an example, you can help your stakeholders see the tangible results you are creating with a peer of theirs already reaping the benefits of working with your team. For more examples of how to do this, look back at the stories that I've included throughout this book.

Invite the Green Monster

Storytelling can also create healthy competition that will show up as you tell more stories, especially to different groups in the organization. There's nothing like a story of someone else's success to draw out the competitive nature of those who want to stand out in their organization. Your stories can create a snowball engagement effect, where they'll be clamoring to be the next on the list to benefit from your team's expertise and support.

I've often used this technique when trying to get new stakeholder groups to adopt our services, and it helped me figure out quickly who my competitive stakeholders were. It all goes back to knowing their WIIFM, which requires you to get to know your stakeholders on a personal level. You must know what they really care about even if what they care about is beating their peers in competition for the next promotion. Make notes in your Stakeholder Engagement Plan as they leave clues in your conversations.

Get the Word Out

Share these stories far and wide through newsletters, town halls, your company intranet, presentations—whatever formats work and at every opportunity you get. It's even better if you can get your early adopters to tell the story from their perspective, instead of you telling it for them. Invite them to your meeting or ask them to share their experience at a leadership meeting where you are asking for more support.

While you may spend several weeks in this stage, building and delivering on your MVP and then even more solutions in future cycles, there's a very important final stage to learn now so you can start thinking about where you're headed. It's the place that helps you stay in tune with your organization and its evolving needs so that your team is front and center in your executives' minds when they are faced with uncertainty, challenges, and shifting business priorities. It's also where you finally see exactly how you're going to get a seat at the leadership table to truly help your organization navigate the journey of strategy delivery.

Keep doing the work you must do in this stage to get that MVP out the door, but continue reading this book, so you know exactly what's coming and how to best position yourself for success.

Trust yourself. Trust the process. It's time to make an IMPACT.

MAKE AN IMPACT

Think: How will you use the change and communication techniques here to lead people through this change?

Do: Revisit your Stakeholder Engagement Plan and IMPACT Communications Plan to consider how to use your communication and change management techniques to bring stakeholders with you through the process. Download the Change Resistance Worksheet so it's handy should you face any resistance along the way.

STAGE

EVOLVE YOUR IMPACT ENGINE

MINDSET

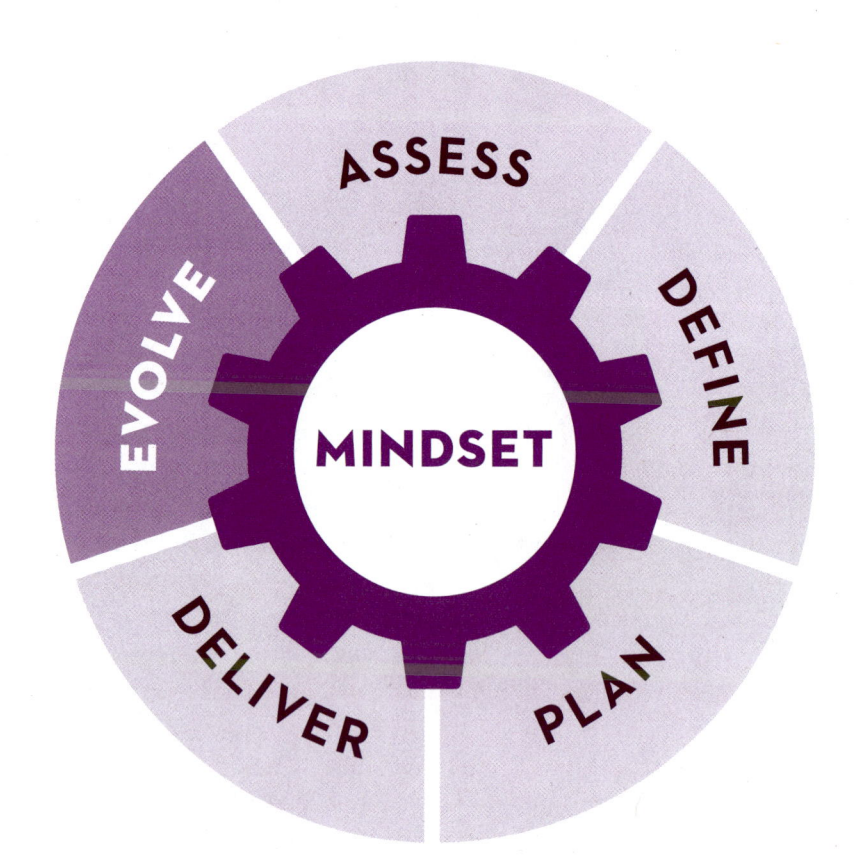

- ASSESS
- DEFINE
- PLAN
- DELIVER
- EVOLVE

Congratulations on reaching Stage Six of the IMPACT Engine System!

You've delivered the MVP version of your IMPACT Engine. Now your goal is to develop a nimble and adaptive value delivery model so shifting business needs don't derail you as you position the organization for ongoing success. That means you're going to look at where you've been and the plans you already have in place, what you've learned from that journey, and what you should focus on next—including what environmental factors may have changed that require you to pivot. That's what the Evolve stage is all about: the work you are doing is an evolution, not a revolution. It's not about one-time big-bang approaches, it's about consistent and persistent progress and growth. This gets and keeps everyone in flow and allows you to always have an answer to "What has your team done for us lately?"

You'll also look at how you are evolving as a leader. As I've been guiding you through this process, I've been weaving in the techniques necessary for you to elevate your role. When we get to the final chapter, we'll explore the transformation that is already taking place and show you exactly how to get your seat at the leadership table.

Let's do this!

13

Drive Continual Value Delivery

ANDREA C. was the leader of the project management office for a large community hospital system. She had applied the IMPACT Engine System to build a strong PMO that her business leaders saw as a critical strategic asset. Now her PMO was facing one of its greatest challenges yet: the global COVID-19 pandemic. As her company grappled with the crisis, Andrea and her team realized that they needed to pivot swiftly.

In the early days of the pandemic, Andrea received the call: they were considered an essential part of the local emergency response team. The PMO quickly activated their emergency incident command and joined forces with the organization's executive leadership team. Daily meetings became the norm as they tackled the emerging challenges head-on. While Andrea's team was in the middle of delivering services in one of their IES cycles, Andrea and her team recognized the importance of adapting to thrive in this new reality. They had to put all of that business-as-usual delivery work on hold to respond to the shifting needs of the organization.

One of their major initiatives was setting up the first drive-through testing site for COVID-19 in the Boston area. With the mayor's announcement and a three-day deadline, they had to move fast, and they couldn't get caught up in burying people in too much process when lives were at stake. Instead, they relied on the foundation they had built to ask good questions to understand the scope, who they would need, and what success looked like to make the impossible happen.

As they went live with the drive-through testing site three days later, Andrea and her team experienced the essence of agility and resilience. They were problem-solvers on the front lines, picking up cases of water, troubleshooting label printers, and ensuring a smooth testing process. Their delivery process became a testament to adaptability, collaboration, and unwavering dedication.

Throughout the crisis, Andrea realized the power of being proactive and anticipating needs before they arose. The trust and credibility the PMO had built in the organization before the crisis struck played a crucial role in making them the "go to" team for this emergency initiative. They didn't have to sell their value; they were already seen as a trusted adviser, ready to contribute to the organization's response.

Andrea's story shows the importance of being agile and responsive when circumstances change. The ability to pivot quickly, leverage existing strengths, and adapt to new challenges becomes a hallmark of success. Andrea and her team were able to navigate the uncertainties of COVID-19 and make a meaningful difference in the community they served. If her team had resisted changing their focus or tried to keep implementing the services that they had been building while the leaders handled the chaos going on around them, the leaders would have found another way—but without Andrea and her PMO. Her team's ability to be adaptive is the reason they continued to thrive. Sometimes you will need to pivot, and building an organization that can adapt to a changing landscape will be key to your success and earning a seat at the table. Andrea had her seat and knew she had to keep it.

Over the years, Andrea has moved on to other organizations, taking the IMPACT Engine System with her every time. She's even become a coach in our Mastermind program so she can help others fast-track their success. Andrea is implementing what she knows to build strong delivery teams that quickly earn her and her team a seat at the table in helping those organizations achieve their strategic goals. And every time, she starts with Stage One to solidify her mindset and get crystal clear on what it's going to take to make an IMPACT. She trusts herself. She trusts the process. And then she drives IMPACT.

The lessons learned from Andrea's PMO are invaluable. They are a reminder that change is inevitable and organizations must be prepared to pivot when needs evolve. When organizations foster a culture of adaptability and equip teams with the tools and mindset to embrace change, they can thrive in the face of adversity. Andrea's journey exemplifies the transformative power of pivoting, proving that through resilience, collaboration, and a forward-thinking approach, your delivery team can not only survive but also thrive even in times of crisis.

In this chapter, your goal is to evaluate the progress you've made with your service delivery and figure out where and how you need to pivot to continue to support your stakeholders' evolving challenges. Your next service could be anything from handling a crisis, to helping the organization scale, to simply making their lives easier.

Evaluate IMPACT

Whether this is your first IES cycle or you've been following the program through multiple cycles, you've already delivered your first service and should have input available on how that's going. Invest the time to do this evaluation process before you start implementing your next services so you can include feedback and results from what you've already done into the planning process for the next cycle. Plus, this is where the success stories live! You need those stories, as you learned in the previous chapter.

What if a service you rolled out isn't being used? Figure out why and fix the issue before you start adding new customers to that service. If the priorities of the organization have changed, you must account for that change. One of the simplest, yet often overlooked, opportunities to improve is intentionally learning from the lessons you've experienced and applying that learning to your plan. Take this approach with the delivery team you're building and the services you provide to the organization. Based on what you now know that you didn't before, figure out what you might need to do differently to increase engagement and utilization of your existing services. By the way, this is also an excellent service you can provide to support project teams. Instilling good practices of collecting lessons learned and then weaving those lessons learned into all future plans can immediately set projects up for success as they are getting started.

What gets measured gets done. Measuring the IMPACT value of the IMPACT Engine gives you insights into what's working and what can be improved. It's like having a compass that guides you toward your goals.

Measure What Matters

Measuring and communicating the value of the IMPACT Engine is like shining a spotlight on the incredible results you're achieving and making sure everyone knows about them. Take the time to look at what's working and what's not so you can keep everyone informed and make the right plans. Your measurements need to capture both the numbers and the stories behind your success.

You already have what you need to do this measurement process because you documented both project- and service-level metrics in Stage Three: Define. In Stage Four: Plan, you created your 30/90 reporting plan, so you know what to measure when and what will be required to pivot. As you deliver the services in this and upcoming cycles, just start measuring on a monthly basis how each of those projects and services are doing according to the metrics you already defined. The secret is making sure you only measure what matters.

Don't waste time on the usual numbers. It can be tempting to track easy metrics such as number of projects, number of project managers, or total budget of the organization, but these metrics bring problems.

1 It's very likely your organization is doing too many projects. If you tie your value to the number of projects you're managing, it will be hard to see that you shouldn't be doing some of them. It might be that you should instead help your business leaders figure out which projects to start later or to cut completely so that your organization's precious resources can be spent on the more valuable projects that can produce a great ROI.

2 When you brag about how much budget you're managing, you're focused on how much you and those projects are costing the organization. It's much more powerful to talk about the ROI or IMPACT your team is driving instead of simply its costs.

3 No one cares. They aren't interested in those numbers. They're interested in what you've done for them lately. Focus your metrics on that. Where and how have you driven value? By creating a value measurement plan that goes beyond project performance or the quantity of projects you're managing, you ensure comprehensive evaluation aligned with what your business leaders really care about.

Go back to your initial metrics that you created in Stage Three. What are they telling you about how the services are being utilized? Have you correctly answered the question "Are we successful?"

For example, if your service was designed to improve transparency so that people were making faster decisions, figure out if people are making faster decisions. If similar teams are popping up in the organization all doing the same project activities but in different ways, and you created a community of practice to better synchronize the way work is being done, is that synchronization happening?

You may find that the metrics you defined in Stage Three aren't yet bearing fruit because it's just too early. In that case, just use some leading indicators of success. For example, if your business leaders were complaining they weren't being given the information necessary to make decisions, and you put a one-page document in place that people now use to capture the answers the executives need to make those decisions, did it help improve the decision-making process?

Sometimes you can just simply ask, "When we talked to you, you told us [insert their words you wrote down from Stage Two] and now you have [service] that solves that challenge. Is it now easier for you to do [the thing they couldn't do before]?" And then when they answer yes, you collect those yeses and use them as anecdotal evidence until you have enough time to measure that the better process is having a positive ripple effect in the organization. If they answer no, then simply say, "Tell me more about that." You might find yourself back in Stage Three doing Root Cause Analysis because you missed something, or it might be that the first pain point is fixed (so you need to make that clear), and because it's fixed, you have uncovered a new pain point that needs addressing next. This is normal and it all counts as progress. Take the win and keep moving.

Remember, this is a journey of continuous improvement. As you measure and communicate your IMPACT, you'll gain valuable insights that will help you fine-tune your road map. If something isn't quite hitting the mark, it's OK! You will adjust so you can keep iterating your way to success. The key is to stay nimble, responsive, and always focused on delivering the most meaningful outcomes for your organization.

Communicate Your Value

Once you've gathered this data about how each of the services is working, it's time to share your success story. Imagine you're sitting down with your biggest cheerleaders—your stakeholders—and you're telling them about the incredible journey you're on. Paint a vivid picture using visualizations, like charts or infographics, to bring the numbers to life. But don't forget to sprinkle in those heartfelt stories and anecdotes that capture the essence of your achievements.

Put your marketing hat on and share stories about what is working well, especially if you don't have enough data yet to show significant 30/90 cycle progress (Chapter 9). You already have what you need from the IMPACT Communication Framework (Chapter 8) to tell you exactly what to say and how to say it.

Take time to celebrate the people in this process. Both the people doing the work and the stakeholders benefiting from the services should be the heroes of this journey. Even when I have bad news to share, it sets a much better tone to first point out what is working, who has been involved in that success, and what they specifically did to contribute to the wins. Show the progress that's been made and then switch gears to talk about opportunities for improvement.

Get ready to shine a light on the incredible value you're creating with the IMPACT Engine. By measuring, celebrating, and continuously improving, you'll not only show the world what you're capable of, you'll also inspire others to join you on this amazing journey. Let's go out there and make a real difference together!

Evolve the Road Map

The next important step is to modify your IMPACT Delivery Road Map based on the insights you've gained. If a new service or capability has become a top priority, update your road map accordingly. Alternatively, if you need to refine and enhance the service or capability you've already introduced, make the necessary adjustments.

Become a Future Predictor

"How do you always seem to know what we need next?" Deanna said.

"It's easy! I'm paying attention," I replied.

I meet with Deanna, the Chief Strategy Officer for a client of ours, every month. When we meet, I walk through the progress we've made with her team, address any challenges that have come up, and listen for clues as to what matters.

Then, when our team is working with their strategy delivery office, I share what I believe the next items need to be on the road map to address the upcoming challenges and opportunities, most of which they don't even realize are coming. Without fail, the minute Deanna

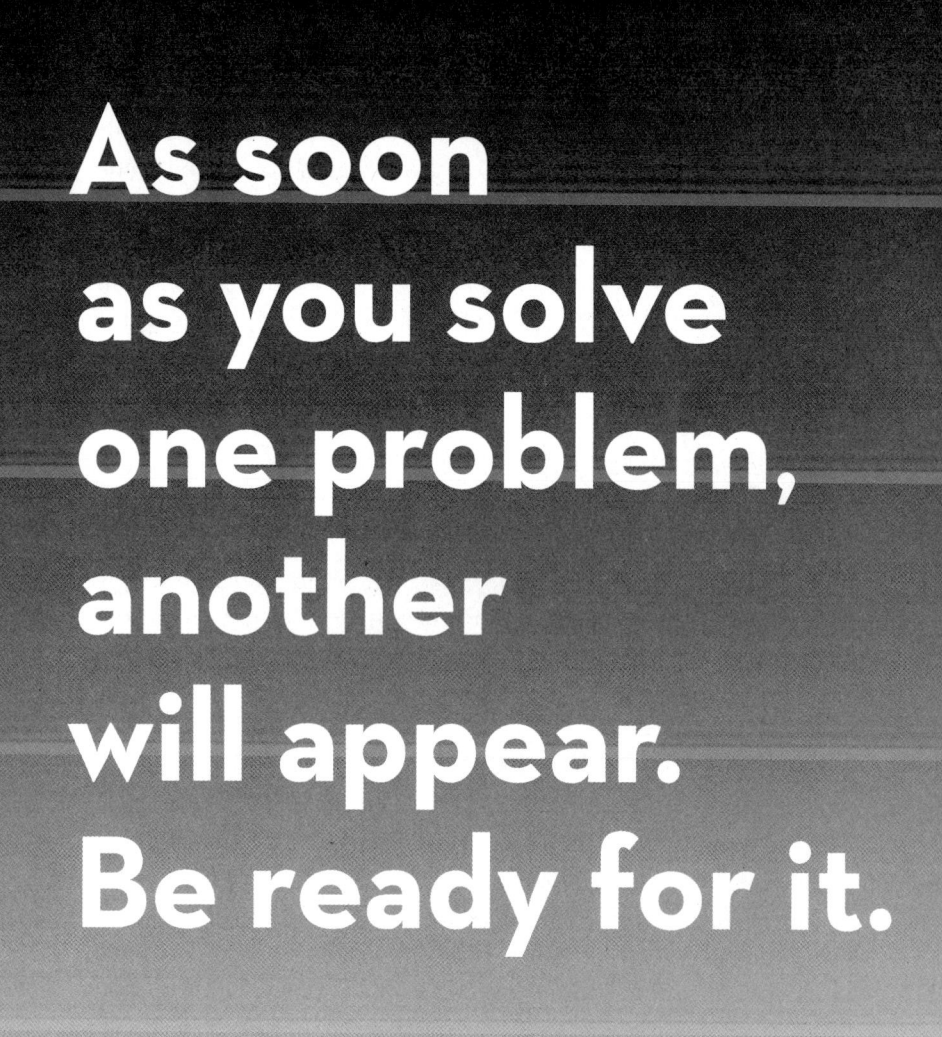

As soon as you solve one problem, another will appear. Be ready for it.

brings up a concern or pain point, the team has already started making preliminary progress on a solution for that problem.

Why? Because I'm a future predictor.

When we work with clients, we make it our job to see where they are now, provide what they need to solve today's pain points, and then know exactly where they will want to go next. As soon as you solve one problem, another will appear. Be ready for it. Get to know your stakeholders so well that they feel like you are reading their mind because you are always one step ahead.

You must pay attention. Listen to what they talk about and the questions they ask, and take time to consider what it's like to walk in their shoes. When you do this, you will easily recognize how far they've come and be able to talk to them about their wins. As soon as you solve one challenge for them, they will grow and face new challenges that you must help them address. Be ready for when the inevitable question comes. Get good at anticipating and know how to address what should happen next. You must become a future predictor.

Stay ahead of the game by predicting where your organization should be heading in the future. Anticipate your stakeholders' evolving needs and align your strategy to meet those needs before they are explicitly requested. By doing so, you can demonstrate proactive leadership and maintain a competitive edge.

Balance Working IN vs. ON Your IMPACT Engine

Through the cycles of value delivery, it's likely that you are doing what our Mastermind group calls building the plane while flying it. As you start putting your services in place, you'll have people dedicated to fulfilling those services while you are focused on creating the next 90-day cycle of service development and delivery. This means you'll need to split your time between working *in* your IMPACT Engine and working *on* your IMPACT Engine.

This balance often gets skewed too far one way or the other, especially if you have a small team. After that initial service is rolled out, you must do the work to deliver and maintain it. At the same time, you'll have a plan for the next service you want to create while you're collecting input from stakeholders on the services they are already utilizing. This feedback will start to create an even bigger list of "to-dos" for you. Know that this is a natural part of the process; you need to be intentional about creating space to do both.

If you have a very small team, or it's only you right now, you'll have to split your time. You can't do what Samantha did in Chapter 1 when she spent months and months building without delivering any services that her stakeholders would find valuable. Your organization's leaders don't have the patience for that. Block time on your calendar each week to go through the steps in the process or it won't happen. Treat that time like a critical appointment and protect it. If you don't, the work you need to do to keep showing value won't happen.

If you have a larger team, go back to Chapter 11 and ensure that you are delegating as much as you can to clear your plate so you have time to think and plan for what's next.

When I was in your shoes, every delivery team I built went through the cycles of building and delivering services and capabilities, and I did this *with* my team. I enlisted their support every step of the way, so it was a team effort, not just me responsible for creating the future state of our organization.

This approach accomplished three goals:

1 They felt very included in the process, knowing that they were a part of the creation, not just the adoption, of what we were building together.

2 We built it a lot faster than if I had tried to create it all on my own. We would ideate together, build a plan together, then divide up the work among team members with one person acting as the project manager for our change cycles. This freed me up to focus on relationships and gaining leadership support, while also having management capacity to support my team as a manager.

3 We ended up with a better result than if I had tried to build it all myself. They were working *in* the organization too, so they had practical experience and a close connection to the stakeholders to know what they wanted.

If you do not have a team, that doesn't mean you need to do this all on your own. Many of our Mastermind students start this way. I teach them to ask themselves "How might we?" Instead of seeing your team as only the people who work *for* you, consider it an opportunity to expand your reach and influence in the organization. There are people in your organization doing project management, even if they don't call themselves project managers. You know who these people are because you have been talking to them since Stage Two.

The best way to get people to support your cause is to solve a problem for them. How can you gather this group together and start talking to them about the pain points they have and what they could really use help with? Create the community of practice you learned about in Chapter 7 to help all the project people in your organization connect with each other, celebrate wins and progress, solve problems together, and share lessons learned.

That forum is a perfect place to enlist support in solving some of the pain points they have together. In fact, if you do the Root Cause Analysis with them, they will see exactly what's causing the pain points they are experiencing. When that light bulb goes off, you better believe they will be excited about fixing it. That's when you enlist their help to do so.

This technique works no matter the size of your team. The more you bring others with you through the change process, the more champions you will have for your cause. You are creating a delivery-focused culture with everyone.

Iterate Your Way to IMPACT

What you've learned in this process is going to help you prepare for what's next. Take the time to celebrate the progress you've made. You'll keep iterating your way through the program every quarter, ensuring sustainable and continuous value and improvements in the organization at every step.

As you prepare for your next cycle of value delivery, there are a few things to keep in mind.

- First, think agile vs. big bang. Evolution instead of revolution. Maintain focus and streamline your services and capabilities in each cycle. Avoid overloading and ensure manageable workloads that can be implemented effectively. Use your 30/90 cycles to measure progress every 30 days and demonstrate tangible results. Continuously measure the IMPACT of all the services you implement.

- When building your team and seeking early adopters and change champions within the organization, prioritize individuals with a business-focused mindset, those who are committed to solving business problems rather than solely project-related issues.

- Prioritize outcomes over outputs. Your business leaders value high-IMPACT outcomes more than perfecting the process of generating deliverables and outputs. Ensure that everything you do contributes to creating significant outcomes for the organization.

- Remember, process and tools should not take precedence. First, address the pain points by identifying their root causes. Often, these root causes exist before projects even commence. If you do implement processes or tools, ensure they are primarily focused on the initial phase of the strategy lifecycle, aiding in proper strategy definition, and setting the foundation for successful project execution.

- Streamline and optimize at every opportunity. Continuously assess whether the services you're implementing will drive faster throughput, deliver high-quality outcomes, and effectively engage people in the process. Simplify and optimize to accelerate IMPACT instead of impeding progress.

- Regularly reevaluate to remain nimble and flexible, while also allowing sufficient time for the services you're implementing to take root. It takes time for the changes you're making to be fully integrated, ensuring that everyone is prepared for the change and understands how to effectively participate in the change process and develop new habits to sustain the implemented changes.

And remember, the reason you are doing quarterly cycles of value delivery is so that you have a reasonable amount of time to make a meaningful change and collect feedback, while being able to show that your services are moving the needle for the organization. It is easier to pivot when you have an adaptive road map. Even with these iterative cycles, you may find yourself wishing you could do more faster, but often that haste does more harm than good.

Pace Yourself for Their Sake

"You're moving too quickly, and we're struggling to keep up. We recommend that you engage in some extracurricular activities *during* work hours."

Wait, what? Did my boss just tell me to stop working so much? Yes, that's exactly what she said.

I was deeply immersed in delivering services for my PMO and eagerly anticipating the next round of services scheduled for delivery. During a routine update meeting with my boss, she dropped the bombshell on me: I was moving too fast for everyone, including my peers.

"We appreciate your hard work, but we need more time to absorb the changes before you add more to our workload," Gina explained.

"So, what should I do while everyone catches up?" I asked, still in a state of mild shock at being told to slow down.

As a high achiever, I was accustomed to receiving accolades for consistently delivering high-IMPACT results. This was the first time I had been instructed to pump the brakes, leaving me uncertain about how to interpret the feedback.

"While your team and colleagues are taking the time they need to assimilate what you've already accomplished, you can channel your positive energy into other meaningful endeavors. How about discussing some ideas with your mentor Margaret?" Gina suggested.

Before I knew it, I found myself nominated for a nonprofit organization's board and assisting with the launch of an internal nonprofit support initiative. Engaging in work where I genuinely felt like I was making a difference gave me a constructive outlet while allowing other people the time to develop the habits that were needed to sustain the changes we had implemented. If I had continued inundating them with new changes during that period, stakeholders would have experienced change fatigue and might have revolted. The organization couldn't absorb the changes I was giving them at the pace that I wanted to roll them out. I had to slow down so they could catch up.

When introducing change to others, remember that you are more familiar with the benefits of the services you are delivering than they are. Your stakeholders need time to break the bad habits, embrace the change, and build new habits. They need time to try out the new service you just handed them. Patience is not my strong suit, but I know that it's important. Self-check your pace and look around to see if people are keeping up.

We often put a lot of pressure on ourselves to deliver, deliver, deliver, and sometimes the internal pressure is preventing us from seeing that those around us aren't as ready as we are for what's next. Consider whether slowing down is necessary to allow your stakeholders to catch their breath and fully utilize the resources at hand before adding too much more to their plate. You can always use this time to apply the One Hour Manager principles—reflect and plan, connect with your team and stakeholders. Be the future predictor

You have built tremendous momentum and you're just getting started.

and start looking at the new problems that are surfacing and where the root causes might be so that you can be ready when they ask you what's next.

You might be thinking, "That's great, Laura, but my executives are the ones pushing me to go this fast!" This is why it's important to give them what they *want* before you give them what they *need*. When you get to the root cause of their pain points, you implement fewer solutions that require fewer changes and enjoy the ripple effect of solving multiple problems simultaneously. For example, when you fix project prioritization, you solve a multitude of issues at once with one solution.

Look How Far You've Come

You have made tremendous progress on your IMPACT journey so far. Take a moment to reflect on your progress. You have:

- ✓ Embraced the IMPACT Driver Mindset and laid a value-focused foundation.
- ✓ Identified opportunities to provide value across the whole strategy lifecycle.
- ✓ Uncovered high-value opportunities through the assessment process.
- ✓ Built strong stakeholder relationships to understand their challenges and opportunities.
- ✓ Discovered the root causes of the symptoms your stakeholders identified.
- ✓ Determined the services required to drive value based on addressing the root causes.
- ✓ Crafted a robust business plan and road map to guide IMPACT delivery.

- ✓ Developed your Communications Plan to clearly articulate the IMPACT your engine drives.
- ✓ Charted a change management journey that puts your stakeholders in the driver's seat.
- ✓ Built an MVP service to address a key challenge or opportunity.
- ✓ Started to cultivate a delivery-focused culture.
- ✓ Addressed any resistance and brought stakeholders with you through the process.
- ✓ Shared authentic and engaging stories of the IMPACT your team is making.
- ✓ Measured initial progress and IMPACT and evolved your road map.

And you did all this in a way that brought your stakeholders with you through the change process, so they were invested in your delivery team and in you.

You have built tremendous momentum and you're just getting started, my friend! Now it's time to keep that momentum going by driving continuous improvement and IMPACT through subsequent cycles. Stay focused on generating value and you will continue achieving great things!

There's one more piece to this puzzle for us to do together—and that's to get you a seat at the table with your business leaders so you can continue to support the organization in achieving its strategic goals long-term. To do this, you'll need to become the Strategy Navigator for your organization. It's time for you to take a seat.

Trust yourself. Trust the process. It's time to make an IMPACT.

MAKE AN IMPACT

Think: What have you learned from delivering your MVP or next cycle solution?

Do: Update your IMPACT Delivery Model, which includes the resources from the Assess, Define, and Plan stages, to reflect any lessons learned or shifts in priorities to support the business. Download your *IMPACT Engine* Book completion badge to celebrate and share your success. When you do, you'll gain access to some secret goodies only for those who made it through the whole MVP cycle!

14

Take Your Seat at the Table

"I JUST PULLED a mind trick on all of you," Shaun said. He was walking the entire program team through what they had accomplished to achieve their business goals in record time.

Whenever I had a tough program with business leaders who were not inclined to follow our program delivery process, Shaun was the specialist I would send in. He instinctively knew how to lead people through change without it feeling heavy or overwhelming. His unique talent was subtly facilitating stakeholder self-discovery—enabling them to organically unlock solutions and reach desired outcomes through an indirect approach that left them feeling in control of the process.

Shaun looked around the room at the team and explained his "mind trick": "I know you said that you didn't want to follow the delivery process we use in the EPMO, but you were following it. You just didn't realize it."

Shaun learned early in the engagement that if he led with the process, the team would resist, so he led them through the change in a way that kept them in charge. They were very proud of what they had made up "on their own" because they "didn't need our process" to guide them. So, when the engagement was complete and he revealed the truth, the room was filled with "Ah... that's what we were doing" moments. They couldn't help but laugh at themselves when they realized the process that they loved was the "EPMO way" after all.

Shaun just looked at me with a knowing smile. It was so fun to watch.

Just like Shaun guided his team to elevate their own leadership skills and competency while they delivered that program, I've been guiding you on a transformation journey. You now have what it takes to be the strategic leader your organization needs.

Before going further, pause and reflect on how much you've grown:

- Do you notice you're having different conversations with business leaders, peers, and team members?

- Are you making decisions in a new way?

- Do you understand and talk about your role and organizational value more clearly?

- Are you more focused on outcomes and delivering value than on process and templates?

- Are you thinking bigger picture about strategy instead of just projects?

I bet your business leaders see it too. They are always observing, even when you think they aren't. They seek those in the organization they can rely on to help achieve their goals and ensure the organization thrives. That's the role I've been preparing you for.

Embracing the Strategy Navigator Role

The ability to bridge the gaps between strategy definition, execution, and realization is a critical skill for anyone aspiring to secure a seat at the table with business leaders. Once honed, this skill enables leaders to play a vital role in driving organizational strategy delivery—a role I refer to as the Strategy Navigator.

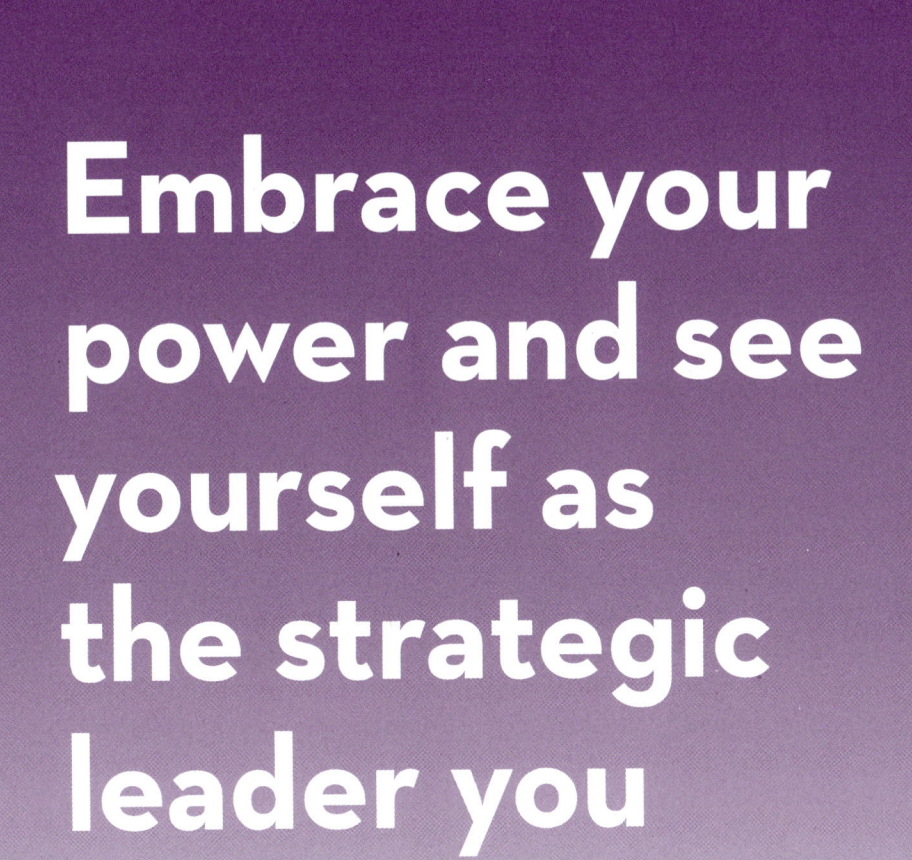

Embrace your power and see yourself as the strategic leader you already are.

Strategy Navigators wear different hats, and you've already been wearing them as you've applied what you've learned in this book.

When you bring your stakeholders with you through the change process and maintain that strong buy-in, you wear the hat of Change Agent.

When you ensure that the work being done in your organization is done in a way that drives the highest ROI or "worth it factor" for your organization, you wear the hat of Investment Manager.

When you show your leaders that they can count on you to solve business problems they care about, not just the typical project problems, you wear the hat of Trusted Adviser.

You're already a Strategy Navigator. By maintaining an IMPACT Driver Mindset as you applied the IMPACT Engine System, you've been positioning yourself this entire time for a seat at the table to help your organization thrive. You simply need to embrace your power and see yourself as the strategic leader you already are simply through the work you've done with this book. Your leaders have pulled a chair up to the table for you. It's time to take a seat.

As a Strategy Navigator, you have all the tools to take your rightful place at the leadership table. You can see the whole chessboard and make strategic moves to advance your organization's goals.

Leverage your ability to build trusted relationships, facilitate change, and guide people through each phase of the strategy lifecycle. Stay above the fray and remain focused on achieving maximum ROI. Make your "worth it factor" clear.

Create a culture of success where everyone understands the strategy and their role in its delivery. Empower your colleagues to make informed decisions that contribute to the bigger picture.

Continue immersing yourself in executive perspectives, aligning to priorities, and delivering value—but with an expanded view of your identity. You can now make the power moves necessary to win and thrive.

Be a Consultant

"You have to step out of the situation and see yourself as a consultant," I said to Melanie as she shared with me the latest political games going on with her leadership team.

Every time we talked, there was another dramatic chapter to the story that was her job as an executive transformation leader. One week it was her leadership team asking her to manage projects while she was running the enterprise transformation group. She was told to "pitch in" to take on several new projects herself while being short-staffed and already working 60 hours a week. She felt like she couldn't keep up. It was no surprise that she kept getting sick, and even then, she didn't take time to rest.

The next week it was reacting to gossip that her team were administrators and "only working 40 hours a week" while everyone else was working more. She spent countless hours just battling and reacting to the rumor mill.

The next it was having to run everything by the COO before she could talk to anyone on his team.

And so it went, week after week. All of it was preventing her from being successful. Reacting to the drama was robbing her of so many hours during which she could have been focused on getting the services delivered, guiding her team so they could navigate the organization and deliver projects, and managing to keep her leadership team bought in to their road map. She had become a pawn on the company chessboard, progress toward her goals was stalling, and her reputation, health, and sanity were at risk.

But while she couldn't control the drama around her, she could control the way she engaged.

I said gently but firmly, "Melanie, it's time to stop being a pawn. Your transformation group is the queen, the most powerful piece on the chessboard, and you need to start playing this game strategically. What power moves can you make to stay focused on driving results and not let the noise distract you?"

Consulting moves help you move the right chess pieces across the board at the right time and in the right order.

This kind of setback has happened to more delivery leaders than we can count. And if it is happening to you, it's standing in the way of your success. It prevents you from getting a seat at the table because you're consumed by reacting to drama and politics instead of doing the important work of delivering on the strategy.

To get and keep your seat at the table, you must get out of the swirl. I realize that may seem like an impossible task, but don't worry! It's easier than you think. It does, however, require you to level up like you learned about in Chapter 4.

I've helped so many of your peers out of the swirl, in a way that did more to help them be seen as peer business leaders in their organizations than anything else they'd tried. It all goes back to mindset.

I taught them how to be consultants.

When a consultant comes into an organization, they can more easily stay out of the drama because it's not their drama. They can see the whole chessboard and all the players on that chessboard. They observe. They don't participate. They evaluate. They don't get consumed by it. They watch the movie. They aren't the characters.

Instead of reacting, they observe, guide, advise, and facilitate. That's what you need to do.

Raise your perspective above the chaos. Stop being a pawn in the game and start determining the moves—not just the next move, but start thinking five moves ahead.

Remember that you can predict what your organization needs and help them get there, as you learned in Chapter 13. That's a consulting move.

If you find that it's taking too long to get services defined, go back to Chapter 3, and get out of the perfection trap.

If you don't have stakeholder buy-in, go back to Stage Two and build stakeholder relationships—for real this time.

If you are facing resistance to the services that you are rolling out, revisit Chapter 5 and give them what they *want* before you give them what they *need*.

If your leaders are asking for more than is doable, go to Chapter 10 and say, "Yes, and..."

If you are only focused on the urgent and never addressing the important, go back to Chapter 11 and dump the busy badge.

If you are feeling like you just have too many priorities on your own plate, revisit Chapter 11 again and pick three.

These are all consulting moves.

Consulting moves help you move the right chess pieces across the board at the right time and in the right order, so you can strategically navigate from where you are today to that leadership table where you can make an even bigger IMPACT.

Accelerate Your IMPACT

Tears streamed down her face as she emerged from the room. Behind her more tear-stained faces appeared from the people leaving the great hall filled with nonprofit leaders and project managers. My heart raced and I froze. Oh no. After all we'd done these past months, we failed.

My mind flashed back to that day only seven months ago—Kendall's exciting vision to elevate project management as a force for social good. Rallying ecosystems of volunteers and sponsors to execute our strategy on that impossible timeline. All those nights and weekends tuning engine parts while perfecting a success formula no one had attempted. And the high-fiving as the gears started to move.

It couldn't end in tears. I rushed over, panic rising. "What happened? Are you okay?" Voices blurred through my tunnel vision.

Then—a smile. I refocused. A woman with glistening trails down her cheeks beamed. "We did something big today. We're changing lives."

The vise grip on my heart released. These were tears of triumph, not defeat! More stories flowed from the room, voices shaking with emotion.

Of clarity emerging from chaos. Nonprofits gaining confidence and walking away with a clear plan. Strategies mapped for maximum social IMPACT despite the "not enough."

Project managers felt the power of their work on projects ranging from feeding the homeless, to housing veterans, to protecting battered women and children, to improving access to clean drinking water. One hundred different stories of IMPACT in one day.

Project management recognized as a force that could change the world!

I stood immersed in the rippling IMPACT as Kendall and Mike joined us. We all embraced the potential we had unlocked that day, my tears mingling with the rest.

The seeds sown at that first PMDoS event grew strong roots that day. We'd gathered in a room with 100 nonprofit leaders, more than 300 project managers, the 40-person PMO team, and a full house of sponsors who had given us the financial backing to make the event happen. The day was kicked off with a speech by the Secretary of Commerce for the United States—even the White House was paying attention! We later determined that the work that we did in the first PMDoS equated to $1 million of IMPACT in our local communities, as a result of the projects that got planned at the day of service and implemented through those nonprofits. And 10 years later, global branches continue to bloom. Ask any PMDoS volunteer—that work stands among their most meaningful.

It lit a spark in me too about the power of aligning strategy, people, and process to create an engine capable of enormous IMPACT—a strategy delivery engine with the power to change the world.

While the focus of that first event was helping nonprofits launch their mission-critical projects, so much more was happening. We were all dedicated to changing the world for the better using the power of project management, and the room vibrated with the electricity of what we were creating together. Each conversation started with the nonprofit leader sharing the IMPACT their work would have. The project managers, moved by these stories, understood how their contributions were making a difference. They knew they had limited time and resources to make the most out of this day, but with a clear line of sight to exactly how what they were doing was going to IMPACT the lives of so many, they immediately got into flow.

That day crystallized for me the power of aligned execution behind an ambitious vision to drive transformational IMPACT. It made me reflect on the example of the Reverend Dr. Martin Luther

King Jr. (MLK), a visionary of his time—one in a movement of many who shared the dream of genuine societal equality and harmony, of a society that could be aware of unjust historical realities without being beholden to them. So why is MLK heralded so much more widely than his similarly talented peers? I believe it is because he was a more effective IMPACT Driver. He didn't just have a dream—MLK had a strategy and a plan; he knew how to lead his followers to deliver on that strategy.

It's no coincidence that the first Project Management Day of Service was held on MLK Day, just a few miles from where Dr. King had delivered his famous "I Have a Dream" speech in 1963. It's no coincidence that the very first PMDoS event was designed not just to deliver a massively high IMPACT to the benefiting nonprofits, but also—perhaps more significantly—to awaken in the project management volunteers the power of their skill set, as evidenced by their "IMPACT tears." And it's no coincidence that I am now calling *you* to drive the highest possible level of positive IMPACT you possibly can.

Dr. King was a change agent, and I am challenging you to be the change agent your organization needs right now. With you as the Strategy Navigator, your organization can transform the way projects are approached and ensure business goals are not only met but exceeded. To accomplish this, you must embrace your power to drive strategy delivery as a true business leader. With every move you make, you are earning your seat at the table. When you lead with purpose, confidence, and a relentless pursuit of value, you are leading by example and inspiring others to join you on this journey.

You've worked through the IMPACT Engine System. Now it's your turn to be an IMPACT Driver—to accelerate strategy delivery so that you can help change the world, one project at a time.

It's time to accelerate your IMPACT. The flag is waving and I can see you coming around the turn.

I am sitting in the stands, cheering you on. I can't wait to celebrate with you in the winner's circle. You've got this!

Acknowledgments

I WOULD LIKE to express my deepest gratitude to the following people for their support, guidance, and sacrifice that made this book possible:

To my son, Grayson—Thank you for sharing mommy with her career and business—from sitting on my lap while I made plans to change the world to helping me in the business a decade later. You are my light.

To my husband, Kurt—Thank you for selflessly putting me and the company first, delaying your own venture while we built mine. Your commitment to our shared dream has been unwavering. I couldn't do any of this without my partner by my side cheering me on every step of the way.

To my mother, Pamela—Thank you for teaching me to never accept "can't," helping me find my voice, and showing me how to go after anything I wanted. Your lifelong guidance and encouragement gave me the confidence to pursue my goals.

To my lifelong friend Bryana—Thank you for being my rock so that no matter the physical distance between us, I never felt alone because a piece of my heart has always been with you.

To my friend Mike—Thank you for creating space for me to write this thing. Your practical support in the business and with this book, challenging me by asking "How might we?" and always making time to listen, made all the difference.

To my friend Kendall—Thank you for teaching and guiding me with your no-nonsense Kendallisms, friendship, and partnership in creating that little thing called PMDoS. Your wisdom has shaped me tremendously.

To my friend Dawn—Thank you for being so giving of your time to help me with this book. I was so lucky to have another set of editing eyes that "gets" what this book needs to be so we can change the world.

To my dream team of troublemaking peers and friends, fellow instigators on this mission to change the world for the better—Stuart Easton, Jesse Fewell, Donna Fitzgerald, Mike Hannan, Andy Jordan, Dawn Mahan, and Amanda Oakenfull—thank you from the bottom of my heart for always saying yes to my crazy ideas, and of course to Andy for always being first to do so.

To Lee Lambert—for your decades of friendship, endless support, and the best hugs, thank you. You are my hero.

To the Project Management for Change and PMDoS volunteers—thank you for helping us change the world one project at a time.

I also want to give a big shout-out to the early readers of this book, whose honest and detailed feedback shaped its pages. This is only the beginning.

And to my IMPACT Engine System students and IMPACT Accelerator Mastermind participants. I am so proud of every one of you for investing in yourself, in your growth, and in making a big IMPACT. I've got your back every step of the way.

Thank you to my publishing team at Page Two for your endless patience working with me to adapt so this book could thrive.

And finally, to my book coach and friend AJ Harper—Thank you for being my steadfast companion on this book birthing journey. Without your wisdom, insight, encouragement, and commitment, this book simply would not have been born. I am forever grateful for your undying support and friendship over the years. You are last on this list not in priority, but because you have been with me from the start of this idea to the very last page.

I could not have done this without each of you. Thank you for everything. I love all of you so very much.

Sources

Chapter 1: Your Strategic Opportunity

p. 17 *about half of PMOs failed to meet their original objectives:* Project Management Institute, *Success in Disruptive Times*, Pulse of the Profession: 10th Global Project Management Survey, 2018.

p. 18 *74 percent of executives don't have faith that their company's transformative strategies will succeed:* McKinsey & Company, "Losing from Day One: Why Even Successful Transformations Fall Short," Survey, December 7, 2021, mckinsey.com/capabilities/people-and-organizational-performance/our-insights/successful-transformations.

p. 18 *only 8 percent of leaders rated their companies as effective at both strategy and execution:* Paul Leinwand, Cesare Mainardi, and Art Kleiner, "Only 8% of Leaders Are Good at Both Strategy and Execution," *Harvard Business Review*, December 30, 2015, hbr.org/2015/12/only-8-of-leaders-are-good-at-both-strategy-and-execution.

p. 18 *50 percent of PMOs fail because they focus too much on processes and tools:* "Trip Report: Program & Portfolio Management," Gartner Symposium/ITxpo, November 15-18, 2010, Sydney, Australia, gartner.com/imagesrv/symposium/sydney/docs/syd10_trip_report_ppm_v3.pdf.

p. 31 *95 percent of the typical workforce does not understand their company's strategy:* Robert S. Kaplan and David P. Norton, "The Office of Strategy Management," *Harvard Business Review*, October 2005, hbr.org/2005/10/the-office-of-strategy-management.

p. 32 *task-switching can cost the organization up to 40 percent loss in productivity:* American Psychological Association, "Multitasking: Switching Costs," March 20, 2006, apa.org/topics/research/multitasking.

p. 32 *In 61 percent of organizations, there's a failure to bridge the gap between strategy formulation and its day-to-day implementation:* Project Management Institute, "Why Good Strategies Fail: Lessons for the C-Suite," an Economist Intelligence Unit report, November 2013, pmi.org/learning/thought-leadership/series/pmo/c-suite-failing-strategiy-lessons.

Detailed Table of Contents

I Wish I Had Me When I Was You 1
The IMPACT Engine System 4
Action Steps Worth Doing 7

Stage One: New Role, New Mindset 11

1: Your Strategic Opportunity 15
The Typical Advice and Typical Results 17
It's Not You, It's the Process 19
Trapped in the Triangle 22
The Real Delivery Gaps 23
Start at the Start 28
Set Up Strategy Delivery for Success 31
How Might We? 34
Make an IMPACT 36

2: You Are an IMPACT Driver 37
The IMPACT Driver Mindset 40
I: Instill Focus 41
M: Measure Outcomes 41
P: Perform Relentlessly 41
A: Adapt to Thrive 42
C: Communicate with Purpose 42
T: Transform Mindset 42
You Are a Navigator 42
Make an IMPACT 45

3: The IMPACT Engine System 47
The IMPACT Delivery Cycle 49
Stage One: Mindset 51
Stage Two: Assess 52
Stage Three: Define 52
Stage Four: Plan 52
Stage Five: Deliver 52
Stage Six: Evolve 53
The MVP Approach 53
Iterate Your Way to IMPACT 56
Mindset (1 Week) 57
Assess (2 Weeks) 57
Define (3 Weeks) 57
Plan (2 Weeks) 57
Deliver (4 Weeks) 58
Evolve (1 Week) 58
The Perfection Trap 59
Experience Not Required 62
Make an IMPACT 63

Stage Two: Assess the Organization 65

4: Bring Them with You 69
You're About to Level Up 74
Identify Stakeholders and Build Trust 75
Your Organization's Change Culture 78
Evaluate Your Stakeholders 81
Lovers, Haters, and Just Don't Cares 82
Who Is Your Sponsor? 84
Evaluate Your Team 86
The Change Resistance Myth 89
Make an IMPACT 90

5: Give Them What They Want 91
Don't Give Them What They Need 94
How to Gather Meaningful Input 96
Don't Say No, But Don't Just Say Yes 102
Use Their Words and Listen for the WIIFM 106
Don't Ask What Your Team Should Do 107
Assess Your Current Capabilities 108
The Bigger-Picture SWOT Analysis 109
The SWOT Analysis with Your Team 111
The Assessment Findings Presentation 114
Make an IMPACT 123

Stage Three: Define High-IMPACT Services 125

6: Solve the Right Problems 129
Find Root Cause with the Five Whys Technique 132
The Five Whys in Action 136
Make an IMPACT 141

7: Create Solutions Across the Strategy Lifecycle 143
Sequence Matters 144
Avoid the Software-First Trap 146
When the Leader Is the Problem 146
Organize the Solutions Across the Strategy Lifecycle 148
Strategy Definition 150
Strategy Governance Framework 152
Portfolio Management Model 152
Portfolio Prioritization Framework 153
Intake Processes and Business Cases 154
Strategy Execution 155
Talent Requirements 155
Project Delivery Framework 157
Tools and Resources 157
Community of Practice 158
Strategy Realization 159

Benefits Tracking 162
IMPACT Metrics 163
Performance Management and Reporting 167
Change Management and Adoption 168
Continuous Improvement 169
Benefits Sustainability and Handover 170
Make an IMPACT 171

8: Determine Your "Worth It Factor" 173
Tie Services to Value 175
The IMPACT Communication Framework 179
IMPACT Communication in Action 183
Make an IMPACT 185

Stage Four: Plan the IMPACT Journey 187

9: Develop the IMPACT Delivery Framework 191
You Don't Need a Charter 193
A Unique Maturity Model 195
Building the IMPACT Delivery Road Map 198
30/90 Delivery and Reporting 201
The Start of Each 90-Day Cycle 201
The 30-Day Mark 202
The 90-Day Mark 202
Make an IMPACT 203

10: Become the Stakeholder Whisperer 205
The Organizational Change Management Plan 210
Guiding the Transition 212
You're a Marketer 214
What Happens If You Don't 217
Present Your IMPACT Delivery Proposal 220
The Power of "Yes, And…" 223
Make an IMPACT 227

Stage Five: Deliver Sustainable Value 229

11: Create a Delivery-Focused Culture 233
Focus On Outcomes, Not Outputs 234
Dump the Busy Badge 236
Pick Three 238
Manage Your Team Effectively 243
Take 15 Minutes to Reflect 244
Take 15 Minutes to Plan 245
Take 15 Minutes to Manage 245
Take 15 Minutes to Make Progress 247
Make an IMPACT 248

12: Lead the Change 249
Adaptive Management Style 252
Directing 253
Collaborating 254
Empowering 255
Evolving 256
Work with the Culture 258
The Marketing Playbook 262
Know 262
Like 264
Trust 264
Try 264
Buy 265
Repeat 265
Refer 265
The Power of Story 267
Invite the Green Monster 270
Get the Word Out 270
Make an IMPACT 271

Stage Six: Evolve Your IMPACT Engine 273

13: Drive Continual Value Delivery 277
Evaluate IMPACT 279
Measure What Matters 280
Communicate Your Value 282
Evolve the Road Map 283
Become a Future Predictor 283
Balance Working IN vs. ON Your IMPACT Engine 285
Iterate Your Way to IMPACT 288
Pace Yourself for Their Sake 289
Look How Far You've Come 292
Make an IMPACT 294

14: Take Your Seat at the Table 295
Embracing the Strategy Navigator Role 296
Be a Consultant 299
Accelerate Your IMPACT 302

About the Author

FOR NEARLY three decades, Laura Barnard has spearheaded efforts to unleash the power of effective project management to help organizations rapidly achieve higher returns on investment for their strategic goals. Her company's groundbreaking IMPACT Engine System empowers organizations to drive transformational outcomes aligned to their vision with unprecedented speed and measurable business IMPACT. Laura's nonprofit, Project Management for Change, is on a mission to elevate the profile of the project management profession while changing the world for the better one project at a time. In 2021, Laura was named World PMO Influencer of the Year by the PMO Global Alliance (now part of the Project Management Institute).

Ready to Go Deeper?

Access our step-by-step training and implementation program, advanced templates, expert guidance, and in-depth resources that will elevate your skills while giving you everything you need to implement the IMPACT Engine System in your organization.

Start accelerating IMPACT at **IMPACTEngineBook.com/IES**.

Accelerate Your Growth with Personalized Coaching

Join the IMPACT Accelerator Mastermind for individualized coaching, powerful community support, and mentorship by seasoned experts from around the globe.

Claim your spot at **IMPACTEngineBook.com/Coaching**.

Become a Certified IMPACT Engine Leader or Consultant

Earn your IMPACT Engine Certification to differentiate yourself from your peers or apply the IMPACT Engine System in your own consulting practice with our support.

Begin your journey at **IMPACTEngineBook.com/Certification**.

Invite Laura to Keynote Your Event

Hire Laura, the visionary behind the IMPACT Engine, to deliver a riveting keynote or immersive workshop that will inspire and equip your audience to accelerate business IMPACT.

Book Laura now at **IMPACTEngineBook.com/Speaking**.

Transform Your Organization with Expert Consulting

Let our team of certified consultants help you accelerate the delivery of your organization's strategy with the IMPACT Engine System.

Ignite your transformation at **IMPACTEngineBook.com/Consulting**.